KT-158-095

Ecology and Society

ECOLOGY AND SOCIETY

An Introduction

LUKE MARTELL

UNIVERSITY OF WOLVERHAMPTON LIBRARY

Acc No. 896845

CLASS

CONTROL 0745610226

333. 7

DATE 19 MAR 1996

SITE RS.

MAR

Polity Press

Copyright © Luke Martell 1994

The right of Luke Martell to be identified as author of this work has been asserted in accordance with the Copyright, Designs and Patents Act 1988.

First published in 1994 by Polity Press in association with Blackwell Publishers.

Editorial Office:
Polity Press
65 Bridge Street
Cambridge CB2 1UR, UK

Marketing and production:
Blackwell Publishers
108 Cowley Road
Oxford OX4 1JF, UK

All rights reserved. Except for the quotation of short passages for the purposes of criticism and review, no part of this publication may be reproduced, stored in a retrieval system, or transmitted, in any form or by any means, electronic, mechanical, photocopying, recording or otherwise, without the prior permission of the publisher.

Except in the United States of America, this book is sold subject to the condition that it shall not, by way of trade or otherwise, be lent, re-sold, hired out, or otherwise circulated without the publisher's prior consent in any form of binding or cover other than that in which it is published and without a similar condition including this condition being imposed on the subsequent purchaser.

ISBN 0-7456 1022-6
ISBN 0-7456 1023-4 (pbk)

British Library Cataloguing in Publication Data

A CIP catalogue record for this book is available from the British Library.

Typeset in 10½ on 12 pt Times by TecSet Ltd, Wallington, Surrey
Printed in Great Britain by T.J. Press Ltd, Padstow, Cornwall

This book is printed on acid-free paper.

Contents

List of Figures and Tables

Introduction

This book introduces green ideas to students of society and politics. Its aim is to outline green ideas at an accessible level to people new or relatively new to them. It is also assertive. It does not just review what other people have said but proposes arguments of its own. It suggests that ecology brings insights to social and political thinking. The latter has to pay attention to non-humans and the way society affects nature and is affected by it. The book also shows how social and political thinking can bring something to ecology, helping to solve environmental problems and explaining environmentalism and environment–society relations.

I think my arguments break with problematic elements in both social analysis and green thinking. Social and political thinkers are poorly attuned to non-humans and the implications of natural environmental factors for the social and political world they study. Many radical greens are one-sided and uncritical in their thinking and make problematic, simple-minded and poorly thought-out assumptions and assertions. My arguments deal with problems in both camps. They do not fit neatly into any school of thought, and I feel they take thinking about the politics and sociology of ecology forward.

Why did I write the book?

There are a number of preoccupations which brought me to an interest in ecology. I found that concerns I had with non-statist socialist politics, animal rights and social constructionist social analysis were raised in the political ecology literature. Worries about the environment and an interest in ecology itself were only part of the reason for deciding to look in more depth at ecological debates.

(1) *New social movement politics*   One concern I had was to find new ideas of socialism which break with statism and economic self-interest yet retain the philosophical principles and political economy of socialism. The new social movements, of which the green movement is one, seemed to offer useful sources for such ideas. Green arguments for decentralized communal living in combination with non-market and non-capitalist institutions and in pursuit of general rather than sectional interests seemed to capture the non-authoritarian non-sectional politics I was looking for. They did this without throwing out the socialist principles and political economy I felt to be of continuing necessity both generally and especially for the resolution of environmental problems. New social movements and the green movement offered exciting ideas about decentralization and civil society politics and addressed oppressions in society other than just class oppression and values other than economic self-interest.

(2) *Environmental problems*   Then there were, of course, environmental problems themselves. Ozone depletion, global warming, acid rain, vehicle fumes, waste disposal and other forms of pollution of land, water and the air seemed to me to be major and escalating problems with serious consequences.[1] Human-made CFC (chlorofluorocarbon) gases – used in fridges, among other things – deplete the protective ozone layer in the earth's atmosphere allowing through radiation from the sun which causes skin cancer and damages food production. Annual holes in the ozone layer over the poles are already thought to let high doses of ultraviolet radiation through to population centres there. Scientists and politicians in Canada, for example, warn parents to keep their children out of the sun at the most affected times of the year. Global warming, it is suspected, is caused by emissions of CO_2 (carbon dioxide) from burning coal, gas and petroleum products (as well as by other gases). CO_2 may act as an insulator, leading to rising temperatures, damaging food production and causing rising sea levels which threaten low-lying population centres. Things are made worse by the destruction of forests. Not only does this cause soil erosion and undermine local human and animal life but it removes trees which absorb CO_2 through photosynthesis and which when burnt, as they often are, produce more CO_2.

Acid rain results from the impurities released when fossil fuels are burnt in power stations, boilers and vehicles. Released into the atmosphere, these come down in rain to damage trees and buildings and poison lakes, and are a health hazard. Acid rain often falls in countries other than those in which it is produced – pointing up the global nature of the problem and the necessity for an international perspective in solving it, something to which I will return in chapter 2. Various vehicle exhaust emissions can affect brain development in children and contribute to global warming, smogs and cancer. Some are poisonous and cause further adverse health effects. Fertilizers, weedkillers, pesticides, disease control agents and food additives which are used in food production go through the food chain and affect plants, animals and humans. Domestic and industrial waste, effluents and sewage are often toxic and contaminate drinking water. Sometimes they are dumped at sea or in poor countries who will take payments to accept them, or they are burned, producing CO_2. Chemicals introduced into the water supply include aluminium which is linked to dementia and nitrate which can cause blood disease in babies. None of this is even to mention problems of resource depletion and over-population which are discussed in chapter 1.

As I will explain, many of these are global problems, caused by industrial and technological processes wrapped up in political and economic relations and tied to social lifestyles and cultural value systems. They are linked to industrial processes which can be stopped, slowed, pursued more selectively or replaced with alternatives. Many pollutants, wastes and additives to the food production process can be halted or reduced. Recycling and the minimization of resource use can reduce waste. There are alternatives to CFCs. CO_2 emissions can be reduced by using tidal, wind, solar or hydro-electric power, more efficient energy use, discouragement of private vehicle use (through, say, a comprehensive public transport infrastructure) and planting rather than cutting down forests. Some (but not all) harmful vehicle emissions can be further reduced by the replacement of pollutants (e.g. lead in petrol) or by the use of catalytic converters (which break down toxic gases) or alternative fuels (e.g. alcohol fuels or electric power). In some areas small advances have been made. Yet governments and capitalists have not shown anything approaching an adequate willingness to tackle these problems or work at possible solutions. Environmental problems, their location in economic, social, political and cultural processes and the need for action by politicians and the business community to solve them was another concern that led me to ecology and to an approach to it that stresses that it is not just a technical or natural science issue but one that is tied up in questions to do with society and politics.

(3) *Biology and nature* As a sociologist and someone interested in socialist and feminist politics, I have always felt uneasy about the rubbishing by sociologists, socialists and feminists of arguments to do with biology and nature. Sociologists have tended to push out

nature because it is perceived to fall outside the remit of the 'social' and to threaten their insistence on social explanations for social phenomena.[2] Socialists and feminists often reject nature because it is seen to justify class or gender inequalities as 'natural', fixed and based in biological traits rather than socially imposed in unequal power relations and open to change. Justifiable as concerns about the evoking of notions of nature and biology may be, it seemed to me that human societies work with natural properties and biological processes, and that these have to come in somewhere to explanations of social life. We are physical creatures with biological characteristics and capacities. The environment outside us, while subject to social transformation, has traits and powers which are the pre-given natural raw material we work with. Issues to do with the environment raise questions about the relevance of natural and biological processes to society and politics that I felt were being pushed out.

(4) *Social constructionism and relativism* A fourth concern, related to the third was with epistemological and ontological issues in sociological theory and the problems of strong anti-naturalist social constructionist and relativist arguments on such issues. Such arguments come up in sociological theory, the philosophy of social science and the sociology of science. But they also arise in the sociology of the environment. Social constructionists and relativists propose that things in the world gain their character from social action rather than independent objective properties, and that our knowledge of them does not have an independent objective basis but is relative to the culture in which it is produced. Yet it seemed to me that in the encounter with ecology and the natural environment social constructionism and relativism have the ideal opportunity to recognize the role of non-social and objective inputs to social life. In ecology more than anywhere else, insights are offered by realist understandings of entities with objective properties independent of, but mediated by, social processes and comprehension. However, as I will discuss, some sociologists of the environment continue to push for strong social constructionism in the face of an external, objective, natural reality.

(5) *Animal rights and vegetarianism* Arguments in green philosophy tapped into issues that, as a vegetarian, I had debated with myself. I had long felt that sentience (capacity for sensory experience), rather than say intelligence, consciousness or capacity to develop, was the basis on which moral consideration should be extended. This led me to opposition to the suffering and killing of animals and to becoming a vegetarian. In debates about ecology these ideas could be worked through and elaborated. In particular, there is a debate in

the philosophy of environmental ethics about the range of entities in the environment to which moral standing should be extended and for what reasons. I felt that moral standing should be extended to animals and that the reason this should be done was because they are sentient creatures.

All five sets of issues came up in the political ecology literature and made me want to look at it more closely. However, writing the book has been a learning process and not all of my initial assumptions have held out. I still think biology and nature should play a role in social explanation, that there are natural limits on, and effects of, social processes which are too much ignored and that environmental ethics should be based on concern for sentient creatures. Yet it will become clear that I am no longer so sympathetic to many of my other initial concerns. I defend in the rest of this book strong state action and global co-ordination over decentralization. Even more unfashionably, I am more worried than I was before about leaving things to the economic and political institutions of civil society. I favour political and socialist strategies for change and collective over private capitalist ownership of the means of production. Much of what I say returns to traditional socialism, the role of socialist political economy, the inadequacy of capitalism and markets and the significance of capitalist class power relations. Before starting work on this book some of these aspects of state action and traditional socialist analysis were things I was trying to get away from. I have found myself less persuaded by elements in green philosophy, green critiques of modernity and green political theory than I expected to be. Some green thinking I have found flawed and dangerous. Some of my initial concerns, in short, have been supported by my work on this book and this is reflected below. Others have been turned upside down the more I thought about green issues.

Radical ecology and other environmentalisms

In discussing environmentalism I deal in particular with one strand in green thinking which is influential in the political ecology literature and has the biggest implications for the social and political world. This is 'radical ecology'.[3] I discuss throughout the book strands in environmental thinking which require, for example, either technological tinkering or fundamental changes in economic structure and value systems or either anthropocentric or eco-centric ethics. It is the most radical strands in which I am especially interested – those that call for structural changes in economic systems, lifestyles and beliefs in the developed world and the extension of intrinsic value, rights and moral standing to entities in the environment beyond just humans or even animals. I will break down environmentalism into different strands as the book goes along and will be dealing with different sorts of environmentalist argument including the more moderate. But I will be using the words green, environmentalist or ecological to apply to radical ecology unless otherwise stated.

My dealing with radical ecology is sympathetic but critical. I sympathize with concern for environmental problems. I share the radical green belief that changes in economic systems, lifestyles and values are needed, rather than just technological adaptation. While I do not think that all entities in the environment are of intrinsic value or inherent moral worth, I do share the radical green belief that we should be concerned about the good of things in the environment other than just humans. I argue in chapter 3 for the intrinsic value and moral standing of animals.

Yet much of the radical ecology literature is one-sided and uncritical.[4] Many radical greens buy the whole anti-modernist case – a hostility to consumption, science and Enlightenment philosophies and advocacy of decentralism, holism and eco-centrism – without critical thought. These planks in the theory are just assumed uncritically to be plainly the case. As a result, big flaws in radical ecology are glossed over; I attempt to deal with these. Some radical greens make simple-minded, ill-informed, arrogant and flawed dismissals of parts of the modernist project which are of social and environmental value or, at the very least, not of the uniformly environmentally damaging character they suggest. Material consumption, modern science, Enlightenment ideas, traditional political theory, the state and humanism are examples. On reflection, many things dismissed turn out to be not so socially and environmentally bankrupt as it is assumed.

Greens may perceive that the arguments in this book devote a lot of space to criticizing radical ecology and not enough to environmental problems with the way industrial societies are run. The book does take a lot of time to analyse ecological deficiencies in industrialism and capitalism and the need for traditional perspectives to take on board ecological insights. But if I do spend time on flaws in radical ecology it is because I assume that the fact that there are environmental problems with industrialism is more generally accepted. The strengths and weaknesses of radical ecology are less well known and more glossed over. Criticisms I make of radical ecology should not be taken to suggest a dismissal of it or of the reality of enormous environmental problems. I accept the case for a more ecological approach to social and political thought and action and many fundamental tenets of radical ecology. In the context of ecological sympathy, however, I am concerned to show the problems in radical ecology as well as its strengths. My concern is to show the case for ecology but to make sure that people, in the first flush of their encounter with its ideas, do not get swept away with its strengths and resistant to acknowledging its weaknesses.

Sociology and the environment

This book deals with the meeting of ecology with economic, social and political life in general and is not narrowly sociological at all. From beginning to end it will be of interest to non-sociologists. But it is in part an attempt to explain the relevance of sociology to environmental questions and of ecology to sociology.

Why is sociology relevant to the environment? The environment is frequently seen as a natural-science issue. Environmental problems involve the pollution of the land, sea and air, all things which natural rather than social scientists know about. It is technologies which use up resources and spill out pollutants, again something which is the preserve of the natural scientist or technologist.

Science has a vital role to play in these areas, and scientists have been key actors in identifying environmental problems which now have such a high profile. But scientific and technological developments which affect the environment are driven by economic and social developments and practices. It is the requirements and practices of societies that lead to technological choices and developments and make demands on the environment. Economic and social factors that stand particularly accused in the green literature include the commitment to economic development and growth, levels of consumption and acquisitive and materialistic values – in short our systems of production and consumption and their social and cultural bases. In sum, structures and processes that are central to the expertise of social scientists are as important to environmental problems as those that are of interest to natural scientists.

This is reflected in a distinction made in the green literature. On one hand there are technocratic environmentalists who see environmental problems as resolvable by the 'technical fix' within existing economic and social practices (recycling, lead-free petrol, banning CFCs and so on). On the other there are ecologists who see such

problems as embedded in economic and social structures and practices and resolvable only by changes at that level (see Dobson 1991:
73–81).

Newby (1991) calls for a reconsideration by sociologists of their
attitude to the environment. He argues they should turn their attention to studying environmental problems, showing how they have a
distinctive and necessary contribution to make to understanding and
resolving them. But in doing so they need to question their assumptions about how they do sociology, taking on board some of the
insights and distinctive approach of the ecological perspective.

This leads to what ecology can bring to sociology. In their explanatory thinking sociologists tend to look more at the internal structures and processes of industrial societies and less at natural factors
affecting their development, or at the effects of their development on
the environment and the reciprocal repercussions of this for society.
An ecological perspective can provide a more complete and realistic
understanding of social and natural factors involved in social development. In their normative thinking sociologists tend to be concerned
with the effect of social structures and processes on humans. Ecology
suggests they should also incorporate environmental criteria and non-
humans in their interest in the effects of social practices.

Catton and Dunlap (1978) suggest that environmental sociology
has received more attention in the USA than other countries. In
their survey of the US environmental sociology literature they conclude that most research has been done on social impacts of changing
environmental conditions such as resource shortages, pollution or
overcrowding. Sociologists have looked at the way these affect lifestyle, psychological well-being, health, values, stratification, conflict,
competitiveness and, to some extent, population levels and choice of
technology. Some studies, for example, suggest that resource
shortages are likely to affect attitudes to nature, levels of inequality,
conflict and competitiveness (Catton 1976; Burch 1970). Sociologists
have also looked at the social impacts of air pollution (Burch 1976)
and of different forms of built as well as natural environment
(Michelson 1976).

But this sort of work is scarce and much of it is done by non-
sociologists. Catton and Dunlap suggest that sociologists have little
to say about the reverse direction of the equation: the social causes
of environmental degradation. They do look at attitudes to the
environment but other aspects of the social bases of environmental
problems – population growth, choice of technology, economic and
social systemic factors and cultural values – have been ignored by
sociologists.

Catton and Dunlap's survey was done some time ago and there have been significant developments since then.[5] Yet when sociologists talk about the environment they are usually talking about the social environment (as in socialization studies) or the built environment (as in urban studies). They do not often look at the natural environment and it is hard to find natural-environmental questions built into mainstream sociology textbooks or courses. Writing in 1993, 15 years after they carried out the survey just discussed, Dunlap and Catton talk of environmental sociology as a 'new and still small specialisation that represents a deviation from sociology's tendency to ignore environmental problems' (1993:1). Reflecting on their attempt to establish a more ecological approach in sociology they ask 'Were we at all successful in this endeavour? The answer would seem to be an obvious "no"' (p. 9). Not one article on environmental problems, they point out, was published in either of the two main American sociology journals between 1970 and 1990 (p. 19).

Why are sociologists reluctant to get mixed up with the environment? A number of reasons have been put forward. Newby (1991:6) dismisses the possibility that sociologists do not subscribe to environmentalist values. Sociologists *are* troubled by environmental problems. But the rise of ecology is comparable to that of feminism as a new and re-invigorating influence in the discipline. It elicits sympathy from sociologists but few deeds in their private or professional lives to match their concern. However, this only redescribes the problem. It does not explain how it has come about.

A second possibility is that, while on a personal level sociologists are concerned about the environment, academically and professionally they find the greens difficult to deal with because of their catastrophic rhetoric. Some of the doom and gloom alarmism of contributors like the Club of Rome and green activists alienates academics who prefer a more sober, balanced and cautious rhetoric. More significantly, sociologists find explicitly normative analysis, alarmist or not, difficult to deal with. Value-freedom and objectivity are important parts of sociological training. Normative analysis – making prescriptive proposals about what things *should* be like rather than analysing how they *are* – may skate too close to political commitment and value-judgement for some sociologists.[6]

Cotgrove (1991) places more emphasis on the dominance of Marxism in post-war sociology. The dismissal of the environment as a diversionary middle-class issue irrelevant to the class struggle and the pointing of the green finger at industrialism rather than capitalism has led to the exclusion of environmental questions from sociology.[7] If Cotgrove is right, this may go some way towards explaining why the environment has been taken more seriously in the USA, where Marxism has been less influential. It may also help explain the rise of environmental interest in the 1970s and 1980s, a period when Marxist thought went into crisis and decline in the social sciences.

A fourth possible explanation for the apparent inertia of sociologists on environmental issues, again one dismissed by Newby (1991:6), is the ageing research community. Age brings wisdom but also consolidation in fields of expertise and, perhaps, a reluctance to break into new fields or question long-held assumptions. The young are less dedicated to long-held views and allegiances, perhaps more open to finding new interests and less restricted by years of socialization into the appropriate parameters for sociological opinion and research.

A fifth possible argument for sociological inertia on the environment, treated as the most likely by Newby (1991) and Fox (1991), deals with these big assumptions that longstanding sociologists may be reluctant to break with. Their argument is that nature is seen to fall outside the traditional boundaries of sociology and as too politically dangerous. It is part, in fact, of an area that sociology has shunned over the years in order to establish its distinctive identity and its case for a discipline studying the 'social' and giving social explanations for it (see Durkheim 1950). Sociologists reject nature because of the protective social exclusivity they have thrown around their discipline. Furthermore they associate 'nature' with politically controversial arguments which justify racism and sexism on genetic and biological grounds. Newby (1991) and Fox (1991) argue that this heritage has made it difficult in the sociological community to advocate what Benton (1991) calls a 'return of the repressed', of biological and natural factors to sociological explanation. It is what makes sociologists leave the environment, against their better judgement, to natural scientists.

If this explanation is correct, then it suggests that sociological encounters with the environment will entail basic archaeological work on the assumptions of the discipline, bringing nature into the sociological remit, taking risks with the specificity of the discipline and skirting with dangerous political issues around biology and nature.[8]

The structure of the book

The book divides into four parts. The first two chapters look at the relationship between practices in industrial societies and the environment. Chapters 3 and 4 look at environmentalist ideology – its philosophical underpinnings and reasons for its increasing popularity in the 1970s and 1980s. Chapters 5 and 6 look at the implications of ecological ideas for traditional political and social theory. Finally, chapter 7 looks at forms of agency and transition most suitable for furthering green change in the future.

The first chapter looks at limitations of analyses of industrial societies which do not investigate society–natural environment links. It shows how the development of industrial societies is affected by the natural environment and has effects on it. It argues that an adequate understanding of such societies needs to incorporate society–environment relations but that at present sociologists fail to do this. It also looks at a classic ecological analysis of industrialism – the Club of Rome's *Limits to Growth* report – and at criticisms of it. Many of the arguments put forward in the report and in critical appraisals of it are typical of those that come up in debates around environmentalism, and a detailed discussion of them here sets us up well for the rest of the book. The chapter concludes with a discussion of the relationship between development and environmental problems in less developed countries.

The book then goes on, in the second chapter, to look at forms of society and politics more appropriate to sustainability. It argues that capitalist and decentralist solutions proposed by economic liberals and greens respectively are not adequate. The chapter argues for state intervention and global co-ordination to solve environmental problems. I deal here also with changes in levels of consumption and forms of technological adaptation which may help halt ecological degradation.

Chapters 3 and 4 go on to examine environmentalism itself. Chapter 3 looks at the philosophical bases underlying environmental concern. It rejects anthropocentrism, the focusing of moral concern exclusively on humans. It argues that animals should also be of moral concern because of their capacity to experience fulfilment or pain. It argues against deep ecologists' holistic and eco-centric arguments which say that ecosystems, species, plants and other living and non-living things in the environment beyond humans and animals have an intrinsic value and moral standing. I argue that such things are not of intrinsic value or moral worth in themselves because they do not have the sentient capacity to experience life. However they do have an extrinsic value and worth for humans and animals. This chapter goes beyond anthropocentrism in extending moral concern to animals but not as far as eco-centrism because it limits the range of entities in the environment which are said to be of intrinsic value.

Chapter 4 moves on from green philosophy to reasons for the rise in popularity of environmental concern in the post-war period. It discusses political, action, cultural and social explanations for the increasing popularity of the green movement, discussing phenomena such as corporatist closure, electoral systems, the role of environmental groups and science, post-materialism and the new middle class. It concludes that explanations of green concern have to be grounded in material economic and social experience and, in particular, in the environmental problems to which environmentalism is a reaction and which it identifies in its discourse.

Chapters 5 and 6 look at the implications of ecology for traditional political and social theory. Chapter 5 looks at the relationship of ecology to traditional perspectives in political theory such as conservatism, liberalism, socialism and feminism. It argues that ecology cannot, as many greens boast, be a new political theory which renders redundant these old perspectives. Such a claim is one-sidedly arrogant and ignorant of the strengths of the traditions. They are still needed to help work out how to solve environmental problems and to make judgements on non-environmental issues. On the other hand, ecology is not, as some sceptics suggest, open to any political conclusions. Some tenets in traditional political theories, *laissez-faire* for example, are not adequate to the resolution of environmental problems while others, socialist political economy for instance, are. Ecology cannot make a political theory, but it does imply some political conclusions rather than others.

Chapter 6 moves from normative political theory to explanatory social theory. It picks up from some of the concerns of chapter 1 in looking at how relations between society and nature could be conceptualized in a more ecological way than they have been in the past. It discusses the 'ecological complex' of American rural sociologists Dunlap and Catton. This incorporates many of the factors involved in society–nature relations. It argues that 'social constructionism' and 'realism' add an understanding of the relative weighting, balance and the nature of the interaction between these factors. Social constructionism, it suggests, gives too much power to human social processes ethically, epistemologically and ontologically. Ethically, environmentalism is not just concerned about the good of humans but also about entities in the environment itself. Epistemologically, environmental concern is not just something we socially manufacture but something which works up, through social mediation, from the objectivity of environmental problems themselves. Ontologically, the environment is not just an artefact of human mental constructs but of the fitting of objective environmental realities into conceptual constructs. Realism, on the other hand, has a scheme within which both social mediation and the objective properties and causal powers of the environment come through in ethical, epistemological and ontological analyses. It retains, however, an awareness of social mediation which is absent in environmentalist fetishizations of nature.

Finally, chapter 7 looks at forms of agency and transition most suitable for pursuing green change in the future. It looks at political strategies such as education, parliamentary and party politics, green consumerism and green communes. It examines possible social agents like the new middle class, the working class, the unemployed and other new social movements and it looks at the idea that there can be a universal agency for green change. I argue that education and consciousness-changing need to be embedded in material experience. Lifestyle politics (green consumerism and green communes, for instance) is useful. However, because green change has to come through political global co-ordination, parliamentary and party politics must be the main plank of green political strategies. All the agents discussed provide possible social bases for green change but I argue for political rather than social agency. The green movement needs to pursue change through political actors, mobilizing as many social agents behind it as are willing, rather than tying the project to specific social groups. Green parties and the green movement, meanwhile, need to form alliances with socialist and social democratic parties in order to gain power and support the political programmes which are best suited to solving environmental problems.

There are a number of main arguments which run through all this: (1) the advocacy of a more realist or naturalistic (and less strongly social constructionist) sociology which does not focus solely on human society or reduce environmental problems or concern to social functions but sees them as embedded in objective natural-environmental processes and problems; (2) a critique of capitalist and green decentralist solutions to environmental problems and an advocacy of state intervention, global co-ordination, political agency and socialist programmes; (3) a critique of both anthropocentric and eco-centric ethical philosophy in favour of a sentient basis for ethical concern; and (4) an assessment of traditional political theory as revolutionized by, but necessary for, green political thought.

Guide to further reading

At the end of each chapter in this book I give some personal proposed next steps for reading for those who wish to follow up issues raised in that chapter. More detailed and in-depth references on specific issues raised are given in the text and endnotes.

There are a number of books which provide accessible introductions to green ideas. Tim O'Riordan's *Environmentalism* (1981) provides a very thorough introduction to the phenomenon written by a leading respected figure in the field. General sociological discussons of environmentalism include Stephen Cotgrove's *Catastrophe or Cornucopia* (1982) and, more recently, Yearly's stimulating *The Green Case* (1991). The latter includes very useful discussions of the socio-economic and technical bases of environmental problems and of environmental problems in less developed countries. In addition it gives an example of a sociological approach to explaining the rise of environmentalism. From the radical green view there is a proliferation of books presenting green ideas. Andrew Dobson's *Green Political Thought* (1990) is one readable example, and Dobson is the editor of a very useful collection of nicely explained and well-presented extracts from green thinkers, *The Green Reader* (1991). Michael Allaby's *Thinking Green* (1989) is another useful reader. Jonathon Porritt's *Seeing Green* (1986) presents green ideas in a racy heartfelt way. These and other green books do not always back up their arguments strongly enough and are prone to lack adequate consideration of alternative views and possible criticisms of their own perspective, but Dobson in particular does provide a clear and readable introduction to green ideas. For well-written, carefully researched and illuminating empirical studies by environmental historians see Cronon (1983 and 1990), Worster (1986 and 1988) and Crosby (1986).

1

Ecology and Industrialism

One of the obvious areas of sociology in which environmental concerns ought to be considered is the sociology of industrialism, the rationality and practices of industrialism being a repeated object of attention in discussions about the environment. The sociology of industrialism is a longstanding and well-researched field (see Kumar 1978 and Badham 1984) in which environmental issues are highly relevant yet largely excluded. This chapter discusses how such issues are relevant to this area of sociology. It looks at the limits of the sociology of industrialism and at an environmentalist analysis of industrialism. This sets us up for the rest of the book, which is concerned with the interaction between the study of society and politics and the ideas of environmentalism.

Environmental issues need to be more considered in the sociology of industrial societies – both in research and courses. However they are at present generally excluded by the focus of these on the internal requirements, contradictions and reproduction of industrialism. In the first section of this chapter I will outline the main preoccupations of the sociology of industrial societies and the way in which they focus on internal social processes at the expense of external natural-environmental factors. In the second section I will discuss why such factors are relevant to a complete understanding of social processes.

The section following that outlines the main claims of a famous and influential ecological study of industrialism, the *Limits to Growth* report, in order to demonstrate the relevance of ecology and environmental factors to the sociology of industrialism. The subsequent section deals with criticisms of the report. The report's arguments are typical of those in the green literature more generally, and criticisms of it are typical of those often made of green thinking.

Finally I will shift the emphasis from developed industrial nations to less developed countries to show how, in this case also, economic, social and political development is interrelated with external natural-environmental factors and how the latter are integral to a complete sociological understanding of the predicament and future fate of the developing world.

The ecological limits and internalist focus of the sociology of industrialism

Sociologists have tended to focus on the interaction of industrial and social development in the formation and reproduction of industrial societies at the expense of attention to external natural-environmental factors affected by and affecting such processes. The sociology of industrialism is limited in ignoring, first, the environmental consequences of social processes – pollution, for example. Second, in a reverse direction, it ignores the range of factors which affect societal development which are natural as well as social – resource availability for instance.

Industrial and social processes have an effect on the environment and natural environmental factors affect industrial and social development. Yet sociologists focus on the internal social processes of industrial societies at the expense of their interrelationships with the natural environment. As such they are unable to gain a full and realistic understanding of the causes and effects of the industrial and social processes they are interested in. The neglect of the environment in the sociology of industrialism is problematic as such, not only for environmental but also for sociological reasons.

Sociology was founded amidst the establishment and gathering speed of industrialism, and its foundation was oriented to laying down a set of concepts and theories intended to make sense of the developing modern industrial order. Alienation and exploitation, the division of labour and anomie, rationalization and legitimacy were all major defining themes in the work of founding figures like Marx, Durkheim and Weber respectively (see Giddens 1971) and are of enduring concern in contemporary sociology.

The concepts and preoccupations that were developed by the founders of the discipline in the nineteenth century reflected this milieu and have imposed their imprint on sociology since. Sociologists of industrialism like Kumar (1978) and Badham (1984) describe this fact. Sociology textbooks like Lee and Newby (1983) reflect it, examining the interpretations of industrialism made by classical sociological theorists and the contemporary application of those early established preoccupations.

What, then, have been the typical concerns of sociological studies of industrial societies? To what extent have they failed to account for environmental factors? And how are such factors relevant to the explanation of the formation and development of industrial societies?

Industry and society

Maria Hirszowicz (1981:1) defines industrialism as 'the new stage of social organisation in which human life is dominated by industrial production'. Sociologists tend to look at aspects of industrial society (the state, education, ideology and class divisions, for example) in terms of the extent to which they reproduce industrialism, cause it conflict or strife or gain their character from the stage of development of industrial production.

One way of understanding the preoccupations of the sociology of industrialism is to think of them as being concerned with the inter-relationship of industry and society – both the effects of the development of industry on society and of society on industry. Let me take these two different directions of causality in turn.

First, sociologists have been concerned with the effects of industrial production and economic and technological change on social structures and processes. They look, for instance, at the effects of the development of mechanization, economic growth and the factory system on work organization, patterns of residence and migration, the degree of community in social relations, changing forms of political structure and shifts in forms of social structure and social mobility.

Secondly and conversely, they have been interested in the way social structures and processes have an effect on industry and industrial and economic development. For instance, the extent to which social structures and processes, as well as gaining their character from the effects of industrial production, contribute to the reproduction of industrialism (e.g. through education, the family, the state or ideology) or cause it conflict or strife (e.g. as a result of class divisions, loss of state legitimation or ideological dissensus) – these are further issues of prime concern to sociologists.

Richard Badham has argued, along these lines, that the central concerns of the sociology of industrialism are the 'social requirements of industrial development, social structures that either facilitate or hinder the efficient pursuit of industry and the impact of industrial development on society' (Badham 1984:2).

Different areas of study of the industry–society relationship

Let me illustrate my argument about the focus of the sociology of industrialism on the effects of industry on social processes and vice versa by looking in more detail at major concerns in the area.

1 The effects of industrialism on social relations   Sociologists work-ing in this area are often interested in the social implications of technical and economic changes such as mechanization, economic growth and the factory system at the time of the industrial revolution and, more recently, developments such as automation and computer-ization. These are seen to have an effect on: the growth and decline of patterns of residence and migration, first urbanization with industria-lization and later deurbanization with developments such as improved transport, communications and information technology; changes in the depth of social relations from pre-industrial community to aliena-tion, anomie and looser forms of association after industrialization, associated with urbanization and the division of labour; changes in the experience of work and social structure and mobility with the decline of old forms of work and the growth of new occupations; the development of bureaucratic and democratic forms of political system and ideologies and forms of family and education suited to meeting the needs of industrialism.[1]

2 The dynamic of industrialism   Sociologists of industrialism are also concerned with explaining changes with the development of industrial societies arising out of technological change and concomi-tant social changes. Some explanations focus on the shift of industrial capitalism in its 'late' or 'advanced' phases from 'liberal' and '*laissez-faire*' to more 'corporate' or 'monopoly' forms and then, in some, back to 'disorganized' forms. 'Convergence' theories propose an endogenously driven logic of convergence towards common sets of social and cultural institutions among industrial societies as a result of their common industrial character. 'Post-industrialists' see industrial societies as moving into a new era – the 'information society', 'knowledge society' or 'service society' – based on the manufacture of information rather than goods, service industry rather than manu-facturing, white collar rather than blue collar work and post-scarcity, technical knowledge and expertise. 'Post Fordists' see industrial socie-ties as moving not beyond industrialism but from a Fordist mode of industrialism based on mass production, standardization and unifor-mity in economic and social life towards greater diversification, flux and flexibility in production, consumption and social lifestyles. All these explanations are concerned to trace the dialectic between technology and social process, between technical change and new forms of economic organization and social structure.[2]

3 The bases of order and cohesion in industrialism Another area of concern in the sociology of industrial societies has been with the ideological and political bases on which social order, cohesion and compliance are secured and maintained. Sociologists look, for instance, at the role of dominant ideologies in securing normative agreement among dominant and subordinate groups in society. And they examine the way in which states secure and maintain their legitimacy among citizens through appeals to their democratic and representative credentials and by attempting to meet the contradictory demands of different groups in society. Once again the focus is on the relationship between industry and society. It examines the requirements of industrial production and capital accumulation and their relationship to social and ideological institutions and norms which meet those requirements.[3]

4 The reproduction of industrialism Relatedly, sociologists also examine the role of institutions like the family and education system in the biological and social production and reproduction of industrialism. They examine the sexual division of labour behind the production and reproduction of the workforce and their socialization in the family and education system into structures and imperatives of hierarchy, division of labour, competition and achievement appropriate to the smooth running of modern industrial capitalist economies.[4] In other words they examine the relationship between the requirements of industrialism, and its productive base in particular, and appropriate social institutions.

5 The impact of industrialism on work and social structure Sociologists have also been interested in the effects of economic and technical change in industrialism on the nature and experience of work and on the shape of the occupational or social structure. They look, for instance, at the impact of the shift from agricultural and skilled craft production to less skilled assembly-line factory work with machines. They have had an interest in the development of techniques such as Taylorism and scientific management and, subsequently, the effect on types and locations of industry and the work experience of automation, computerization and the information revolution. Job satisfaction or enrichment, degradation and deskilling have been important concerns. Sociologists have been interested in shifts between different sectors of industry – agricultural, manufacturing and service, for instance – and the implications these have for the occupational and class structure in society – the decline of the male, manual, manufacturing worker, for instance, and the growth of white collar and part-time temporary work and the feminization of the labour force.[5]

The main point about these different areas of preoccupation in the sociology of industrialism is that they focus on the relationship between industry and society, whether they perceive causality in one direction or the other. They fail to break out of that relationship to a conceptualization of the relations between industry and society on one hand and the external natural world on the other: how they impact on the external natural world with resultant effects back again and how that external natural world imposes constraints and limits in its own right. I have focused so far on the ecological limits of sociological explanations of industrialism. The same sort of limits exist in relation to criticisms of industrialism.

Critiques of industrialism

Sociologists have not been uncritical of industrialism. From Marx, Weber and Durkheim on they have questioned the capitalist or socialist, individualist or bureaucratic forms that industrialism has taken. They have looked sorrowfully at its centralizing, bureaucratic and alienating tendencies, at division and conflict and at what has been lost as well as gained relative to the past (see Giddens 1971).

But the critique of industrialism has been 'internalist' and has rarely looked at industrialism in its external context. The first sense in which it has been internalist relates to the range of empirical factors of which its conceptual framework extends to taking account. The second relates to the range of theoretical alternatives it incorporates.

The empirical point first: critiques of industrialism have been mostly within a concern with the industrial or social forms industrialism has taken. Exploitation, bureaucratization, anomie and so on all describe phenomena internal to industrial and social relations. The critiques do not generally break out of the industry–society relationship to a framework which assesses the relationship between industry, society and the wider natural environment.[6] This is the first empirical sense in which critiques of industrialism are internalist. They are empirically uninclusive of the range of relationships involved in industry–society–nature processes when they try to build critical appraisals of the merits and limitations of industrial societies.

The second way in which critiques of industrialism are internalist concerns more the range of theoretical alternatives accounted for in criticisms of industrial societies. In addition to not taking the external natural world into account, they have, after some initial hankering for a pre-industrial past, become increasingly focused on alternative paradigms within an acceptance of industrial production and growth to the exclusion of alternatives outside the industrial paradigm. Critiques have been around socialist or capitalist, liberal or collectivist alternative forms of industrialism. They exclude attention to evaluations which come from outside industrialist assumptions and can question industrialism itself as well as the different forms of it. So in a theoretical as well as empirical sense their focus is internal to industry society factors and the paradigm of industrialism and does not extend to a conceptualization of relations external to the industry–society relationship and to alien non-industrial paradigms of reference and evaluation.

Ecology and the sociology of industrialism

Let me summarize the usefulness of ecology for a fuller and more realistic sociology of industrialism, capable of conceptualizing the range of factors involved in the formation and development of industrial and social processes. There are three points: the first concerns the meaning of 'ecology'; the second the traditional focus of sociology; the third the relevance of natural factors identified by ecologists to societal processes of interest to sociologists.

First, 'ecology'. This is usually taken to mean the study of the relationships between humans, plants and animals and between them and their wider environment. In other words it looks not only at the internal societies of species but also at how their character and development forms in interaction with other species and in relation to broader environmental conditions.[7]

Secondly, sociology, on the other hand, is not a particularly ecological discipline in the full sense of this word, because it analyses the internal structures and processes of human societies in isolation from the external natural environment and without paying attention to the relationship between society and external natural factors in the way that ecologists do. Sociologists do look at individuals in their social environment. There has even been a branch of the discipline – human ecology – dedicated to a fuller ecological conceptualization of social

life in the wider context of its physical surroundings.[8] But few sociologists have stretched out to a conceptualization of social life in the
natural environmental context.

These two points so far suggest that sociology does not take full
account of the range of social and non-social factors which impinge
on the formation and development of human societies and that ecology can bring back into sociology a fuller account of such excluded
external natural factors.

This brings us to the third point. What sort of relationship with
society have I suggested that external natural factors have? There are
three ways in which such a relationship can be seen to occur: the first
involves the impact of nature on society; the second the impact of
society on nature; the third the effect of society's impact on nature
back on society again.

First, external natural factors limit the way in which societies
develop. Sociologists have been well aware of the significance of
technological developments, cultural conditions, the existence of specific social groupings and political choices in society as facilitating and
driving social change. Marx, for instance, put great emphasis on the
development of productive forces, the role of emergent class groups
like the industrial bourgeoisie and on dialectical contradiction as
driving through change. Weber complemented this with an emphasis
on the role of ideas, religious ideas in particular, in historical development. Nowadays historians impress on us that directions of change
are not socially predetermined but that within the range of economically and socially permitted alternatives there are political choices
which are another factor in change.[9]

Yet ecologists would want to add the role of natural limits such as
resource availability and finitude as factors affecting societal development. The initial availability of resources will affect a society's industrial and social development. Certain industries are only possible if the
resources on which they rely are available and accessible. This applies
to the early days of British industrialization as much as to the route
that the oil-producing nations and developing third world countries
take now.

In the third world, one factor affecting divergent experiences of
different nations is varying access to resources. In addition, third
world ownership of resources, bio-diversity for instance, is an important source of power in the relationship of less developed countries
with the developed world, which in this example requires access to
bio-diversity for its drugs industries. The availability of specific
resources can, in short, be one determinant of a society's industrial

and economic future, its political power and the social circumstances of its citizens.

Furthermore, the long-term finitude of resources, as well as their initial availability, can cause societies either to choose certain courses of action or be forced to adopt them. This is the issue environmentalists are keen to press on politicians and industrialists in the developed world. As they see it, the finite availability of currently used resources must compel us to find alternative energy sources and perhaps, as a result, different paths of economic development and social lifestyle, an issue to which I shall return in the next chapter. In short, there are natural as well as economic, technological, cultural, social and political limits and influences on societal development.

So natural limits on societal development are one element constitutive of the society–nature relationship from which an 'internalist' sociology distracts us, but which a sociology corrected in its rubric by a more ecological input could bring back in. A second issue is one in which the direction of effect goes not from nature to society but society to nature. Society is not only affected by natural limits but also has an effect on nature in the form of, for example, pollution and the depletion of resources. The pursuit of particular paths of industrial development can lead to the pollution of the air, sea and land. High-profile examples of this might include: CFC and CO_2 emissions involved, respectively, in ozone depletion and global warming; the dumping of sewage and toxic wastes in the sea and in landfill sites and the use of pesticides, fertilizers and such like, all of which affect the land, water and plant and animal life; not to mention car fumes and acid rain and many other examples of the environmental effects of social processes.[10]

Pollution and resource depletion obviously affect 'nature'. They pollute and deplete it! Yet they also have a reciprocal effect on human societies and this is the third area in which the relationship between society and nature can be seen to be operative. Not only does nature place limits on societal development, not only does societal development affect nature, but the effects of societal development on nature rebound on human societies again.

Resource depletion, for example, leads to limits on certain sources of fuel for industrial production. Others may have to be sought out, and production and growth may have to be run down or redirected into areas which can be supported by new forms of energy or resources. This can have an effect on social lifestyles which are shaped in part by patterns of production and growth in the economy. On pollution, ozone depletion is thought to remove ozone protection from the sun's ultraviolet rays which can cause skin cancer. Global warming, caused by CO_2 emissions, is likely to lead to rising sea-levels, loss of land and other climatic effects on the quality of life for humans, such as the accentuated pollution from car fumes in cities. All the other forms of pollution mentioned affect food production or create health risks for humans in a variety of other ways.

In short, the society–nature relationship is constituted by natural limits on society, society's effects on nature and the effects of society's impact on nature as they rebound on society. A sociology which excludes attention to such factors is unable to explain in a complete and realistic way the full effects and causes of societal development, whether in the past, present or future. A sociologically as well as environmentally adequate sociology would have to be more ecological and look not only at the internal structures and processes of human societies; it would also have to look at them externally and in their full ecological context.

The Limits to Growth thesis

Let me look now at a classic ecological analysis of industrialism – the Club of Rome's *Limits to Growth* report (Meadows et al. 1983) – the debate around which is covered only briefly in some of the secondary introductory literature. I hope to illustrate two things: first, the sort of thing a more ecological sociology of industrialism could be getting up to; second, ideas central to environmentalism and typical criticisms of it, both of which are well represented in debates around the report. In other words, a discussion of the report will allow us to see along what lines a more ecological sociology of industrialism could develop and introduce us to some of the main tenets and areas of criticism of environmentalist thinking. My book is centrally about environmentalist ideas and their relation to the study of society and politics. Spending some time on a piece of work which illustrates issues surrounding both is of interest itself and also useful for introducing wider issues which are the concern of this book.

The Limits to Growth report was first published in the early 1970s, when capitalist liberal democracy was plagued by internal crises and criticisms and concerns for civil liberties, peace and the environment were on the rise. At the time, other works significant in the evolution and establishment of environmentalism were published. *Limits to Growth* focused on the predicted results of continuing levels of resource depletion, pollution and population growth.[11] An issue of the green journal *The Ecologist* focused on proposals for alternative, more environmentally friendly forms of society (Goldsmith et al.

1972). E. F. Schumacher's *Small is Beautiful* (1974) combined practical proposals and analysis of third world development with alternative philosophy. It gave to green thinking Buddhism, where *Limits to Growth* brought it computer modelling.

An Italian management consultant, Aurelio Peccei, concerned about the global and interdependent nature of contemporary problems and the inadequate, short-term and national focus of policy-makers, founded the 'Club of Rome', a group of industrialists, business advisers and civil servants with similar concerns. The Club turned to the Massachusetts Institute of Technology (MIT) in the USA, where Jay Forrester and other technologists and systems analysts were developing computer modelling techniques capable of analysing complex interdependencies between variables and projecting different scenarios of change, assuming changes in different variables within the whole (Forrester 1970).

The authors of *The Limits to Growth*, Meadows et al., commissioned by the Club of Rome, adopted such techniques to make predictions about the consequences of continued growth in industrialization, resource depletion, pollution, food production and population growth. They extrapolated from growth in each factor as it had occurred between 1900 and 1970, showing how it would grow if it continued at this rate until the year 2100. They then altered in turn assumptions about how each of the variables would grow, feeding the projections into their computers and seeing what the outcome of each scenario would be.

They found that that the factors they analysed were highly interdependent and that changes to single factors often merely pushed problems on to others. Technical innovations to modify or deal with the consequences of growth in each of the factors, they concluded, could slow but not halt crises which could only be prevented by actual halts in growth.

I will outline the different scenarios they projected before moving on to lessons they drew from such projections and then to criticisms that have been made of the research.

The computer runs

There are seven different permutations that Meadows et al. considered, each of which assume alterations to growth in different combinations of the factors considered: population growth, industrial output, food production, pollution and resource depletion. In each run they assume a solution to the problem that precipitated overshoot and collapse in the previous run.

The first permutation is their 'standard run', in which they assume continued growth on 1900–70 trends in all of the factors. The prediction on this simulation is for dramatic exponential growth in all the variables, leading to 'overshoot and collapse'. High levels of industrialization lead to resource depletion. Depletion and the diversion of capital from investment to the search for resources leads to the collapse of industry and of service and agricultural sectors dependent on it. Lack of food and health services leads to population decline. Halts in growth happen in all these areas well before 2100.

In the second run Meadows et al. assume technological developments which will double resource availability, depletion having been the key factor in collapse on the first run. This time high industrial output leads to unabsorbable pollution levels. Pollution and lack of food lead to an increased death rate. Industrial growth, elongated by the extra resources, still leads eventually to resource depletion.

In the third run they add the assumption of technological developments which can double resource availability (e.g. nuclear power, new techniques for sea-bed mining and the use of low-grade ore) *and* cut resource use to a quarter of present levels (e.g. through new techniques of recycling and reclamation). However unlimited resources does not prevent the same key problem of the previous run – unsustainable pollution levels. The lives of industrial output, food production and service industry are elongated but still eventually collapse, and population is hit again by this.

In the first run depletion was the key problem. The second and third runs assumed solutions to this, but these led to collapse caused by pollution. The fourth run assumes technical solutions to pollution: nuclear power and recycling (which cut down on some polluting emissions) and pollution control, for example. It is assumed these will add a fourfold reduction in pollution to the extra resource availability of the previous run. Resource depletion and pollution crises are averted and population and industrial output rise. However, the latter two factors lead to the exhaustion of arable land through overexploitation and appropriation by industry. This leads to a food shortage crisis. Capital is diverted to agriculture to solve the problem but this leads to the collapse of industrial output. Population falls as a result of food shortages.

The next two runs assume technical solutions to food production and population levels to tackle the food shortage crisis of the last run. The fifth run assumes land yields are doubled by developments such as high-yield grain. Once again this is added to the assumptions about resource availability and pollution control made on the previous runs. Increased food and industrial outputs, however, increase to levels so high that pollution levels rise despite the controls and are again the source of collapse for the same reasons they were in the second and third runs. In the sixth run voluntary birth control which prevents the birth of all unwanted children is assumed. But even this only slows and does not halt population growth, so leading only to the postponement of the food crisis.

The seventh and final run assumes a combination of all the solutions so far outlined: resource availability, pollution control, food production and population control. The result is still overshoot and collapse as a result of land overuse and food shortages, resource depletion and excessive pollution leading to a food production crisis and rising death rate. As with previous runs, solutions on one factor often only push the problem on to another (runs 1–4) and technological solutions slow but cannot halt growth (runs 5 and 6), which still, on Meadows et al.'s calculations, leads to collapse before the year 2100.

Lessons from the Limits to Growth report

I will come to criticisms of the *Limits to Growth,* but let me look first at some general implications which come out of it. In the projected trends identified and the results of the computer runs four main conclusions arise which define the argument of the report and have become of central significance in environmentalist thinking: the first on interdependency; second, the natural limits thesis; third, the notion of exponential growth; fourth, the significance of social as well as technical solutions.

First, interdependency. Meadows et al. argue that the character of a system and each of its parts is constituted by the interdependent relationship between the parts. Different elements are affected by others and each element affects others, often with a reciprocal effect back on itself again. The structure of a system is as much constituted by relationships and the dynamic interactions and 'feedback loops' between different parts of the system as by the parts themselves in isolation:

> Of course, none of the five factors we are examining here is independent. Each interacts with all the others . . . Population cannot grow without food, food production is increased by growth of capital, more capital requires more resources, discarded resources become pollution, pollution interferes with the growth of both population and food. (Meadows et al. 1983:89)

Figure 1.1   *The* Limits to Growth *computer runs*

Standard Run (1): assumes growth in all factors
Industrialization -> resource depletion -> capital diverted from investment
to search for resources -> collapse of industry -> collapse of dependent
service and agricultural sectors -> lack of food and health services ->
population decline

Run (2): assumes problem of depletion solved by high resource
availability
High resource availability -> high industrial output -> high pollution ->
increased death rate -> eventual resource depletion

Run (3): assumes problem of depletion solved by technical developments
High resource availability -> high pollution -> eventual halts in industrial
output, food production and service industry -> high death rate

Run (4): assumes pollution solved by technical developments
Rising population and industrial output -> overexploitation and exhaustion
of arable land -> food shortages -> capital diverted to agriculture ->
collapse of industrial output -> population falls

Run (5): assumes technical development increases land yields
Increased food and industrial outputs -> higher pollution -> higher death
rate -> eventual resource depletion

Run (6): assumes voluntary birth controls reduce population
Voluntary population controls -> insufficient reduction in population ->
food production crisis -> population falls

Run (7): all solutions combined
Land overuse -> food shortages -> resource depletion -> excessive
pollution -> food production crisis -> rising death rate

The MIT team found that each time they altered one variable there
was still eventually a crisis even if after a longer delay than there
would have otherwise been. Sometimes this was because technical
solutions only slowed rather than halted growth, so postponing but
not preventing crises. But at other times it was because solutions on
one factor only offloaded problems onto another where crisis led to
overshoot and collapse. In other words, the different variables were
interdependent and a resolution of problems in one often led to
problems in another. Resolving resource availability problems, for
example, as in the second and third runs, leads to pollution crises

caused by resource-driven industrial growth. Resource availability combined with pollution control, as in the fourth run, also only loads the problem onto another area when over-intensive agriculture and use of arable land for industrial expansion leads to food production problems.

The significance of interdependency is also illustrated in the natural limits thesis, where development in society is seen to be constrained by limits in the natural world and in the social versus technical solutions thesis where problems in the natural environment are seen to have causes in processes in the social world. Not only are different socio-economic processes interlinked, implying the need for interdisciplinary social science, so too are natural and social processes, suggesting that interdisciplinarity should spread also to relations between the natural and social sciences.

So one thing that comes out of *The Limits to Growth* is that problems are not isolated but are part of a bigger context and related to other issues and problems. Changes in one part of a system are linked to changes in another. The emphasis on interdependency runs through explanations and prescriptions in green thinking in general and is by definition what 'ecology' is all about. In some cases interdependency between parts leads to a stronger, holistic position which sees the whole as more than the sum of the parts.[12] The ontology of interdependency is reflected in Meadows et al.'s choice of method. They use a systems analysis approach and computer modelling capable of comprehending and charting complex and multiple changing links and relationships. It is also reflected in their prescriptions, which are geared to interdependence and are distinctively global and co-operative in character especially when compared to decentralist self-sufficiency proposals such as those of Goldsmith et al. (1972).[13]

Meadows et al. put particular purchase on the necessity for a long-term and systems understanding of problems when so many of us in everyday life and policy-making take a short-term immediate perspective, both over space and time. We look for short-term solutions to the most proximately obvious problems rather than longer-term solutions with an eye to the relation of proximate problems to others less immediately pressing on our attentions yet no less objectively important.

The second important issue to come out of the Club of Rome report is the natural limits to growth thesis. Perhaps the main conclusion of the report is that growth in industrial societies is not compatible with the finite nature of the planet's resources and ability to carry population and absorb pollution. The report points to the unsustainability of present levels of growth in 'population, industrialisation,

pollution, food production and resource depletion' (p. 23). The food
and resource needs of people cannot be met indefinitely over certain
population levels because land runs out or is made infertile by
overuse and non-renewable resources are exhausted. Waste produced and pollution caused by production to meet human needs
cannot be absorbed and transformed into safe forms by the world's
ecosystem beyond certain limits. The resource and food supplying
and pollution and waste-absorbing capacities of the earth are
naturally finite. Population and industrial output pursued indefinitely
will exhaust natural limits in all these respects because of human
food and resource needs and pollution that comes with growth in
these factors. You cannot, in short, pursue infinite growth in a finite
world.

Some of the computer simulations described by Meadows et al. fail
to avoid crisis because resolutions to problems in one area create
problems in another, as highlighted in the discussion of interdependency above. Sometimes, though, it is because technological solutions
only take the edge off problems of resource depletion, pollution, food
production, over-population or industrial output and stall crisis until
later. Problems are about growth beyond certain limits, and technical
solutions slow growth and delay the date at which limits are reached
rather than bringing growth down to levels compatible with finitude,
since this requires halting growth altogether.

All this is a major theme in wider environmentalist thinking. Greens
emphazise the absoluteness and unavoidability of natural limits and
the futility of continuing with growth on a planet where there are
natural and unavoidable limits on how far it can go.

The third issue to come out of the Club of Rome report is the idea
of 'exponential growth'. This is a notion that lies behind Meadows et
al.'s analysis of existing trends and on which many of their extrapolations are based. The report gives a startling illustration to explain the
meaning of the term.

> Suppose you own a pond on which a water lily is growing. The lily plant
> doubles in size each day. If the lily were allowed to grow unchecked, it
> would completely cover the pond in thirty days, choking off the other
> forms of life in the water. For a long time the lily plant seems small, and
> so you decide not to worry about cutting it back until it covers half the
> pond. On what day will that be? On the twenty-ninth day of course. You
> have one day to save your pond. (Meadows et al. 1983:29)

This can be read as a metaphor for the planet-wide situation, the pond
symbolizing the planet and the lily, say, pollution. Linear growth
involves growth by a constant amount over a constant time period,

the lily growing by a metre square each day, for instance. It occurs incrementally and by the same amount in each same time period. But exponential growth occurs when a quantity increases by a constant percentage of the whole over a constant time period – the lily, say, doubling in size each day. This can produce immense numbers very quickly and in quantities which escalate more and more massively at each stage. Meadows et al. argue that population, food production, industrialization, pollution and resource depletion are increasing in an exponential manner.

At each stage growth jumps dramatically and at each stage the size of the jump itself grows fantastically bigger. Final collapse can come very suddenly with a huge exponential leap soon after the rate of growth seemed to be way off causing crisis – the syndrome of the twenty-ninth day. Current growth levels can appear deceptively less problematic than they are, and when growth is curving up exponentially curbing it is something you cannot leave until you are quantitatively even halfway to crisis as over time this may be the eleventh hour. The concept of exponential growth explains the vision of sudden catastrophic crisis in much green rhetoric and the alarmism in the face of apparently easily containable problems that many greens are criticized for.

The fourth and final outcome of *The Limits to Growth* which is of note is the emphasis on social rather than technical solutions. Greens have continued to emphasize the report's stress on the inadequacy of technical fixes – technological solutions formulated within existing economic and social practices, values, lifestyles and levels of growth which are not compatible with natural limits. On the runs 3–7, summarized in figure 1.1, a number of technological solutions to problems such as resource depletion, pollution or food shortages are proposed. In each case crisis still occurs because the solutions only sustain growth for longer and so stall overshoot, rather than running down growth which is the real problem.

Technical solutions to resource depletion in runs 3 and 4 merely allow growth to continue in other sectors (industrial output, pollution, population and food production) which leads to collapse due to pollution and its effects or food shortages. In run 5 technological developments which increase food production create pollution problems due to growth in the other areas as a result of food holding up. In fact pollution becomes so inflated as a result of the new boosts to resource availability and food production that even technical innovations of the sort proposed in run 4 cannot contain it. In this case not only is crisis pushed into a second area by technological innovations which sustain growth in the first, but in the second area technology is inadequate to containing the problem. The same goes for run 6, on which the birth control fixes proposed are simply not sufficient to bring down population and avert a food crisis.

In short, technical solutions fail either because they sustain growth to overshoot in other areas (e.g. fixes on resource availability, pollution and food in runs 3–5) or because they are ineffective in holding back growth where they are supposed to (e.g. pollution and birth controls in runs 5 and 6). In both cases the problem proves to be continuing growth in a finite system. Technical solutions which attempt to sustain growth or vainly try to curb it are inadequate to the resolution of problems of resource availability, pollution, food production, population and industrial output because they do not deal with the root problem, which is growth itself in a system in which there are natural limits.

There are optimists who have faith in human abilities to produce technologies which have not yet been developed but which could sustain growth without the resource depleting and polluting effects of older technologies. These are regarded by Meadows et al. and others like Trainer (1985) with caution. Relying on the faith that environmentally friendly technologies can be developed on a scale that would allow us to continue existing lifestyles without the existing problems of growth is seen to be a risky business. A surer solution is seen to be attacking root causes: social systems and values based on growth. The restraining of growth to levels compatible with the planet's supplying, carrying and absorbent capacities is required. This requires the rolling back of economic objectives and social life-styles on which growth is based – social rather than technical solutions.

These, then, are four main principles of central significance in *The Limits to Growth* and in environmentalist thinking in general: that problems are interdependent and require across-the-board thinking and action; that growth is exponential and so in need of earlier rather than later remedies; that there are natural limits to growth which cannot be avoided by solutions which try to prolong growth; and that technical solutions are inadequate without social changes also.

The ideas of natural limits to growth and social rather than technical solutions to environmental problems are of particular significance for sociology. The first suggests that natural environmental factors are relevant to the study of society and the second that sociology has a role to play in the resolution of environmental problems. The natural limits thesis suggests that sociologists could provide a more realistic and complete analysis of the range of factors affecting the development of social systems if they paid more attention to natural as well as economic, social and political factors. Furthermore, if environmental problems have social as much as technical origins, then social scientists have as much to offer in their resolution as natural scientists and technologists. The analysis of the patterns of social life which prop up industrial growth or which would be appropriate for greater sustainability calls out for sociological expertise. At present, however, sociologists are reluctant to include nature within a wider ecological conceptualization of the range of factors relevant to the study of society or to treat environmental problems as an appropriate area for sociological study.

Criticisms of *The Limits to Growth*

Let me turn now to criticisms of *The Limits to Growth*. These are instructive for two reasons. First, they expose limitations in the report. Given the compelling nature of the report's findings and its influence, it is important to give critical appraisals of it serious and open-minded consideration. Second, criticisms of the report are typical of those made of wider environmentalist thinking. It is worth dwelling on them as criticisms of environmentalist thinking as a whole because they bear on the concern of this book with this more general phenomenon.

There are many places in which criticisms of the Club of Rome report are covered or made.[14] Some criticisms address a distortion of its arguments rather than what it really says. Some are as one-sided, lacking in open-mindedness and loaded with ideological bias as they accuse the report of being. Others, though, are more balanced, open and objective, and I will focus on one such response, Cole et al.'s (1973) *Thinking About the Future*, although misrepresentation and ideological closed-mindedness creep in even here at moments.

There are six areas of criticism of the report that I will address. These concern: (1) the timescale within which it predicts disaster will strike; (2) its pessimism and fatalism; (3) the limits of systems dynamics and computer modelling; (4) flaws in the data used in these methods and their presentation as scientific by Meadows et al.; (5) the class interests and ideological bias behind its conclusions; (6) the aggregative way in which it analyses global averages and is insensitive to regional differences and the specific situation of less developed countries.

The first problem can be dealt with swiftly as it has been widely accepted as valid by greens and the Club of Rome. Meadows et al. predicted crisis by the year 2100 and probably within 100 years of the date of publication of the report in the early 1970s. The Club and most greens now accept that while they think crisis could occur in one of the scenarios outlined by the report if avertive action is not taken promptly they do not think it will come anything like as soon as this.

Perhaps the most frequently and forcefully put criticism is of the pessimism of the report, the second criticism mentioned above.[15] The extrapolative method used by Meadows et al. focuses on physical limits and assumes existing rates of growth and technological innovation. It excludes humans' technological and political capacity to adapt. This is seen by critics to lead to pessimistic and fatalistic conclusions which are factually implausible yet encourage self-fulfilling prophecy by spreading fatalism, gloom and inertia rather than spurring action.

Meadows et al. extrapolate from rates of growth between 1900 and 1970 and assume growth continuing at similar rates into the future. They then calculate what the consequences of such continuing growth would be. As we have seen, their conclusions are that there would be crises of overshoot and collapse whatever way the different variables are altered to create changes in the system. However, the growth areas and feedback loops affecting growth rates which they incorporate into their calculations do not include technological development or political action – human-led feedbacks which could alter rates of growth. Different technological changes are assumed in the runs but human creativity and adaptation and improvements on existing technological responses are not built in as feedback loops. This leads, according to critics, to a set of conclusions which are inevitably doom-laden and fails to take account of human ingenuity and determination to alter rates of growth as they are assumed in the different variables calculated.

It is argued that a similar lack of technological optimism was evident in the predictions of Malthus and other eighteenth- and nineteenth-century economists. Yet the crises these figures predicted were averted by changes in birth control, colonization, trade and technical progress which it was beyond the capacity of someone living in their historical context to foresee (Cole et al. 1973:140–1, 153–4).

In short, pessimism and fatalism and a lack of faith in human adaptive capacities are built into Meadows et al.'s extrapolative method and the factors chosen to include as feedback loops. This is seen to have led to negative conclusions. Such conclusions, it is argued, have potentially disabling consequences for policy solutions. Pessimism and doom-mongering may lead to a feeling among people that nothing can be done and subsequently to a self-fulfilling inertia and lack of action (Cole et al. 1973:ch. 14).

There is truth and error in this criticism. It is certainly true that Meadows et al. exclude adaptability from their calculations and even that the authors are unconvinced that adaptation will occur. But the very purpose of their research is to show what will happen if it does not. This is not to say that adaptation will not occur but that the consequences, if it does not, will be of the sort outlined. Meadows et al.'s models are warnings rather than predictions. Critics (e.g. Cole et al. 1973:209–10) are mistaken to read into predictions about the outcomes of modelled variables based on what are deliberate assumptions, predictions about what will necessarily happen in reality. In reality political and technological feedbacks may avert crisis. The models give predictions about what will happen if adaptation does not occur. In this sense critics miss the point when they accuse Meadows et al. of not building into their models social and technical ameliorative feedback loops (Cole et al. 1973:213). Such an exclusion is the whole point of the exercise.

In a level-headed assessment which deals with what *The Limits to Growth* actually says, Page argues (Cole et al. 1973) that the MIT models

> are not attempting to predict The Future, but to show the possible consequences of present trends and relationships continuing without drastic change. Indeed the message of most of the doomsday authors is not that forecasts are necessarily expected to materialise – but that they could do so if appropriate action is not taken now. (Cole et al. 1973:172)

The same could be said of green espousals in general. They are not usually deterministic predictions of doom (although sometimes they are) but warnings of what will happen if we do not act. They are calls to action rather than resignation to the lack or ineffectivity of it.

A third area of criticism is of the systems dynamics and computer modelling methods used by the *Limits to Growth* team. While models can be misused or go askew when based on poor data, there are some inherent problems in using them in the first place. Models are simplified constructions which pick out particular features and ignore others in order to create a manageable picture to analyse and deal with. The problem is whether the selectivity and exclusions involved create a simplicity which outweighs in the results it can deliver the imperfection and distortions it creates (Cole et al. 1973:23–4). Because of the interdependency in systems outlined by Meadows et al., a conglomeration of many tiny exclusions from a model could accumulate to lead to simulations which go far away from what would happen in reality when the effect of complex details that have been left out is amplified many times (Cole et al. 1973:30). Similarly inclusions may become overweighted with an effect on the conclusions out of proportion to their actual significance in reality (Cole et al. 1973:31).

These are problems inherent in any attempt to use modelling techniques for analysing systems. A fourth set of criticisms focuses not so much on modelling itself as on putative problems in the way in which Meadows et al. built or present their modelling method. There are two criticisms here, the first referring to the adequacy of the data used and the second to the way in which Meadows et al. present the scientificity and accessibility of their method. On the first criticism it is argued that, regardless of the intrinsic virtues or lack of them of systems analysis and modelling, these techniques in the hands of Meadows et al. are flawed because they are based on inadequate data and empirical information (Cole et al. 1973:28, 31, 109, 177). Furthermore, systematic rounding and approximations in numerical values might accumulate to lead to significant miscalculations in the final results (Cole et al. 1973:30). These problems become particularly amplified when extrapolations are made on the basis of the data along exponential rather than just linear lines so that what might only be small imperfections in numerical values at first become much bigger when multiplied exponentially (Cole et al. 1973:32).

One test of the accuracy of forecasting is to look at previous attempts at forecasting and the extent to which they have been accurate. Cole et al. argue that population forecasting has always been inaccurate and that there is no reason to suggest that modern attempts are going to be any more successful (Cole et al. 1973:171–2). The problem with forecasting is that it can only be based on extrapolations from present trends with no attention to possible future interactions which cannot be foreseen. As such we can only predict what will happen if humankind continues to act as at present (Cole et al. 1973:189).

In defence of the MIT team it has to be repeated that this less ambitious project is all they were trying to do. It was not their intention to predict the future fate of humankind, but only to say what it is likely to be if existing trends continue without changes we could foresee or not. The critique of forecasting is fair as a critique of forecasting but not as a criticism of the Club of Rome report.

So the first criticism of the way in which the MIT team used their models is based on the accuracy of data. A second criticism on this question concerns the public presentation of systems dynamics and computer modelling by Meadows et al. There are two points here. One is that Meadows et al. give an overly scientific appearance to research which essentially leaves out adaptive capacities, is oversimplified, empirically inadequate and involves a lot of subjective value judgement (Cole et al. 1973:12). Computers, numbers and graphs are used to give a scientific appearance to the work. Far too many complex interactions are included, most of which are unnecessary and obstruct accessibility but give the appearance of a systematic scientific thoroughness (Cole et al. 1973:28). The second point on Meadows et al.'s presentation of their research method is that they falsely present as accessible, transparent and publicly testable a mode of research which is actually not easily available to the non-numerate or those unused to computers (Cole et al. 1973:213–4).

The point about the false scientificity with which Meadows et al. present their research is linked to the related fifth criticism that their research is, firstly, value-laden rather than objective and detached and, secondly, that it reflects the particular interest of a certain stratum or class grouping in society.

Cole et al. argue that far from being the detached objective scientific thing they make it out to be, the computer modelling used by Meadows et al. is run through with biased value judgements and assumptions. For instance, the variables which Meadows et al, choose to feed into their computer runs reflect their pessimistic bias. If the initial assumptions are altered and different ones fed in, the result of the computer runs can look quite different and more positive for the future (Cole et al. 1973:133–4, 176–7). The pessimistic bias in particular was influenced by the context in which they were working, one in which there was a widespread millennial mood of discontent with the extremes to which advanced industrial societies had gone (Cole et al. 1973:214). This is accentuated by instances where data on growth are insufficient to allow trend analysis and so have been substituted for by subjective estimates (Cole et al. 1973:190). Furthermore, it is argued that not only is their historical analysis informed by pessimistic bias but that their prescriptions for the future are influenced by prior ideological preferences for non-material values and pursuits which are out of line with scientific neutrality and objectivity (Cole et al. 1973:207). The allegation that environmentalism is an ideological project concerned with politics that has been disguised as science concerned with the natural world has become a typical criticism of environmentalism as a whole.

The bias of Meadows et al., however, is seen to consist of more than an expression of a generalized pessimism about the march of advanced industrialism fed into computers. More damning than this, it is seen to reflect also the class interests of a particular social stratum in society.

One criticism dealt with by Cole et al. (1973:139, 142–3, 154–6) is that environmental concern and hostility to growth reflects the biased interests of the materially well-off. To be concerned with the environment and non-material concerns which break with growth, development and material well-being reflects the interests of those who already benefit from the latter. It is not sensitive to the needs of those who would benefit from growth more than environmental protection – the poorer sections of industrial societies or people in less developed countries. Furthermore, proposals which emphasize the need for controls on population rather than consumption, and so place the onus of change on third world countries with high birth rates rather than on the high-consumption nations of the 'North', further bolster the idea that concern for the environment is a luxury of the rich of the developed world.

Two issues come out of this which are relevant to environmentalist thinking in general. The first is the idea that environmentalism is, as a matter of empirical fact, very much the concern of middle-class people and that, therefore, it is they who are likely to be the main agent of change in the future politics of environmentalism. I will discuss this contention further in chapters 4 and 7. The second issue concerns the implications that environmentalist ideas and proposals have for equality, both within industrial societies and between industrial and less developed countries. I will return to this in the last section of this chapter. But as with the previous points Cole et al. again raise in relation to the Club of Rome report criticisms and controversies which are central to debates around environmentalism as a whole.

The sixth and final set of criticisms link issues to do with method and equality. Meadows et al., it is argued, have an over-aggregated model of world trends which makes them insensitive to regional differences and the specific situation of third world countries (an oversight acknowledged in later Club of Rome sponsored work by Mesarovic and Pestel 1975). Furthermore proposals for no-growth, it is argued, are also over-aggregated and do not differentiate on the basis of what the composition and distribution of growth should be.

The trends that Meadows et al. fed into their computer runs and from which they extrapolated about the future were based on aggregated world average rates of growth (Cole et al. 1973:27–8). In other words they calculated growth across the world but did not distinguish between differences in growth rates in different parts of the world.

This is empirically problematic because it does not allow for sensitivity to local conditions – famine or drought, for instance – which may have a specific effect on growth in some areas and not others and so affect local and general growth rates. Cole et al. calculated quite different results from dividing up growth regionally in different ways (Cole et al. 1973:119–21).

Furthermore, on prescriptions for change, no-growth proposals are seen by critics to avoid real, more complex problems about the composition and distribution of growth. Some forms of growth, for instance, may not be environmentally problematic and in need of curbing. Growth in some services – health or education, for example – may be less environmentally problematic than growth in some sectors of manufacturing industry. In addition, growth in some regions – e.g. the affluent 'North' – may require rolling back while in others – e.g. less developed countries – social considerations may dictate that it should continue and expand. In addition to physical questions about natural limits there are social and political issues to do with social choices and equality, choice of areas of growth and the distribution of growth. The focus on physical limits and no-growth does not allow us to take these into account.

These criticisms raise three points which are central to environmentalism as a whole. First, environmentalism is often regarded as insensitive to the particular needs of third world countries where growth needs are acute. Third world politicians are frequently incensed by calls to curb growth which has adverse environmental effects when they come from environmentalists in countries which have already developed industrially using environmentally problematic practices and can now afford to find less environmentally problematic solutions. As such, physical issues to do with the environment raise social and political issues to do with equality.

Second, no-growth proposals are also seen to be insufficiently complex in other respects – ignoring the varying environmental implications of different forms of growth as well as the different growth patterns and needs of different social groups.

Third, and continuing from the implications of the first point about the third world, environmentalism often involves prescriptions about desirable forms of economic, social and political organization on the basis of stipulations about natural limits and without sufficient attention to non-environmental social and political choices. We may want to choose certain social and political preferences (growth to alleviate poverty, for example) which are environmentally damaging, and radical ecology often does not allow for this. I shall return to this in chapters 2 and 5. My view is that environmentalism is necessary but insufficient for defining what a sustainable society should look like. This is because this involves social and political choices about issues like distribution and liberty, which are not specifically environmental, as well as attention to physical factors which are. There can be a green input into political theory but because thinking about how society and politics should be organized involves more than environmental criteria there cannot be such a thing as a green political theory, a political theory built on ecological stipulations alone.

Implications for the sociology of development

Sociologists of industrialism tend to focus on the developed industrial nations at the expense of their place in the wider global context, in particular their relationship to the less developed world and the way this relationship shapes the fates of both. However, there is a subbranch in sociology, the sociology of development, which does look at this question and, in particular, at industrialization in the third world (see Harrison 1988). The sociology of development is a well-established and important area of sociological study and, I wish to argue, one in which attention to ecological issues is very illuminating.

One criticism made of environmentalism, as I have mentioned, is that it is something that only the developed world has the luxury to be concerned with. Less developed countries have enough on their plates trying to foster development and growth and eradicate poverty, starvation and inequality without worrying about environmental consequences. They have too many pressing material concerns on their hands for them to worry about non-material issues.

Take one example. Developed countries want to phase out chlorofluorocarbons (CFCs) which are used in, among other things, aerosols and fridges. When CFCs are released into the ozone layer and exposed to the sun's radiation they decompose and release chlorine compounds which break up this layer. This is worrying because the ozone layer screens the earth from the sun's radiation which, in sufficient doses, can cause skin cancer and affect food production (Yearly 1991:12–16). However, critics of green fears argue that poorer nations like China and India need more fridges and cannot afford expensive alternatives to CFCs. They do not have the luxury that the richer developed nations have to worry about such environmental issues.

There is a vital point here about the importance of development and material improvement which no-growth or low-growth greens in the developed world have to take seriously. Yet some greens would defend their concern with environmental problems in the face of criticisms about the greater importance of third world development needs. Many greens are in fact active in political struggles over North–South relations and in third world-concerned activities like 'The Other Economic Summit' (see Ekins 1986). Others would argue that environmental issues rather than being a distraction from development and the well-being of less developed countries (LDCs) actually have a very important bearing on these.

Three reasons why this is the case might be mentioned. First, ecological crises such as the greenhouse effect and the depletion of the ozone layer are so global and potentially so grave that they affect everyone, North and South, and could be more serious and less trivial than criticisms from LDCs imply.

Second, developing countries also need to pay particular attention to environmental questions because of the environmental effects of industrialization. Countries North and South are suffering the results of the developed world pursuing industrialization blind to its environmental consequences. Now that knowledge of some of these consequences and their causes is available, planning alternative paths of industrial development with a long-term view which takes account of them makes sense from the point of view of LDCs themselves.

Third, the environmental effects of industrial development are accentuated in the third world by the dependent position of many LDCs and have serious impacts not only on the environment and local populations but also on development itself.

I will say more about the third point below. All three points, though, suggest that ecological insights are important to the sociology of development, to explaining the position of LDCs and to planning development.

I will focus now on the link between the dependent position of LDCs and environmental problems they face and on the way in which these problems have implications for development. First, I will mention specific issues such as environmental protection regulations, waste disposal and pesticides. I will discuss how these and other issues tie in with economic relations of dependency. Aid and debt are also relevant to this question. I will then say something, with reference to examples of soil use and deforestation, about the way in which environmental problems can affect development in the third world. Finally, I will move on from explanations of environmental problems in LDCs to proposals on development which attempt to be sensitive to environmental degradation.

Explanations of development and environmental problems in LDCs

The dependent position of third world countries on the North makes them especially vulnerable to the adoption of environmentally damaging practices. Dependency theorists emphasize that, despite the ending of direct colonial political rule, economic, political and cultural dependency on, and domination by, developed countries continues in the third world.

Less developed economies depend, for instance, on investment from the North. One way they can attract it is with relaxed environmental regulations. Companies find this congenial because it cuts down on pollution control costs and means they can avoid having to make awkward changes to meet tighter regulations in the North. Many businesses may choose to stay in the North and tighten up their practices or try to evade regulations there. Where they do relocate to less developed parts of the world it may be to do with factors such as low labour costs or the availability of raw materials rather than looser environmental regulations. But looser regulations may still be one incentive that LDCs use, and they mean that once companies are there, regardless of what determined their decisions about industrial location in the first place, they and indigenous companies are freer to neglect the environmental impact of their practices (Yearly 1991:157–61).

Many third world countries, because of their comparatively loose regulations and the tightening of standards in the North, have become dumping grounds for hazardous toxic waste from the North. In fact some LDCs may positively encourage the importation of waste and drastically undercut disposal prices charged in the North because it is a source of much-needed foreign exchange (Yearly 1991:36). A similar situation exists in the case of fertilizers and pesticides, where restrictions on the manufacture and use of agro-chemicals is loose in many third world countries. These chemicals get into the land, water, animals and local people and ultimately into the stomachs of people in the North through the food they eat. Chemicals which people in the North have banned are still used in the South creating a 'circle of poison' where people in developed countries still end up eating them in imported third world cash crops (Yearly 1991:168–9; Weir and Shapiro 1981).

Yearly (1991:174–7) also points out how the web of dependency spun by third world aid and debt creates environmental problems. The financial interests of first world creditors and the development needs of debtors combine to ensure that loans are usually dedicated to big projects geared to rapid industrial development, with little thought for environmental impact. Furthermore, debt has to be paid off in foreign exchange so third world countries are keen to develop industries like cash cropping and mining where production can be exported to bring this in. These, of course, are industries which have a large environmental impact because they involve the use of soil and resource extraction.

Industrialization is an environmentally messy business at the best of times. But LDCs are dependent on attracting investment and foreign exchange from the North. This dependence may lead to the relaxation of environmental regulations and the promotion of damaging forms of production, so making LDCs especially prone to ecological degradation. This rooting of environmental problems in dependency is one reason why some greens are keen to advocate economic self-sufficiency, a point to which I shall return below.

All this is not only an environmental problem. It is also a development problem because environmental degradation can hit development strategies. The dependence and poverty of many LDCs lead them into, for example, agricultural practices which degrade the soil and ultimately damage crop and food production. Agribusinesses move into third world countries because their climate is favourable for the production of certain crops for export. They tend to go for maximum production with little regard for its effect on soil fertility. When yields fall on degraded soils, the companies can move on to new soils, but the locals are left with infertile land (Yearly 1991: 166–8).

Conroy and Litvinoff (1988) argue that major environmental problems in the South are deforestation and soil erosion. Food production which depends on indigenous natural resources is a major activity for rural third world people, and industries are frequently based on timber, paper, rubber and cotton textiles. As such the degradation or hyper-exploitation of these resources to the extent that further production becomes undermined is not only an environmental problem but also undermines economic development. Poverty leads the rural poor to over-exploit and degrade their environments, as do the high consumption levels of the rich North which puts heavy pressure on the third world's natural resources for development.

Proposals on development and environmental problems in LDCs

I have focused so far on explanations which analyse the relationship between development problems and environmental degradation. Let me turn now to proposals put forward to overcome these and foster what is known as 'sustainable development'. I will mention four: no-growth strategies, de-development of more developed countries, self-reliance and appropriate technology.

The first proposal is for the global slowing or halting of growth in line with natural finitude. Green no-growth proposals are much criticized by advocates of the needs of LDCs. On the explanatory side aggregated world average data in the *Limits to Growth* report failed to distinguish between different rates of growth and development needs in different parts of the world. This is also the case with no-growth proposals on the normative side (see Barkenbus 1977). Critics argue that developed countries with the highest rates of growth should shoulder the burden for slowing growth, whereas LDCs with greater development needs have a case for pursuing higher rates of growth within a context of globally slowed growth.

This leads to the second proposal for rolling back growth in a way which is sensitive to the development needs of third world countries. The proposal here is for the restriction of no-growth strategies to the developed world, while allowing growth to continue in LDCs (see Daly 1973). This proposal rests on a belief that the problem of third world development lies with the overdevelopment of the rich North rather than the underdevelopment of the South and that environmental problems are primarily due to high consumption in the rich countries rather than, say, population growth or the drive to develop in the South. The solution is to involve an accent on the North's de-development to allow for development in the South (see Caldwell 1977; Trainer 1985).

Greens challenge the idea that LDCs should be striving to reach the same levels of material consumption as the developed North (see Trainer 1985). These levels create problems for both development and the environment. On development, poverty is a result of affluence. Natural bases for development are damaged by over-exploitation of resources to provide goods for consumption by the rich. On the environment, the natural limits thesis suggests that only certain levels of growth and consumption are compatible with the finite resources of the planet. Natural limits will not permit all countries in the world to sustain consumption and growth at the levels at which they occur in the developed world.

Modernizers argue that the solution to global inequality is more growth and a bigger cake. Greens argue that the global ecosystem cannot sustain a bigger cake. There are natural as well as social limits to growth and the planet cannot carry all the world's population consuming at the Western rate. An answer which is compatible with globally moderated growth but also allows for development in the third world and a distribution of shares in finite goods is for the developed world to consume less or 'de-develop'. The point is for all to consume at a sustainable level and not for some to consume at such a level that natural limits do not allow the others to have an adequate share.

However, there is a problem with this which leads to the third proposal for reconciling development with protection of the environment. The problem is that restricting no-growth strategies to the developed world while allowing growth to continue in LDCs fails to account for the dependency of LDC development on growth in developed countries. LDCs rely, for instance, on markets for export earnings and on the attraction of capital, management and technology from the developed world.

The third alternative which deals with this and is increasingly popular is a combination of 'sustainable development' (development which in the words of the Brundtland report 'meets the needs of the present without constraining the ability of future generations to meet their own needs'[16]) with self-reliance. Self-reliance is needed to break with the dependency problem of the second proposal (see Barkenbus 1977).

Self-reliance is also a central objective of the fourth proposal for overcoming development and environment problems in LDCs – 'appropriate technology' (Schumacher 1973). This involves the use in development strategies of technology which is appropriate to the needs, culture and abilities of local populations and sensitive to their environment, rather than built according to the abilities and interests of outside parties who import it and, because they can move on, are not hit by the local environmental effects of their practices. Advocates of appropriate technology argue that development in LDCs based on imported Western technology, culture and practices is inappropriate because it is not fitted to the specific abilities, strengths and skills of indigenous LDC populations. Their development continues, therefore, to be dependent on first world interests, paternalism and expertise. Yet first world paternalism tends to obstruct as much as foster development because it relies on factors such as low third world labour costs and, as we have seen, is over-exploitative of third world environments, so in the long term undermining development.

Appropriate technology, on the other hand, is sensitive to the environment in two related ways. First, it fosters indigenous self-reliance. Local populations should be able to develop without dependence on outside help. Therefore they will bear the effects, environmental or social, of their choice of technology and will have an interest, in a way that an external unaffected body does not, in pursuing socially and environmentally benign paths of development and technological choice. Second, it is argued that appropriate technology which fits local circumstances and abilities will usually be smaller in scale and less disruptive of localities.

These last few points have taken us from explanatory critiques of industrialism to normative proposals for sustainability. Let me now move on more fully to this concern in the next chapter. Here I shall discuss environmentalist proposals for the sustainable society and how this may be a relevant area for study and discussion in sociology and the social sciences.

Guide to further reading

There are both advocacies and criticisms of *Limits to Growth* in which the authors have clearly not read the report. Why this is the case confounds me because (for all its flaws) the book is brief, readable and stimulating. The best way to read further is to read the report itself. Some critiques of the report suffer from overdoses of ideological rage. The best critical assessment is Cole et al.'s *Thinking about the Future* (1973) although even here there are moments of misrepresentation and prior ideological antipathy creeps in. The first part of the book deals with technical criticisms and the latter part with ideological assumptions. Especially useful are chapters 1, 2, 9 and Pt II, a readable and mostly level-headed set of discussions. Chapters 5 and 1 of Yearly's *The Green Case* (1991) provide very good introductions to the political and economic dimensions of environmental problems in LDCs. I have found Barkenbus's article (1977) on slowed growth in Pirages's *The Sustainable Society* collection a useful discussion of the implications of lower growth proposals for third world countries. Adams's *Green Development* (1991) provides a more recent survey of the literature. Michael Redclift has written widely on sustainable development from a left-wing point of view, for example in *Development and the Environmental Crisis* (1984) and *Sustainable Development* (1987). Influential contributions which have inspired followers and critics include the Brundtland Report's globally oriented *Our Common Future* (WCED 1987) and Schumacher's more locally oriented advocacy of intermediate technology in *Small is Beautiful* (1973).

2

The Sustainable Society

The *Limits to Growth* thesis suggests that there are natural as well as social factors constraining and shaping the way that society develops, to which sociologists need to be sensitive. It also suggests that present rates of growth in the developed world will have to be rolled back whether by choice or by necessity caused by exhaustion of the earth's carrying, supplying and absorbent capacities. Restrained rates of growth are a social as well as a technical and scientific issue because they involve not only natural capacities and technological development of interest to natural scientists and technologists. They also involve the social relations and patterns of social life appropriate to the running down of growth and the institutionalization of sustainability.

Sustainability requires technical decisions about choice of technology, energy use and forms of production. Yet it also requires restrictions on growth, resource extraction and pollution and implies radically changed social lifestyles and values, whether taken on by choice or necessity or by some combination of the two. The social lifestyles and values suitable for sustainability are something on which sociologists are eminently well-qualified to comment, since they touch on issues to do with consumption, community and economy in which sociologists have a longstanding interest.

In this chapter I wish to look at the forms of social lifestyle and values appropriate to sustainability. In looking at green proposals in these areas I will be distinguishing between the social and the environmental arguments in favour of them. This chapter discusses three areas: consumption, community and economy. I wish to argue for global and interventionist approaches to solving environmental problems rather than decentralized or capitalist solutions favoured by many greens and economic liberals.

I shall be taking issues which sociologists are used to describing and explaining and looking at them along a normative dimension. The last chapter which dealt with the sociology of industrialism looked at explanations of what society is like. This chapter is geared to discussions about what it *should* be like. It discusses issues relevant to a normative sociology of the sustainable society.

Consumption and frugality

Perhaps most notably, sustainability is said by greens to require reduced levels of consumption and changes in associated values to do with material fulfilment and acquisition.[1]

Resource depletion, production and pollution result from consumption and the materialist values underlying it. Resources are extracted and industrial production carried out to provide goods for consumption. Pollution results from extraction, production and consumption, both from the polluting technologies used in these processes and from the waste they produce. Levels of consumption are now so high and growing that they are leading to the depletion of some resources and the earth is unable to absorb current levels of some forms of pollution without serious and dangerous detrimental effects on the natural environment and human beings. Consumption is, thus, at the basis of depleting and polluting processes. Reductions in levels of consumption can lead to lower levels of extraction and production and so to reductions in depletion and pollution. All these links show that sustainability relies not just on more environmentally friendly technologies in extraction, production and consumption (although those technologies which are non-polluting or can exploit renewable energy sources are very important) but on changes in social lifestyles (lower levels of consumption) and their underlying social value systems (acquisitive materialism).

Greens find the proposal for decreased consumption difficult to sell to the public because of the frugal lifestyle it implies. It also raises another question which is difficult to sell because of emotions associated with children and liberal issues to do with rights – the question of reducing population levels and having fewer children.[2] Greens argue that current population levels, let alone the rates at which they are growing, are unsustainable because of the amount of waste, consumption and resource depletion they impose. Levels of consumption are bumped up not only by the amount individuals consume but also by the numbers of people consuming. They can be reduced by lower rates of individual consumption but also need to be lowered by reductions in population. The figures vary but many greens argue that the British population, for example, needs to be halved, while the world population needs to be brought down by a similar proportion – from about 5,000 million to around 3,500 million (Dobson 1990:94).

Few greens suggest the coercive measures that many people associate with reductions in population levels – legal limits on family size, forced sterilization etc. But even some of the most liberal financial sticks and carrots proposals put forward by greens are troubling. Irvine and Ponton (1988:23), for instance, suggest financial incentives (e.g. for non-pregnancy, small families or sterilization) and the withdrawal of child-related benefits. These, however, would not affect the ability of the rich to continue to make choices about having children but would restrict the choices of the poor. Proposals for the cessation of fertility research and surrogate motherhood would lead to infertile couples being prevented from having children while the fertile could continue to do so. On both liberal and egalitarian grounds these sorts of proposals are pretty hard to stomach.

The necessity for lower levels of consumption and more frugal lifestyles is a thorny issue because exhortations to roll back levels of material consumption and live more frugally lack popular appeal. Greens reply that the pay-off is that a reduced concern with material acquisition will lead to a proportionate increase in people finding fulfilment through post-materialist intellectual and spiritual concerns and the intrinsic rewards of work. A decrease in quantity can lead to an increase in the quality of life.

The green case for reduced levels of consumption for environmental reasons is powerful.[3] But the social argument about post-materialist sources of fulfilment is more problematic. The environmental arguments for reduced consumption are stronger than the social arguments for it. Let me say something about the problems of the latter.

First, greens perhaps sometimes undervalue the extent to which material acquisition and consumption can be a source of personal fulfilment.[4] Clothes and buying things for the home, for example, are vital aesthetic sources of personal identity and the definition of self for many people. People define and express themselves through the way they present themselves to the world and their efforts to give a specific appearance and meaning to the place where they live. This is not the case for all of us. But for many, acquisition is not always the shabby, personally impoverishing form of behaviour greens suppose it to be. Nor is it clear who is in a position to define whether spiritual or intellectual activities are more lofty or fulfilling than acquisitive consumption.

Second, advances in material standards of living are as likely as frugality to further intellectual and spiritual fulfilment in that they can free people from the mundane compulsion of the reproduction of everyday existence. Equally, a reduction in material standards of living and the labour-intensive and simple lifestyle many greens advocate may reduce opportunities for intellectual and spiritual fulfilment as much as increase them.[5]

I distinguished in the last chapter between technocratic and structural environmentalism. Let me make another important distinction here between environmental and social dimensions of ecology. The environmental case for reduced levels of consumption is strong. In so far as environmental degradation is rooted in high levels of consumption there is a strong environmental case for reducing it. However the social case, based on not strictly environmental arguments but gelling quite nicely with them, about the social preferability of frugality over acquisitiveness is more problematic.

Greens are often criticized for questioning a modernist project which has vastly improved the economic, social and political quality of human life in the developed world and for advocating a return to the dark days of our pre-industrial past. On strictly environmental grounds greens have a case for questioning aspects of modernism which appear to undermine life-support systems. But the nicely compatible social ecological case that green frugality is not only environmentally sound but in principle preferable to modernist materialism is more problematic. Tactically it may not help greens to question whether a more environmentally friendly society will really improve our quality of life as well as safeguarding the natural world. But for the sake of truth and accuracy it is worth thinking about more carefully.

I do not wish to reject outright the social case but to put it into question as a complex and contradictory problem. Nor do I wish to suggest that, should the social case collapse, the environmental case is not strong enough on its own to carry through arguments for greater frugality and reduced consumption in specific spheres.

In this instance it may not be as important to separate off the environmental and social arguments for frugality if the green case can be carried on environmental grounds alone. However, in the case I wish to discuss next – green arguments for decentralization and self-sufficiency – it is an important distinction to make. My argument is that on environmental grounds decentralization and self-sufficiency have as many disadvantages as advantages. Consequently the green case for proposals along these lines rests more heavily on social arguments about the intrinsic desirability of such arrangements, arguments which coincide with green concerns but are not themselves specifically green.

Decentralization and community

Ecological considerations imply not only reduced levels of consumption and greater labour intensity but also, greens have argued, a number of stipulations about appropriate levels of organization of social relations – self-reliant, appropriate in scale, decentralized and bio-regional.[6] Green arguments for self-sufficient, human-scale, decentralized and bio-regionally organized communities appeal to their environmental advantages. But greens also appeal to nicely compatible social arguments about the independent social desirability of such types of communities. I will take environmental and social arguments in turn.

Environmental arguments for decentralized community

Greens argue that local production and self-sufficiency are environmentally sensitive because they cut down on the environmental damage wreaked by the transport infrastructure that trade requires. For example, road building, fuel consumption and traffic pollution would decline. All these at present deface the countryside, deplete resources and pollute the air. Other infrastructure required by communities, they argue, such as chemically poisonous sewage treatment, declines with reducing concentrations of numbers. Less concentrated sewage output can be dealt with more easily without so much use of damaging human-made chemicals.[7]

Kirkpatrick Sale (1974, 1980, 1984, 1985) advocates a 'bio-regional' concept based on ecological criteria for determining levels of community most appropriate to fostering sensitivity to the environment.[8] Many sociologists will find Sale's analysis difficult to accept. This is, first, because, as I shall explain, Sale belongs to the 'lessons from nature' school of environmentalism which goes beyond natural limits ecological contextualizations of societal development to a stronger normative naturalism based on the accommodation of humans to the rhythms and boundaries of nature (see also Lovelock 1979). Second, some greens will find Sale's relativist political tolerance unacceptable in that, as I shall outline, it implies there is no green social or political theory or system. Some sociologists will also have problems with it; this is because of the implied prescription that we should put up with systems we regard as morally objectionable in deference to more important principles to do with the toleration of diversity and a greater humility before the 'laws' of nature.

Sale argues that we should become 'dwellers in the land' and gain a greater knowledge of nature by living in and accommodating to it, particularly through our immediate physical surroundings.

> We must somehow live as close to it as possible, be in touch with its particular soils, its waters, its winds; we must learn its ways, its capacities, its limits: we must make its rhythms our patterns, its laws our guide, its fruits our bounty. (1974:224)

This would be less environmentally damaging. Learning its rhythms and accommodating to the natural world implies minimizing resource use and pollution and opting for adaptive rather than interventionist systems which damage the environment, for instance harnessing wind energy sources rather than extracting fossil fuels. Going with the environment rather than against it, in other words, is better suited to preventing environmental problems.

Another reason Sale gives for 'dwelling in the land' derives from an awed and humble respect he has for nature. Sale is highly impressed by the remarkable self-stabilizing patterns and complex harmony of the natural world. He also has a beatific vision of what the natural world is like and of the spiritual fulfilments to be gained from living close to nature and being at one with its wonder as American Indians are said to have been.

Another reason is that Sale is a strong liberal and values tolerance highly, both of diverse political systems and of the natural world as we find it. What makes Sale different from traditional liberals is that he extends the ethic of toleration to nature as well as human beings and argues we should take nature as it is rather than messing with it.

The specific way Sale sees us living in nature – and this is where decentralized community comes in – is by accepting its physically demarcated territories – bio-regions – and understanding and accommodating to the natural boundaries in our immediate physical surroundings. Sale argues that the earth's surface is composed of bio-regions with natural rather than human-imposed boundaries. These can be vast areas defined by native vegetations and soil contours or on a smaller scale defined by watersheds, river basins, valleys, deserts, plateaus or mountain ranges. Becoming more part of nature rather than against it, in the organic and holistic terms I mentioned earlier, involves constructing human communities on the basis of such naturally defined boundaries.

Sale argues that living in bio-regions fulfils in one principle that greens admire – getting close to nature – another that they frequently advocate – self-sufficiency. He believes that bio-regions contain within their own boundaries all the resources that their inhabitants could require: energy, food, shelter, etc. As I have already mentioned greens like self-sufficiency because it cuts down on the environmental effects of transport and trade and the impact of growing infrastructure with increasing scale. Green analyses of the third world see dependency as being at the root of economic, social, political and environmental problems and so they also value self-sufficiency as a solution (Schumacher 1973). They argue that autonomy cuts communities off from the dictates of external political forces and economic circumstances. Autonomy and local-scale can foster the conditions for community and democratic participation and control. It can provide for simplicity and accessibility of tasks that go against bureaucratic expert monopolies. Most importantly, on specifically environmental reasons for preferring decentralized community, it allows for a sensitivity to local environmental circumstances and the importance of sustaining the environmental base of development.

Social arguments for decentralized community

This brings us on from mainly environmental reasons for preferring self-reliance, appropriate scale, decentralization and bio-regionalism to social reasons which coincide with the environmental ones but are separate from them.

Goldsmith et al. (1972) argue that small-scale communities where everyone knows one another foster communal responsibility while in mass communities people are more anonymous and feel less cohesion and responsibility to one another. Small-scale can lead to an increased sense of citizenship, membership and belonging to a community, and of integration and obligations to it. This is good for individuals as well as the community. Individuals feel less atomized, anonymous and required to defend and assert their individuality through competitive individualism. In small communities relationships are deeper and less superficial. All these factors are seen to add to our spiritual life and compensate for the loss of material luxuries and consumerist satisfactions which the sustainable society demands.

Politically, decentralized communities are small and homogeneous enough for people to participate in decision-making and negotiate common agreements relatively harmoniously and unhindered by irresolvable differences. This conduciveness to participation adds to the attractiveness decentralization gets from its putative communality. Beyond their social and democratic merits, greater community and participation are seen as conducive to people making publicly-minded decisions and feeling involved in carrying them through, both of which are important ingredients in the agency and transition of radical green change.[9]

Problems with decentralized community: appropriate scale and interrelations

There are many problems with green advocacies of decentralized community. Debates could be had over the desirability of participatory democracy or strong community, or the forms these should take or the adequacy of decentralized community for facilitating them. Other issues are connected with the realism or social implications of decentralization. It is difficult to see how nations and communities heading for at least semi-autarky could extricate themselves from the complex webs of interdependency they are entangled in. And if this were possible, could the accumulation of excessive inequalities between different communities be avoided? Decentralization would result in communities with the best resources and skills benefiting more than those without. This could not be ameliorated without centralized or co-ordinating forums able to redistribute resources. These are important issues. However I will assume here that decentralism is possible and sidestep the issue of desirability to focus on the adequacy of decentralism for the resolution of environmental problems.

Many greens put two qualifications on their advocacy of decentralization. First, some say that what they argue for is appropriate scale rather than decentralization but that the latter is what is implied by the former (Schumacher 1973; Sale 1980). Second, they argue that they are not in favour of decentralization in isolation but of decentralized communities operating in a context of mutual interrelations and co-ordination (Goldsmith et al. 1972; Sale 1980).

However, these qualifications expose a limitation in the green advocacy of decentralized communities. Decentralization is inadequate to solving environmental problems. Such problems require centralized global action. The advocacy of appropriate scale undermines the case for decentralism because on criteria of appropriateness centralization often seems as well suited, if not better, to the resolution of environmental problems. The advocacy of interrelations undermines decentralist proposals because it fails to specify the mechanisms through which interrelations can be developed and begs the question of the need for centralized agencies to accomplish such a task.

Among red and green thinkers the reaction to the failure of state socialism has been to look for non-statist forms of a green or socialist society. I wish to argue that the reaction to statism, however, should be the democratization of the state rather than its dismantling, whether by the *laissez-faire* of the right or the radical decentralization of the left. Environmental necessities show how important it is to retain the strong state and centralized co-ordination. Decentralization is inadequate because of the need for centralized solutions to environmental problems. The advocacy of appropriate scale and interrelationships highlight this problem. Let me expand on these points, first in relation to the advocacy of appropriate scale and second with regard to interrelations between decentralized communities.

Appropriate scale first. Greens are not dogmatic, blinkered advocates of decentralization. Many of them recognize that in diverse contexts and for varying purposes different scales are appropriate. In other words, they argue for the best suited scale, rather than smallness, and sometimes for balance and mix rather than decentralization all over. Schumacher (1973) is, perhaps, the most notable advocate of this perspective. What greens are arguing for is not decentralization *per se* or the replacement of giantism by smallness but appropriate scale. This, in the context of present levels of economic, social and political organization and environmental problems, implies greater decentralization.

However, this appropriateness qualification does not so much give the argument for decentralism as undermine its relevance to solving environmental problems. There are two reasons why. First, taken by itself the advocacy of appropriate scale only half supports proposals for decentralism and more supports a mix of mechanisms. Decentralized communities might offer the most appropriate scale for certain activities, objectives and people but not for others. The ideal society would be one based on a mix of scales capable of meeting the needs of all people and different objectives rather than a reversion to a single uniform scale throughout society. This would also, of course, be more in tune with the ecological principle of diversity (Eckersley 1992: 175).

Second, taken not just in the abstract but in relation specifically to environmental problems, appropriate scale could be seen to require not just a mix of mechanisms but a positive bias to centralization. Many environmental problems are caused by the combined behaviour of plural actors. Acid rain, for example, is often caused by pollution in one country but falls in another. There is nothing that the state in the affected country can do by itself to solve the problem. Ozone depletion and global warming are caused by CFC and CO_2 emissions in different countries rather than in just one or a few. Reductions by any single state would not solve the problem. Resolutions to these problems require combined action by many states, co-ordinated and agreed between them. Decentralizing powers would undermine combined action to deal with environmental problems because it would take power away from combinations of nations or international agencies and give it to local bodies. Decentralization of powers away from combined or centralized agencies undermines the resolution of problems which have to be dealt with at such higher levels.

This leads to the second problem to do with interrelationships between decentralized communities. Greens might say that decentralization does not undermine combined co-ordinated action between communities because those communities could voluntarily combine and negotiate solutions. They advocate decentralization but not to the point of isolation and introversion. They see small-scale communities being the prime location of production, social relations and political authority in the sustainable society but within a context of interdependence, global consciousness and co-ordination between communities. Greens shun the deferring of decisions up to external centralized authorities. But they do envisage decentralized communities collaborating in voluntary combinations, networks or federations and attempting, through these, to solve common problems.

> Although we believe that the small community should be the basic unit of society and that each community should be as self-sufficient and self-regulating as possible, we would like to stress that we are not proposing that they be inward-looking, self-obsessed or in any way closed to the rest of the world. Basic precepts of ecology such as the interrelatedness of all things and the far-reaching effect of ecological processes and their disruption, should influence community decision-making and therefore there must be an efficient and sensitive communications network between all communities . . . We emphasize that our goal should be to create community feeling and global awareness, rather than that dangerous and sterile compromise which is nationalism. (Goldsmith et al. 1972: 15–16)

However, just as the 'appropriate scale' qualification on decentralization undermines the latter and implies centralized solutions, so is this also the case with the 'co-ordination' qualification just outlined. The difficulty here is that while the problems of an isolationist decentralization and the need for co-ordination are recognized by greens the mechanisms through which decentralization can be combined into co-ordinating networks are not outlined. The extract from Goldsmith et al. quoted above, for example, is an expression of an aspiration about the combination of localism or globalism rather than an explanation of how to achieve it.

Greens are vague about the mechanisms for integrating decentralized self-sufficiency with global interdependence and it is not clear that the influence of people living in small-scale autarkic communities would not undermine a wider consciousness or more integrated structures of co-ordination. Small-scale autarkic organization may well foster internal at the expense of other-concerned co-operation. Greens are never very clear about how communes are to be linked into wider external relationships which will prevent internal communal feeling turning into an externally defensive sectarianism or a stifling, parochial inward-lookingness. 'Acting local', in other words, may actually inhibit 'thinking global'.[10]

Why do greens leave out the mechanism for linking decentralization with co-ordination? This could be for one of two reasons. The first might be that decentralist greens adhere to a strong ecological model of the natural or spontaneous development of co-operative relationships between separate units. Maybe they see co-ordination as following naturally from the co-presence of decentralized communities.

On this, it is certainly impossible for communities to be completely autonomous and divorced from interrelations with other communities. Relations between communities will be mutually constitutive of the different communities' identities and actions. However, this is a different thing from saying these interrelations will, or are likely to, be co-operative or co-ordinated. While relations are inevitable, the form they may take is open and they could be antagonistic, competitive and unco-ordinated as much as co-operative and co-ordinated.

The second possible explanation for the lack of a specified mechanism for linking decentralized communities into co-ordination is mere optimism or omission. This seems more likely to me as an explanation for the gap in the theory. Whatever the explanation, my argument is that the lack of a specified mechanism begs the question of the need for centralized agencies charged with engineering such co-ordination and undermines the arguments of greens for a decentralized society.

I have suggested that there are a mixture of social and environmental arguments put forward in the green proposal for decentralized communities. Other proposals for global co-ordination or centralized authoritarianism[11] are at least as likely to further environmental objectives, and it is problematic for greens to give decentralized communities exclusive right to the label 'Green' (see Dobson 1990: 81–5,

122–9). Often their preference for decentralist alternatives over others is social rather than strictly green. Their social preference for decentralism may well colour their interpretation of its environmental advantages over other possibilities. And decentralization may, I would guess, turn out in practice to be a lot less 'green' in the strict sense of the word than centralized co-ordination.[12]

Global co-ordination and environmental sustainability

Let me look now at the global co-ordinating strategies I have argued are more suited than decentralization to resolving environmental problems. Table 2.1 gives four models of social and political organization. There are varying degrees of centralization and decentralization in structure. And there are different degrees of voluntariness or formal institutionalization of co-ordination between communities, the latter requiring, rather than leaving to them, co-ordinated relations between communities.

I have already argued that greens like Goldsmith et al. (1972) see strong autarkic models such as 1 as in table 2.1 as too far out from the sort of co-ordination required to solve environmental problems. With respect to model 2 I have argued that, while its aspirations are right, it fails to replace its rejection of the sort of centralized authority

Table 2.1 *Centralism and co-ordination in resolving environmental problems*

Type of community	Decentralized or centralist system	Voluntary or institutionalized co-ordination
(1) Autarkic decentralized	Decentralized	No co-ordination
(2) Decentralized with voluntary co-ordination	Decentralized with centralism	Voluntary
(3) Decentralized with institutionalized co-ordination	Decentralized with centralism	Institutionalized
(4) Centralized independent body	Centralized	Institutionalized

envisaged in models 3 and 4 with another mechanism for fixing global co-ordination. In this section I will look further at the way in which the limits of 1 and 2 demand structures of the sort envisaged in 3 or 4. I will discuss the way these are intended to overcome the limits of decentralism and install structures of global co-ordination for overcoming environmental problems.

(1) The first approach shuns co-ordination. Greens could defend it on the grounds that co-ordination will not be necessary if autarkic communities are green and globally minded. Co-ordination is unnecessary if communities already behave in the environmentally friendly way with which it is intended that they should be brought into line. And it is globally minded and green communities that greens are thinking of when they propose decentralized communities in a sustainable society.

There are two problems with this – the first relates to the role of co-ordinating authorities as legislators and the second to their role as co-ordinators and managers. The first problem is that the position just set out starts from way-out assumptions of ecological optimism. Decentralization does not mean eco-centrism. Decentralizing powers to local communities does not mean they will then operate in green ways. Starting off from the assumption of decentralized communities which are green starts off much too late, and ways need to be worked out in which such communities are persuaded to be green in the first place.[13] Centralized co-ordination in pursuit of green objectives would be one such way, one purpose of centralized co-ordination being to bring decentralized communities into line on environmental objectives. In the case of model 1, then, centralized authority is needed to secure environmental objectives from autarkic communities which do not adhere to them.

A green reply to this could be that decentralization would be on such a small scale that even supposing communities were not all environmentally friendly, any environmental harm they caused, whether by accident or lack of environmental concern, would be minor compared to the size of a similar environmental blunder committed on, say, a national level (e.g. see Sale 1985:95). The problem with this is that it separates out too atomistically the individual decentralized community. Great environmental damage would result if many decentralized communities pursued environmentally damaging practices, and looking at individual communities as if they would be isolated examples of this is too narrow.

The second problem with the argument about the irrelevance of co-ordination in a context of green globally minded communities is that co-ordination bodies are about more than securing environmental behaviour from lower down bodies. They are also about overseeing decentralized behaviour, identifying where it goes wrong and seeing what combined paths of action across communities are best suited to resolving environmental problems. Having external co-ordinating authorities is about more than exerting authority. It is also about co-ordination, management and planning, as well as sanctions and regulation, and it is informational as well as motivational in function. Even if all decentralized communities thought green, centralized bodies would still be needed to co-ordinate them. Overseeing the actions of many different communities an overall co-ordinating body could see how much action would be required by all communities, ensure consistency and cohesion and avoid contradictory policies or unnecessary duplication and repetition of errors (see Goodin 1992:164–8).

(2) The second model assumes that voluntary co-ordination will be forthcoming among decentralized communities. But, as I have argued, without a theory of natural co-ordination or the specification of a mechanism to bring forth co-ordination in the absence of its spontaneous development this model is unrealistic or at least too optimistic to be gambled on.

There are, however, some hopes for model 2, and while I wish to suggest the *institutionalization* of co-ordination should be pursued I would also argue that the pursuit of informal voluntary co-ordination should not be passed by. One obstacle to voluntary co-ordination is that communities are unlikely to pursue environmental objectives unless other communities will do so as well. This is because: (1) in terms of dealing with the *causes* of environmental problems, lone action would be ineffective because causes are combined rather than locally specific; and, (2) in terms of the *effects* of environmental problems, lone actors would have to carry the burden of the cost of environmental friendliness yet still be subjected to environmental problems caused by other communities not doing the same.[14]

Two solutions to this would be the formal institutionalization of agreements or the imposition by a central authority of environmentally friendly behaviour from above. However, these fit into categories 3 and 4 respectively and so do not constitute a solution within the voluntary non-institutional category 2 where communities go for co-ordination out of their own volition rather than because of institutional requirements to do so. Within category 2, though, change could rest with moral leadership from a single community or group of communities. This would be self-sacrificial in the first instance but

based on the hope that it would spur and mobilize combined voluntary co-ordination incorporating other communities in the future.

(3) and (4) Moral leadership is however something to hope for; it is
too uncertain to base a strategy on or to rely upon. While any attempt
to build global co-ordination should include work within category 2,
by itself it is unreliable. The main thrust of a strategy for global co-
ordination would have to rest with categories 3 and 4; co-ordination
institutionally agreed by incorporated communities or imposed from
above by a recognized democratic central authority. Both of these
imply a world governmental agency, in 3 of an inclusive corporatist
sort, in 4 of an independent external sort, both imposing mutually
beneficial enforceable international strategies, with teeth, for environmental protection.

The advantage of models 3 and 4 over 2 is that while they rely
initially on voluntary effort to get them off the ground they do not
rely in the environmental agreements they set up on voluntary good-
will and participation. They rest on formal, institutionalized enforceable agreements. Where they differ from each other is on the fact that
3 envisages an inclusive forum which incorporates communities in
decision-making; 4 however is independent and external, not inclusive of all communities but a separate central institution sending down
orders from above.

The obvious objection to 3 and especially 4 is, of course, on the
grounds of liberal fears of potential tyranny and totalitarianism.
However, there is no reason why these should be the result of such
arrangements. To start with, the proposed bodies are for environmental regulation and their remit extends no further than that, although
they would have to be part of wider bodies like the United Nations
because environmental issues are too heavily interrelated with others
for them to be separated off. Furthermore, bodies under 3 and 4
would not have powers of military coercion and would enforce environmental protection through legal channels and with the support of,
the economic and moral authority of member communities rather
than coercive force or might. They should also be restrained by liberal and pluralist checks and democratic accountability. They should
have their scope of authority formally and legally delimited and pre-
scribed. They should operate within the context of a world made up of
plural and diverse independent power centres, governmental and non-
governmental, which would have the cultural and financial weight,
political authority and social legitimacy to stand up against them if
they overstretched their remit. Finally they should be democratically
accountable. In the case of 3 this is written into the model by the

inclusion of communities in the forum's structures, making it like an environmental council within a beefed-up UN. In the case of 4 the body is external and independent but could be elected and democratically accountable. In other words, 3 and 4 involve mutual coercion by mutual consent (Hardin 1977), the latter institutionalized in democratic accountability and limits and restraints on their power. In fact, given the experience of bodies like the UN, the worry would be that such bodies would be too feeble than too strong.[15]

Both 3 and 4 rest on initial voluntary efforts to set them up. But they assume, unlike 1 and 2, that mutual voluntary co-ordination may not be forthcoming without a superior centralized authority to build co-operation and enforce it from above.

I argued above that communities are unlikely to pursue environmental objectives unless other communities do so as well. They will perceive that lone action will be ineffective because the causes of problems are combined rather than locally specific. Furthermore, they will have to bear the cost of environmental friendliness while being subjected to environmental problems caused by other communities not doing the same. However, co-ordinated action engineered by centralized bodies can ensure that responses will be collective. Actors can be assured they will not be lone actors, ineffective in tackling alone problems caused by the combined actions of many communities and subject to the effects of environmental problems caused by others who do not work for solutions to them. They can be motivated into taking environmental action knowing that combined action appropriate to supra-local causes will be enforced and that there will not be free riders avoiding the costs of protection and continuing to inflict harm.

The economy and technology in the sustainable society

I have looked so far in this chapter at low consumption and decentralized and global community as components of a sustainable society. I will turn my attention now to the economic structure and technological aspects of sustainability. The main issue I will discuss around economic structure is whether environmental problems can be solved within capitalism. On technology I will discuss whether changes to more environmentally friendly forms of technology can be sufficient to foster sustainability. I have argued that global as well as decentralized strategies favoured by many greens are needed to solve environmental problems. I wish to argue now that interventionist rather than *laissez-faire* or capitalist approaches, of the sort favoured by economic liberals, are also required.

Can capitalism solve environmental problems? Capitalists, consumers and markets

There are three main issues on whether environmental problems can be resolved within capitalist structures. (1) Can capitalists be expected to pursue environmentally sustainable courses of action? Is it in their interests to do so? (2) Can environmental sustainability be built on consumers voluntarily adjusting their behaviour within market structures? (3) Can environmentally friendly behaviour be fostered within markets by modifying them?[16]

I will suggest that, while some advances can be made within these constraints, it is unrealistic to expect that sustainability can be achieved within capitalist and market structures and through voluntary consumer action. Environmental sustainability will have to be tackled through the building of a much bigger non-capitalist sector in the economy geared to public-interest goals, through action at the level of production as well as consumption and through non-market interventions as well as financial incentives for voluntary adjustments of behaviour within markets. Collectivist intervention rather than economic liberalism is necessary for securing sustainability.

1 Capitalist interests   Let me look first at the issue of whether capitalists can be expected to pursue sustainable courses of action voluntarily. Is a liberal approach of leaving capitalists be and trusting to their voluntary action adequate, or do more coercive interventionist measures need to be taken to make them respect environmental measures in the public interest?

In recent years there has been a burst of published guides not only on green consumer behaviour but also on good green behaviour for business and producers (see Elkington and Burke 1987). These guides rest on the premiss that businesses can adjust their behaviour in accordance with more environmentally sustainable patterns of behaviour. More significantly, they assume that it is realistic to expect that they actually might do this and that there is a market for books which explain how to go about it. There are also environmental audit agencies who aspire now to do more than tell businesses how to come into line with legislation on health and safety – for instance on asbestos replacement in workplaces or conformity to pollution regulations.

They also aim to give guidance to those who want to take further voluntary steps in pursuit of wider and bigger environmental aims.

The pro-capitalist argument starts off from the basis that the pursuit of capitalist self-interests does not conflict with wider goods in the public interest, environmental sensitivity for example. Pro-capitalists argue that the pursuit of capitalist self-interest will not lead to greed in production at the expense of the consequences for, say, resource depletion and pollution. Capitalists can be persuaded to show regard for the environment on the basis that it is in their interests to do so. Depleting resources, for example, will undermine their capacity to produce for profit in the future when resources run out. What are environmentally unsound activities that go against the public interest are also economically unsound activities for capitalists.

It is also not in the interests of capitalists to pollute because they will suffer the consequences as well as the public. In addition to this, there can be adjustments to markets such as pollution taxes and green consumerism. These provide further incentives within capitalist structures for capitalists to take measures voluntarily and in their own self-interests. Critics say that there is a contradiction between capitalist self-interest and the general interest of the population in environmental protection. Pro-capitalist greens, however, say that the two are connected, that the pursuit by capitalists of their self-interests is compatible with the general interest of the population as a whole.

2 Green consumerism   Critics of capitalism say that the system is based on capitalists profiting through the production of more and more goods, rising consumption to increase profits and the creation of new needs in people to buy new products when the market for the old ones has been saturated. This produces levels of production and consumption which use up immense amounts of resources and create pollution in production and consumption. However green capitalists say that this sort of thing can be compatible with solving environmental problems if consumers use the power they have over producers – 'consumer sovereignty' – by refusing to buy products which are not environmentally friendly. This gives capitalists an incentive to concentrate on the production of environmentally friendly products in order to make a profit.

Moreover, pro-capitalist greens can say, this not only works in theory but is also what has been happening in practice over recent years in developed countries. People who are environmentally concerned, of whom there are said to be rising numbers, have started buying environmentally friendly goods: Ecover washing powder, lead-free petrol, bio-degradable goods, aerosols without CFCs and organically grown products in which pesticides have not been used, for example. Capitalists produce more of these and fewer of the old environmentally damaging products. And there is now a plethora of green consumer guides. These themselves can be seen as a capitalist response to green consumer concern, selling information on the environmental credentials of different companies and products to a market which exists for it. They are both symptomatic and facilitative of the rise of green consumerism (see Elkington and Hailes 1988; Button 1989).

The British Body Shop Company exemplifies both the phenomena so far discussed: green capitalism and green consumerism. The Body Shop is a chain of cosmetics outlets which has spread across Britain and beyond from small beginnings in Brighton. It sells products which have been produced in less depleting and polluting ways than competitor products. They are not tested on animals and are marketed as having been produced in a way sensitive to the needs of the 'indigenous' populations of the countries from which they are derived.[17] The Body Shop has been a capitalist success, making a profit and expanding from selling environmentally friendly products. People who buy at the shop want to be green consumers, continuing to consume luxury products but in an environmentally friendly way. Pro-capitalists could say that the Body Shop shows how sustainability can be pursued through the entrepreneurial pursuit of capitalist interests, within the imperative to gain competitive market success, led by consumer concerns and without cutting back on consumption levels, even of 'luxury' products.

Green consumerism implies you can have capitalist consumerism *and* be environmentally friendly. You can have your cake and eat it. Acquisitive lifestyles can be compatible with an altruistic concern for the environment if consumption is adjusted in environmentally friendly directions. Green consumerism is a real boon for greens who have often argued that we need to sacrifice our materialist lifestyles to protect resources and prevent pollution. This is a demand which, in acquisitive industrial societies, where elections are won and lost on ability to deliver economic prosperity, is not a very popular message, publically or electorally. To be able to say you can be green and consumerist is much more appealing.

3 Market values Finally, green capitalists argue that markets, rather than being necessarily blind to environmental problems, can be compatible with their resolution. Competitive markets, far from being oriented to the pursuit of economic success against all else, can also be sensitive to other objectives such as social welfare and environmental sustainability.

Socialist and green opponents of markets argue that the only thing capitalists take into account when making and selling things is the monetary value of their products – how much it costs to produce them and how much of a profit they can be sold for. Factors which do not have a market value are not taken into account in their calculations. It does not make sense to include things other than exchange value in markets which are geared around this factor. Anything which does not appear on the balance sheet is excluded from production decisions. Free natural resources and the effect of industrial processes on the environment have no monetary value and so are not included in market calculations. In fact economists call things like social or environmental factors which do not appear on the balance sheet 'externalities' (see Mishan 1969).

Not only do these sorts of things not appear on the balance sheet, they are also free and so there are no financial disincentives to using or affecting them. You do not pay for a view of the Downs, for the service provided by the ozone layer, for rainwater, for rainforest diversity or for coal. You pay for the labour and capital which goes into the processes which make some of these things available for human consumption – the water or coal industry, for example. But you do not pay for the natural resources themselves. And if they are free, there is strong motivation to use them up without restraint.

However, green pro-capitalists like David Pearce (Pearce 1991; Pearce et al. 1989) argue that markets can be sensitive to environmental problems and that having a market system is not incompatible with caring for the environment. If the market is modified and parts of the environment are given values equivalent to how precious they are, then capitalists and consumers will have to take the environment into account in economic calculations about production and consumption.[18]

The value of environmental services should be incorporated into the costs of production or selling price of goods and services which are produced using them. This would provide market incentives for capitalists and consumers to pay attention to the environment. If part of the environment is given a price value then it will cost. It will show up on the balance sheet and will have to be included in production calculations rather than being regarded as an 'externality'. Furthermore, because it involves a cost, there will be a financial disincentive to using or affecting it.

Monetary values can be introduced into markets through resource depletion charges or pollution taxes. These would involve interventions in markets to modify their workings rather than non-market regulation or direction. Their two big advantages are that (1) they are compatible with the existence of markets rather than requiring their replacement and (2) they rely on voluntary action rather than coercion. They involve economic disincentives rather than political compulsion. They are compatible with markets rather than replacing market forces with state force. This is a big advantage for liberals. They leave action on environmental sustainability to the voluntary action of capitalists and consumers rather than pressing them into line by coercive state legislation from above.

Why capitalism cannot solve environmental problems

I want to discuss now why I believe the proposals outlined above are not adequate for environmental sustainability. I do not think that capitalist measures are totally ineffective. Within capitalism some of these can and should be pursued. It is conceivable that on occasions capitalist self-interests will be best served through the pursuit of environmentally friendly practices. Green consumerism can engender more environmentally sustainable production decisions. Market values on environmental goods can provide an incentive for capitalists and consumers to behave with more of an environmental consciousness. However, these strategies alone cannot ensure sustainability for reasons I will outline.

1 Capitalist interests The argument that it is in the interests of capitalists to pursue environmentally sustainable practices is vulnerable on at least three grounds to do with adaptation, short-termism and future generations.

The first problem revolves around the perception that capitalists are an innovative and adaptive breed. Historically they are seen to have been able to switch production to new areas when old areas of production are exhausted. The green criticism of capitalism here says that there is nothing to say that they will not be able to do this if resources run out or if they over-exploit and despoil environmental services. In other words, environmental damage is not necessarily against the self-interest of capitalists if they can adapt, as they have shown in the past they can. This does not pose a problem for anthropocentric environmentalists because, while parts of the environment are depleted or destroyed, capitalist adaptation to new bases for production ensures that environmental damage does not hinder human well-being, at least in narrowly economic terms. For eco-centrists, though, or those concerned with humans who see their well-being as being entwined with environmental preservation rather than just economic prosperity,[19] it is worrying because it means environmental damage can continue to be inflicted.

A second problem is that capitalists are often said to have a short-term rather than a long-term perspective. They tend to exploit something until it does not deliver a profit any more and then move on. Often they do not plan far enough in advance to calculate whether resources will run out or what they will do when they do. They are happy to exploit them while they are still around. This is bad for both anthropocentric and eco-centric greens because it implies capitalists will continue to exploit the environment as long as there is a fast buck in it, without an eye for what the implications of environmental damage will be for humans later.

There is a third and less standard problem with the view that self-interest will stop capitalists from damaging the environment. The problem here is that, in the cases of most of the large-scale and worrying environmental problems we are aware of, it is likely to be the interests of future rather than present generations of capitalists who will be most affected. If it is their own self-interests and not those of future capitalists that present-day capitalists are concerned about, then they will not be too bothered about environmental problems whose most serious effects are going to hit capitalists who are born later.

2 Green consumerism   There are strengths and weaknesses in the case for green consumerism. I do not wish to throw the whole idea out of the window, so let me say something about some of its positive aspects first. There are four points to do with: the case for modern industrialism, third world interests, political effects and individual activity.

First, green consumerist arguments show that green rhetoric about the need to stop growth and consumption and about the evils of industrialism often fail to take into account increases in standards and quality of living that industrialism and consumerism have produced. Furthermore they suggest that some growth and consumption patterns may not be environmentally problematic and can be continued. They suggest that there have been positive benefits to the modernist project and that no-growth proposals need to be more disaggregated and discriminating, taking into account the benefits of consumption and areas of consumption which are not environmentally problematic.

The second positive point follows from this. Massive cut-backs in growth would not only lower standards of living in industrial societies but, as I suggested in chapter 1, would also hit third world countries who rely on first world consumers to provide markets for their goods. The argument for continuing consumption and growth where it is environmentally sustainable, rather than seeking across the board cut-backs in these, is important for increasing third world standards of living as well as protecting those in the developed world.

Third, green consumerism can have a beneficial political effect. It makes it clear in patterns of purchasing behaviour that there is an environmentally concerned constituency and brings this to the attention of governments as well as producers. Governments then have an electoral incentive, like the producers' economic incentive, to react to consumer demand.

Fourth, green consumerism gives individuals who are alienated from political and other power structures something to do. For many people an involvement in green consumerism maintains their motivation for environmental protection and is a first step to a broader and deeper understanding of environmental issues.

However, there are limits as well as positive aspects to green consumerism (see Irvine 1989). I will mention five problems to do with: non-material fulfilments, work, information, expense and levels of consumption. The first two involve social criticisms of green consumerism and the next three environmental problems with it.

First, anti-consumerist greens might argue that green consumerism reinforces a focus on material acquisition. This leads to the one-sided development of human personalities in which acquisition and material comforts become overdeveloped and non-material intellectual, spiritual and psychological development is ignored. Second, another criticism can be that while consumerism is supposed to improve our leisure it often leads to a work culture in which people have to work long hours to earn money to obtain consumer benefits that they never have the time or energy left to enjoy.

Third, there is a problem in green consumerism with acquiring accurate information on the environmental friendliness of products. In practice, green consumerism is often based on poorly informed choices, and companies peddle products as green which are not all that environmentally friendly. Information on environmental friendliness is not always understandable, accessible or reliable.[20] Fourth, green consumerism is expensive. Organic food, catalytic converters, green washing powders and home insulation cost a lot, and green consumerism will not be effective as long as it is too expensive for many people to pay for it.

Fifth and most serious, anti-consumerist greens argue that there is a problem in green consumerist arguments in that levels rather than types of consumption are the real problem. The implication here is that there are not enough sorts of consumption which can be made more environmentally friendly for green consumerism to replace low consumption as a strategy for sustainability. Natural limits demand reduced rather than just different forms of consumption. Numbers of consumers and levels of consumption taken together suggest the need for cutting rather than redirecting consumption patterns.

3 Market values To recall, this proposal is that if market values are put on environmental services (1) they can be included in market calculations and (2) there is a financial disincentive to despoiling the environment. There are two problems here: the first concerns consumers and the second producers. I will discuss these and then link them in with general problems to do with liberal ideas about freedom and coercion.

The first problem is that added values may be passed on by producers to consumers in the form of higher prices. There are two reasons why this is undesirable. The first, on grounds of social justice, is that it means that one group of people will have to pay for the actions of another group, to which they were not party and for which they should not be responsible. That is, they will pay for the decision of producers to pollute and pay rather than to pursue more environmentally responsible paths of behaviour. The second, on environmental grounds, is that it means producers can continue to degrade the environment by finding a way of paying to do it.

The second problem on market values is that they still leave businesses free to continue environmentally damaging practices. Even if consumers do not pay, producers may choose to. It is the deliberate liberal intention of market values proposals that companies are not coerced. But this means that the proposals are weak environmentally if businesses are willing and able to continue to pursue environmentally problematic courses of action. They can do this by paying the added values to deplete and pollute. As well as being flawed on environmental grounds, this raises problems to do with equality and justice because companies that are rich can pursue environmentally damaging practices, profiting in the marketplace as a result, while less well-off firms cannot.

An economic liberal might give two responses to this criticism. The first might be that liberal concerns outweigh environmental concerns. In other words, it is more important for producers to be free to choose than for environmental objectives to be achieved. This does not work, however, if the environmental problems resulting from this curb human freedoms. This could happen through, say, the lack of resources available for the pursuit of certain paths of development or the adverse effects on human health of pollution. This may limit peoples' freedom to live a healthy life and be free to do things for which health is a necessary prerequisite. Liberals focus their fire on political coercion but an avoidance of political coercion may lead to greater coercions in the future resulting from environmental factors.

A second liberal response might be that if the added market values are not sufficient to deter companies from pursuing environmentally damaging practices then those values can be increased until they are. Market values on environmental services can be pushed up so high that no firms would be able to afford them.

However, the argument for market values against state regulation is that the former avoid the coercion on firms entailed in the latter. Proposals on market values combine environmental concern with liberal freedom. If market values become so punitive and prohibitive that no one could afford to pay them, then they effectively involve forcing environmental responsibility on firms just as much as state coercion. We may just as well then go for non-market restrictions on environmental harm such as state regulation.

Let me summarize on market values here, linking in the points I have made with general issues to do with liberal theories of coercion and freedom. First, if liberal concerns leave it up to firms whether to halt environmental damage or pay to continue it, then they run the risk of being ineffective on environmental grounds in the name of liberal freedoms. Second, if liberal approaches are ineffective on environmental grounds they may prove ultimately to increase rather than diminish coercion and so end up inadequate on liberal grounds also. The state could have to intervene later in a more authoritarian way than it would have done earlier in order to halt big reductions in human opportunities imposed by resource depletion or pollution. Failing that, depletion and pollution themselves may become so acute as to create environmental necessities which impose on human well-being and freedoms. Third, if market values are so severe that they cause firms to pull back from environmental degradation, then they could be seen to be coercive because they force firms to alter their behaviour unwillingly. In this context the argument for market values against state regulation on the basis of the former's greater liberalism no longer holds up.

All these points highlight problems in liberal theories of freedom and coercion. These theories are obsessed with the threat of state coercion. In being so they open up the way for other forms of compulsion – those of natural necessity or market forces – which are perversely excluded from the range of sources which liberals say diminish freedom. State coercion to safeguard freedom from environmental necessity or economic circumstances is ruled out when it may be a force for protecting both the environment and liberty. Environmental problems and greater coercions in the form of heavy values on environmental services or emergency state action or environmental necessity are stored up for the future because of liberal fears of the state in the present.[21]

Green technology?

I have discussed proposals for solutions to environmental problems within existing capitalist and market structures. Another proposal for solutions within existing structures and without having to change them involves the idea that new forms of environmentally friendly technology can be introduced which will diminish or rid us of the problems we presently face without us having to make widespread societal changes in economic structures or social lifestyles.[22] If what causes environmental problems is technology, then we do not have to change the economic system that underpins society. We can change the technologies we use and keep capitalism.

Let me give three sets of examples of how technological solutions under capitalism could be pursued: non-polluting technologies, the use of renewable resources and recycling.

First, non-polluting technologies. There are technologies which pollute. Many of these are associated with heavy manufacturing industry. Burning coal, natural gas and petroleum, for example, creates carbon dioxide. CO_2 emissions are a direct threat to human health and are thought to be a factor in global warming. CFCs, meanwhile, which are used as propellants and coolants in aerosols and fridges, among other things, are thought to cause depletion of the ozone layer. Ozone protects us from radiation from the sun which, as I have mentioned, causes skin cancer and damages food production.

However, these can be replaced by cleaner non-polluting technologies. Nuclear power is a target of much environmental criticism because of the dangers of radiation. However, governments argue that nuclear power is environmentally friendly because it is a source of energy which does not involve CO_2 emissions. CO_2 can also be reduced by the use of other alternative sources of energy – tidal, wind and solar – the reduction of vehicle emissions and forest burning and massive tree planting. Aerosols and fridges can be produced without CFCs although at present the alternatives are expensive. The

Montreal Protocol (1987) is an agreement aimed at phasing out CFCs and related substances by the year 2000.

These are technological changes which can cut down on pollution. Technical change can also deal with resource depletion problems. This brings us to the second technological change under capitalism. There are technologies that use up a lot of non-renewable resources – coal, oil and gas for example. These are resources which once they are used are gone forever.

The solution is to introduce new technologies which exploit renewable resources which cannot be used up and depleted. This might include the use of wind, sun and wave in wind-powered, solar-powered and water-powered machinery or the conversion of waste to liquid and gas fuels. Sun, wind, wave and much waste will always be there, however much we use them up to create energy. Another set of technical solutions to resource depletion involve more efficient ways of storing and retaining heat and energy so that less energy needs to be used in the first place.

Third, there is recycling. This involves technological developments which allow us to recycle goods for reuse rather than disposing of them. This cuts down on resource depletion for the production of goods that can be produced using recycled waste – paper, glass and certain metal products for example. It also sometimes reduces the polluting effects of extractive and manufacturing processes.

However, many greens, while keen that clean technology be developed to diminish environmental degradation, are not convinced that technical solutions alone can solve environmental problems. There are two issues here: first, whether technologies exist or can be developed which could beat environmental problems; second, whether technological solutions are always clean enough themselves.

There are two ways of approaching the first issue. The first is to look at whether technological solutions exist which can overcome environmental crises. The second is to try to judge, if such solutions do not at present exist, whether humans are skilful and adaptive enough to develop ones that will.

The first issue is fairly clear cut. Technological solutions, some of which are mentioned above, do exist to many environmental problems and the issue now is to make them economically cheap enough to be usable and to mobilize political will behind their wider proliferation. However, there is relative unanimity among greens and technocrats that technological solutions adequate to resolve existing problems do not yet exist over a sufficiently widespread range of such problems. Where technological optimists pin their hopes is on the ability of humans to come up with technological solutions in the future.

Greens argue that the main problem with technical fixes is that environmental problems are at root social rather than technical (Meadows et al. 1983; Trainer 1985). They are caused by high levels of consumption and production underpinned by acquisitive values and materialistic lifestyles rather than by the technologies through which production and consumption are pursued. Ecologists reject the idea that ecological problems can be resolved by technical fixes or reforms within existing economic and social practices. It is fundamental value systems and practices of industrial societies which are at the basis of ecological problems and introducing new cleaner technologies will not solve environmental problems if levels of production and consumption remain excessive.

The second way of approaching the issue of existing or potential technologies to beat environmental problems is to say that while technologies that can solve environmental problems do not yet exist on a large enough scale they can do in the future. Humans are an adaptive intelligent species who can develop technical ways of combining existing lifestyles with ecological sustainability (Cole et al. 1973). In the past we have proved technologically adaptable and we should extrapolate to the future on the basis that we will continue to be so.

However this optimism, even assuming it is well placed, worries many greens because it is so risky. As of yet we have not developed sufficient technological solutions to environmental problems, and to continue with present rates of growth and consumption in the confidence that we will is a risky business.

> How good are the grounds for thinking that sufficient technical break-throughs will occur? . . . we must be given good reason to think that solutions to each and all of the serious problems ahead will be found. Would it not be much wiser and safer to undertake social change to values and structures that do not generate any of these problems? (Trainer 1985: 208)

The second issue mentioned above is that environmentally friendly technological developments may themselves not be as clean as they are thought to be. Some enthusiasts for the post-industrial or information society look optimistically at the environmental implications of a shift from heavy manufacturing industry to service and information industries based on computerization and information technology.[23]

However, many of the processes that go into the manufacture of computer technology are actually very dirty chemically. I have already mentioned nuclear power. This does not produce CO_2 emissions, which is the green argument in its favour. However, environmental defences of nuclear power rest on the assumption that highly dangerous substances can be stored safely and kept secure. Furthermore there is medical and scientific evidence on untypical incidences of health problems among workers in the nuclear power industry and communities close by. Renewable resource technologies and recycling, meanwhile, are still parts of industrial production processes. The machinery which can harness renewable resources and recycle is developed industrially, and recycling itself is an industrial process.

This chapter and the last have discussed environmental problems under industrialism and changed patterns of economic, social and political life which could be compatible with sustainability. A more complex version of the low-consumption prescription of greens – one which discriminates between environmentally damaging and harmless forms of growth and consumption – is environmentally powerful, although I have expressed doubts about some of the social benefits claimed for it. Green strategies for decentralization and economic liberal hopes for capitalist solutions are problematic. My discussions have suggested the need for global and interventionist approaches. Technological change is important but not without reductions in acquisitive values and levels of consumption in the developed world.

In the next two chapters I want to look at environmentalism as a set of ideas and a social movement. What are its main philosophical bases and what has contributed to its greater popularity in recent years?

Guide to further reading

Andew Dobson (1991) collects radical green views on sustainability in the sections on 'The Green Society' and 'Green Economics' in *The Green Reader*. His discussion in chapter 3 of *Green Political Thought* (1990) is similarly an accessible outline of the radical green view. Pirages's *The Sustainable Society* (1977) is a useful collection as is Daly's *Towards a Steady-State Economy* (1973). Goldsmith et al.'s 'A Blueprint for Survival' (1972) in the journal *The Ecologist* is an influential and classic manifesto, especially for the decentralist case. Schumacher puts the 'appropriate scale' argument for decentralization in *Small is Beautiful* (1973). Kirkpatrick Sale puts the 'bioregional' case for it in books like *Dwellers in the Land* (1985) and *Human Scale* (1980). Irvine and Ponton provide a short, fierce and unapologetic version of the radical green vision in *A Green Manifesto* (1988). Irvine has also written a useful critical discussion of green consumerism in his 1989 Friends of the Earth pamphlet *Beyond Green*

Consumerism. A more favourable presentation of what green consumerism can be like is laid out in Elkington and Hailes's *The Green Consumer Guide* (1988). Pearce et al. in *Blueprint for a Green Economy* (1989) make the influential case for a market solution to environmental problems. Jacobs provides an important recent discussion of many of the economic issues in *The Green Economy* (1991). See also Ekins's edited collection *The Living Economy* (1986).

3

Green Philosophy

In the book so far I have concentrated on the relationship between industrial systems and the environment and the way such systems could be made more sustainable. In the rest of the book I will look at environmentalist ideas and their implications. I will focus in this chapter on philosophical principles which underlie environmentalist thinking before looking at other aspects of environmentalism as an ideology in the chapters that follow.

The main issues in green philosophy are on the ethical basis of environmental concern.[1] (1) How far should obligations and moral concern be extended to entities in the environment beyond human-kind and (2) for what reasons should they be extended? What should be the scope and basis for our ethical concern vis-à-vis the environment? These two points are linked because the bases on which obligations are due has implications for which entities they are due to. Because deciding *why* we care for things environmental determines *which* we care for, philosophical discussions on environmental ethics are more than just academic. They have implications for policy.

There are a number of issues and positions in green philosophy to deal with. (1) Should we care only about humans in the wider environment? Should it be because of the adverse effect of environmental problems on humans that we protect the environment? (2) If we are concerned about humans should we care about future as well as present generations of the species? (3) Should we extend rights and obligations to other 'sentient' beings (beings with the power of sensory perception), namely animals? (4) Should our concern be focused not only on sentient beings but also non-sentient beings whether living (e.g. plants) or non-living (e.g. sand and stones)? (5) If we extend obligations to different groups should they be entitled to equal consideration or should obligations be weighted differently for different groups? If the latter, how and on what basis?

These are important questions. We need to decide why we care about the environment and which parts of the enviroment our care should extend to, according to the reasons why we have chosen them. Positions 1 and 2 above are usually seen in the literature as coming from 'shallow' or 'anthropocentric' (human-centred) perspectives. Position 3 is usually associated with animal rights arguments, although by no means all such arguments focus on 'sentient' criteria for caring about animals.[2] Position 4 is associated with the 'deep' ecology movement in which nature beyond sentient beings is seen to have 'intrinsic value' (value in itself) regardless of its instrumental benefits for humans or other species.[3] Let me start with the first position.

Anthropocentrism

Anthropocentrism – the placing of humans at the centre of our pre-occupations – is the basis on which environmental concern is most often publicly argued for (on anthropocentrism see Dobson 1990:63-72). Causing damage to the environment has awful consequences for humans. Resource depletion leads to crises of production and consumption in human societies and pollution is a health hazard. It is because of these human consequences that we should do something about environmental problems.

However, anthropocentrism is more complicated than this. Let me give two reasons why. First, anthropocentrism is often the public political face of an ecological perspective which is deeper down more non-anthropocentric in its philosophy (see Dobson 1990; Porritt 1986). Political ecologists tend to argue in public in favour of caring for the environment for the sake of humans. It is thought that this excites peoples' self-interested motivations more than saying that we should care about the environment because it has a value in itself.

The second complication is that there are two sorts of anthropo-centrism (see Dobson 1990:63-72). The first is an epistemological anthropocentrism which says that the source of values which involve care for the environment is the human mind. We may say the environment should be cared for because it has a value in itself rather than because to do so is good for humans. But, despite the fact that value is seen to reside in the environment and not in its functions for humans, this is still anthropocentric because the value is ascribed by humans. This argument on anthropocentrism is half right and half wrong. It is half right in the sense that the intrinsic value of the environment is only 'operationalized' once it is attributed by humans. Where it is wrong is in the fact that the value is not just dreamt up by humans but is attached to objective properties in the environment. Without the objective properties in which it resides, value could not be attributed. In other words, value in the environment is not just an invention of the human mind but has an objective basis.

Critics of intrinsic value positions (in which things are said to have a value-in-themselves rather than a value in their functions for other things) could argue that it is impossible to get away from anthropocentrism because of the fact that value is always attributed by humans. This argument does not work, not only because value resides in objective properties but also because it is possible for humans to attribute value to the environment without that value being in the instrumental benefits it has for them. You can have a reason for caring about the environment which is non-anthropocentric even if the reasoning behind it is human-derived. This leads me to my second point on complications in the meaning of anthropocentrism.

The first meaning of anthropocentrism suggests that values attached to the environment are derived from human consciousness. The second is ethical rather than epistemological. It says that the reason for caring for the environment is in the positive benefits for humans of doing so. It is not so much about whether the value attributed to the environment comes from the human mind but about the imputation that it is not intrinsic to the environment but derived from its instrumental benefits for humans.

Anthropocentrists can be concerned for the environment. But being concerned for it for anthropocentric reasons has implications for which parts of the environment fall within the remit for protection. It is only where environmental protection has benefits for humans that it can be argued for. Where the environment does not have such benefits it is not protected by an anthropocentric environmental ethic. This is where 'shallow' anthropocentrists fall out with 'deep' ecologists because the latter think that parts of the environment have a value in themselves and should not be messed with, even if it can be shown that to do so does no harm to humans or even benefits them.

It should be mentioned that some writers argue it is possible to have a non-anthropocentric concern for the intrinsic value of the environment without being anti-humanist.[4] In other words anthropocentrism is not the only form of humanism, and a concern for human well-being and flourishing is not necessarily anthropocentric. To put it another way, being against the instrumentalism involved in anthropocentrism need not entail downgrading concern for humans, their special qualities and development. Eco-humanists argue that the

division between anthropocentric reasons for caring about the
environment and those which stress its intrinsic value involve too
radical a dichotomy. In fact, the well-being of humans and the
environment cannot be divorced. Valuing the flourishing of all beings
allows an eco-humanism which (1) sees humans developing as one set
of entities in a context where all entities in the environment which can
flourish have a value in themselves, and (2) in which human flourishing is an instance not only within, but also facilitated by, the wider
development of all things. Ecology and humanism can be compatible
where ecological flourishing includes human flourishing and where
human life is improved by wider ecological well-being.

My argument below, against anthropocentrism, will be that what
gives humans' lives value – their capacity to gain a sense of well-being
from their experiences – is something which animals share. This being
the case, we should give animals moral consideration too. I will argue,
against many environmentalists, that although plants and non-living
parts of the environment have a value, it is for humans and animals
rather than intrinsic. Plants and stones do not have nervous systems
or brains. They do not have the capacity to experience well-being or
suffering and it is such capacities which are of value and worth in
themselves.

But before I get onto arguments for extending ethical concern to
non-human entities such as animals, plants and the land let me stay
with humans and discuss how ecological thinking extends obligations
further within the human world – to future as well as present generations of human beings.

Future generations

Ecological thinking has particular reasons for wanting to extend
obligations to future generations.[5] Our actions on the environment
have an effect on those still to be born as well as people living now.
Resource depletion, pollution, over-population, land exhaustion,
ozone depletion and global warming are examples of prominent environmental problems. They have effects on present generations. But of
equal concern is their likely effect on generations of people not yet
born.

The argument for extending moral consideration to future generations can start off from the point that we currently extend it to existing
people we do not know. We believe we should be concerned about
other humans even if they are strangers. It can be argued that it

follows that we should extend similar consideration to future people we do not know. If consideration is to be extended to strangers who are alive now it should also be extended to strangers yet to be born. We have obligations to preserve resources and eco-systems and keep them clean for future generations even if at costs to ourselves, say not pursing resource-intensive or polluting activities that could increase our own material standards of living. Similarly, we should not go around exhausting and despoiling the resources and eco-systems of other peoples in the world even if at the expense of depriving ourselves of resources which would make our own lives better. Just as remoteness over space in the case of contemporary strangers does not lessen our obligations to them so it can be argued that remoteness over time should not lessen them to future generations.

Some thinkers apply Locke's rule on private property to the consideration of future generations. We should leave enough and as good for those that follow us (see Kavka 1978). We should leave enough for future generations to be able to maintain standards of living comparable to our own. Non-renewable resources, for example, should only be used so long as technologies are available which make possible replacement renewable resources which provide for an equal standard of living in the future.

Problems with future generations arguments

Let me look at seven arguments against the idea that we should consider future as well as present generations. (1) *Entitlements*: as long as we have justly acquired something we should not be obliged to share it with someone else. (2) *Present generations*: concern for future generations can squeeze out concern for the needy now. (3) *Non-existence*: someone cannot have rights if they do not exist. (4) *Reciprocity*: we cannot be expected to have obligations to future generations because they cannot reciprocate. (5) *Shared responsibility*: our responsibility for future generations can be reduced because we share it with our successor generations. (6) *Future wants*: we cannot be expected to have obligations to the needs and wants of future generations when we do not know what these will be. (7) *Risk and optimism*: we are justified in taking risks that may affect future generations if the risk is low or if we have the capacity to develop solutions which will rectify the effects of present practices.

1 Entitlements Most of these criticisms relate to the futurity involved in obligations to future generations. The first problem, though, revolves around having obligations at all, whomsoever they are to. This view, a version of which is in Nozick (1974), says that as long as what we have is justly acquired we are entitled to it and have no obligations to others with respect to sharing it or what we do with it. Why should anyone else have claims on money I justly earn from writing this book or on money I justly acquire and pass on to my children freely and fairly?

This does not work, though, because obligations should be about more than just acquisition and transfer. We have obligations to others on criteria which go beyond how just our acquisition of a good was: another party's neediness and our capacity to remedy it, for example. If I justly acquire wealth and have the capacity to help those who through no injustice or fault committed by them are in need, then I have an obligation to help them and would be doing a wrong not to. Similarly, just acquisition is not the only factor which determines what I do with property. The effects of its use on other people must also be taken into account. Justice and obligations, in short, are not contained only in the past historical acquisition and transfer of property but also in the implications of the distribution and use of that property for the well-being of third parties, present or future.

The entitlements argument attempts to reduce the scope of obligations generally. Other criticisms of future generations obligations assume we have obligations on a broader scale than Nozick acknowledges, but say that the temporal location of future generations reduces the extent to which we have obligations to them.

2 Present generations   A second problem is that arguments for future generations represent the concerns of those in rich developed nations for their children and their successors and exclude a concern for the poor in the third world today. A concern for future generations gives insufficient weight to obligations due to the present-day poor.

One problem with this criticism is that a concern for future generations does not distinguish by region or affluence and must be at least as concerned with the poor and third world populations as the rich because the former make up as much, if not more, of future generations as the latter. Future generations arguments must be as much concerned with the third as the first world because third world populations are part of future as well as present generations.

This deals with the issue of preference for the rich over the poor but not the weight to be given to future over present generations, among whom the needy are a group with special claims to attention. The criticism here can be that a concern for future generations is biased to the future over the present and marginalizes a concern for the poor today. If the basis of our concern for future generations is the equal consideration of all individuals, those of future generations are more numerous than those of presesnt generations and so get greater weight.

There is, though, an answer to this problem which shows that within a concern for future generations people now living should give special attention to solving the problems of the contemporary poor. Successor generations cannot do anything about present generations but can do things about their contemporaries and successors. This being so, all responsibility for people now living rests with present generations. Present generations, therefore, have more of an obligation to others today than to future generations for whom their responsibility is more widely shared. This does not mean that consideration of future generations no longer stands. The argument I have made has implications for the *weight* of our attentions. It does not remove the principle that we should respect the obligations due to others who follow us in what we do now. But it does mean we shoulder an extra-large burden of responsibility for people alive today. I will return to the sharing of responsibility with successor generations in a moment.

3 Non-existence A third criticism which can be made of arguments for future generations is that it does not make sense to say that people who do not even exist can have rights (see Kavka 1978). This is a weak argument because even within its own terms of reference it can be seen that when people do exist they will have rights and our actions now may transgress those rights then. Thus even if it is agreed that people do not have rights unless they exist it can be seen that actions in the present can transgress those rights in advance of their foreseeable materialization. We can transgress now rights that will exist later.

4 Reciprocity The non-existence criticism tries not just to downweight consideration of future generations but to deny obligations to them altogether. A fourth criticism also tries to deny obligations to them on the basis that reciprocity is a condition for obligations to be owed (see discussions of this issue in Barry 1977 and O'Neill 1993b). Obligations, it is argued, arise out of membership of a community in which they are held reciprocally. Future generations are not in a position to reciprocate and so we do not have obligations to them.

There are two problems with this: first, with the idea that there can be no reciprocity in relations with future generations, and second, on the question of whether in the absence of reciprocity obligations are due. On the first problem it could be argued that future generations can reciprocate with obligations to past generations. We often feel obligations to people who have died. We feel obliged to ensure they are remembered accurately or favourably. We do some things in particular ways because that is how they would have wanted them done and not necessarily because it is the way we may feel they should be. We feel obligations to carry on their work. Future generations can fulfil obligations to previous generations and if reciprocity is a condition for obligations to future generations then it can be seen that reciprocity from them is possible.

The second problem is that reciprocity or shared membership of community should not be a condition for owing obligations. I owe obligations to the unjustly poor or oppressed if I can help them, even if I am not part of the same community and do not expect, or am unlikely to receive, reciprocal obligations from them. I have obligations to future generations because they are feeling beings whose circumstances of life can be affected by my actions and not because they owe me obligations back.

5 Shared responsibility   A fifth problem which I have already touched on is the idea that we can disown some of our responsibilities to future generations because we share these with successor generations. Where we can continue to do things in the sure knowledge that later generations will pay the obligation, it is fair for us to share it out and leave some obligations to later.

There are two problems here. One is that we cannot be sure that successor generations will fulfil their obligations, in which case we should try to do so ourselves. Another is that some things we do, resource depletion or pollution for example, will adversely affect future generations whatever successor generations do, and so we alone shoulder the obligation for curbing such actions. So in terms of taking positive action we should take it ourselves because we cannot be sure later generations will do so. In terms of limiting harmful actions we should limit them now because by their very nature it is doing them now rather than, or as well as, later generations doing them that causes the harm. On both counts the argument for lessening responsibilities to future generations by sharing them over time is diluted in its power.

However, note that I have argued above that present generations hold special obligations to their contemporaries. For the reasons just given we cannot absolve ourselves of responsibilities to future generations. But our obligation to our contemporaries is bound to put demands on our attention which will dilute and counterbalance what we can do for people not yet born.

6 Future wants A sixth criticism of arguments on future generations proposes that we cannot owe obligations to future generations
if we do not know what their idea of the good or wants or needs will
be (see Kavka 1978; Golding 1972). We do not know what to have
obligations to do or not to do because future generations' needs and
wants may come to be different from ours with changing historical
and social circumstances. Ignorance as to future generations' wants,
therefore, is put as a reason for holding back on our obligations to
them.

This is weak. As well as changing with circumstances, there are
common needs across humanity and we can have a pretty good idea
of what future generations will need at a basic level or even, in a lot of
cases, what they will want and an even better idea of what will be bad
for them. In such circumstances we owe obligations on the basis of the
knowledge we do have. As Barry (1977:273) puts it, 'Of course we
don't know what the precise tastes of our remote descendants will be,
but they are unlikely to include a desire for skin cancer, soil erosion,
or the inundation of low-lying areas as a result of the melting of the
ice-caps.'

7 Risk and optimism Finally, an oft-repeated criticism is that we
are justified in pursuing paths of action if there is only a risk rather
than a likelihood or certainty that they will affect future generations
badly. Nuclear power is a good example of a risk sometimes deemed
worth taking on such grounds.[6] Or we can pursue paths of action
which will be harmful if continued at present rates, and in the
present absence of alternative solutions, because of the proven capacity of humans to adapt and find solutions even where they do not
at present exist (for such technological optimism see Cole et al.
1973).

The merits of taking risks and being optimistic have been questioned in chapter 2. At present human societies gamble with practices such as nuclear power generation in which there is no
unanimity on the risk involved and with problems such as resource
depletion on which faith in future technological solutions is far from
widely held. Risks as they are taken have, in such cases, potentially
enormous implications should the calculations prove to have been
faulty. Optimism is optimism and relies on the record of the past.
The potential costs of miscalculation in instances such as those
noted are enormous.

Non-humans

I have discussed ethical concerns for the environment which focus on
obligations to humans. Ecologists argue that what is distinctive about
environmental ethics is that it extends rights and obligations beyond
humans to other entities in the wider environment: animals and other
living and non-living non-sentient beings. Anthropocentric arguments
justify protection of parts of the environment – resources, animals,
wilderness, bio-diversity and such like – for the practical or aesthetic
value they have for humans. Many environmentalists argue that such
parts of the environment should command obligations in themselves.
They should be protected regardless of, and in cases where they do not
have, value for humans.[7]

Coming to conclusions on where value resides or obligations are
due has implications for which parts of the environment we protect. It
may mean, for instance, protecting parts of the environment which
have little value for humans but have value in themselves. Intrinsic
value in nature broadens our policy responsibilities.

I wish to discuss here arguments for extending obligations to non-
humans, why we should do so and to what range of entities. Some
environmentalists want to include animals. Others want to include
living non-sentient entities like plants or even non-living things like
rocks and stones. I will be making three sets of distinctions between
(1) different sorts of value; (2) different bases for attributing value and
moral standing; and (3) different sorts of being to which value should
be attached.

The first distinction is between intrinsic and extrinsic value. Intrinsic value is in something itself regardless of its value for other things.
Humans could be said to have a value in themselves in their capacity
to experience pleasure or flourish or in their nature as conscious
intelligent beings. Humans have a value in such properties regardless
of their use or value for other things. A spanner has extrinsic value. It
has a value which derives from its objective properties but it is not
intrinsic in the spanner itself but in the use it has for humans by virtue
of its functions. Its value comes from its objective properties but is a
value for something else.

Another distinction is between the differing bases on which non-
humans have value or moral standing. These are listed under 2 in
figure 3.1. Finally, there are different entities in the world, as under
3 in figure 3.1. I wish to discuss to which of these entities in 3 the
reasons in 2 suggest value and concern should be extended and
whether this value is intrinsic or extrinsic as distinguished in 1.

Figure 3.1 *Value in and obligations to the non-human environment*

1 Sorts of value
  (a) intrinsic
  (b) extrinsic
2 Bases for attributing value or moral standing
  (a) sentience
  (b) capacity to flourish and develop
  (c) preservation of diversity
  (d) preservation of species and systems
  (e) membership of community
3 Entities to which value or moral standing attached
  (a) humans
  (b) non-human sentient living beings, i.e. animals
  (c) non-human non-sentient living beings, e.g. plants
  (d) non-human non-sentient non-living beings, e.g. rocks

Using the distinction between the two different sorts of value, let me proceed to category 2: different arguments for attributing value and being concerned for, or holding obligations to, things. Which arguments are favoured determines which entities are attributed value or moral standing.

1 Sentience I will start with sentience – having the power to experience a sense of well-being or suffering.[8] We should extend obligations to entities in the world that have such a capacity. It is wrong to cause suffering to a being or curtail its ability to experience well-being. Using sentience as a basis for extending obligations incorporates animals alongside humans as a group to whom these are due. Animals, like humans, have the capacity to feel pain and pleasure and so on sentient criteria should also command obligations. At present we keep many animals in conditions that cause pain, distress or discomfort or we curtail their ability to lead a pleasurable life by killing them for sport or food. As such, animals are often not given the moral respect sentient arguments say they are due.[9]

Other living beings like plants or non-living things like rocks and stones do not, as far as we know, have the capacity to experience pleasure or pain. On sentient criteria, therefore, they do not have value in themselves and cannot command moral concern or obligations. They do have a value but that value is for beings who can experience well-being or suffering from the existence or flourishing of plants or stones. They should be preserved for their value to such beings. But they cannot have a value or command obligations in abstraction from sentient experience which comes only in their relation to other sentient groups.

For many of us, our emotional feelings and intuitions are that there *is* an intrinsic value in the being, life or development of plants or rocks. But, as I argue below, we should not trust our intuitions. It is hard to see a value in just being, living or growing. Value is in the experience of these. Plants and rocks do not have the capacity to experience being or growing or gain well-being from them. But experience or well-being, which *are* of intrinsic value, can be felt by sentient beings – humans and animals – and it is in them that intrinsic value lies.

2 Flourishing The debate with sentience is based not so much on a rejection of sentient arguments (although this sometimes features as I will discuss below) as on the argument that they are not enough. It is argued that sentience is part but not all of what gives a being value and a claim to rights and obligations. There are beings who do not have sentience, plants for example, but have a claim to rights and obligations because of other capacities they have which can pin down such claims – the capacity to grow, develop and flourish, for example. We should respect the rights of, and hold obligations to, anything which can flourish and develop and should restrain from actions which interfere with such capacities.[10]

A problem here is that arguments for the capacity for flourishing as a criterion on which obligations are due distinguish too sharply between it and sentience. What makes it of value is the joy of flourishing, not just flourishing by itself. Where it brings suffering it is not of value and we may not want to give rights and obligations to entities if their growth has ill effects. Think of locusts or plants that strangle other plants. We should judge flourishing according to the experiences it is wrapped up in. It is they which are of value.

The value in non-sentient flourishing beings is not intrinsic, as it is in its implications for things other than flourishing itself. Values and obligations of an extrinsic sort can be extended to non-sentient flourishing beings. They have a value but in the well-being which derives from their capacities rather than in those capacities themselves. They evoke well-being not in themselves because they are non-sentient but in other sentient beings. This is why their value is extrinsic (for other things). Intrinsic value is located in sentient rather than non-sentient beings because it is sentience which is of value in itself. Intrinsic value is not divorced from flourishing because sentient experience is wrapped up in it. But it is experience which is the locus of value and not flourishing independently of the experience it is associated with.

We should, in sum, be responsive to the capacities of flourishing beings to flourish. But obligations go to sentient beings because it is the sentient experience involved in their own or others' flourishing which is of value. Flourishing itself cannot be a basis for commanding respect and obligations. First, it does not by itself have the weight commanding of respect that it has when wrapped up with sentient experience. Second, it could involve flourishing with ill effects to which we would not want to give value, respect or obligations.

3 Diversity So far I have considered two characteristics of entities which might make them of value and deserving of respect or obligations: sentience and the capacity to flourish. I have argued for the former. Let me now turn to three other arguments in environmental ethics for giving value, obligations or respect to entities in the world. The arguments I want to consider now do not, on the face of it, turn so much on the characteristics of individual beings as on structures or principles which are seen to be of value: diversity; species or systems; and community obligations.

Diversity can be seen as a value in itself. It is of positive value and it is because it is good that we should value and extend respect, rights and obligations to diverse things in the world.[11] We should respect the place of all things in the world not so much for the sake of those things but because diversity is desirable. Plurality rather than the entities of which there are plural instances is what should make us want to respect them. In ecology diversity has a special ring to it because diversity and interdependence are said to be functional for the smooth running of ecosystems.[12]

There are a number of problems here. The first is on the functions of diversity for the system. If it is this that is desirable then it is the system, rather than diversity which is of intrinsic value and which we should want to protect. Diversity only has extrinsic value and we would not want to respect it where it fails to fulfil its systemic functions. It is not diversity itself which is of intrinsic value. The argument made for it here is better covered under the valuing of systems which I will discuss below. We should not extend rights on the basis of a respect for diversity if it is the system which is of value and not diversity, which could potentially be of disservice.

On the other hand, if it is a concern for the individuals in the system which makes the functions of diversity for the system valuable then the environmental ethic is concerned about individuals rather than diversity. The value of individuals is covered by the discussions above on sentience and flourishing or by properties of value such as consciousness, intelligence, control or autonomy which individuals have.

Functions apart, one of the things which makes diversity of value is the fulfilment that living in a diverse world brings to beings with the sensory capacities to experience it. It is that diversity has such consequences rather than just the existence of diversity in abstraction that is behind our convictions when we say the world is better for being pluralistic. It is not diversity which is of value but the benefits it brings. What is of value is the experience facilitated by it. Gaining this experience is based on having a capacity for sensory experience – sentience. In itself it is difficult to see why diversity – just having lots of kinds of things – is good on its own. What is good about diversity is in its connection with the experience it contributes to and it is of value where it does so positively but may be a principle which we do not wish to respect or value where it does so negatively.

4 Species and systems   In much environmental thinking value is put on the preservation of collective entities like species or ecosystems. These are said to have an intrinsic value in themselves. The death of the last member of a species is worse than the death of a member of a not endangered species. A species is seen to have a value in itself over and above the value of its individual members.[13]

One of the arguments on species comes from the case for diversity just discussed. We should preserve species because if one is lost there is a loss of a type of thing and a loss, therefore, to the diversity of things in the world. However, I have already explained why I think arguments on diversity are weak in abstraction from arguments for individual well-being. They are strengthened by being linked to well-being but then become based on the value of well-being rather than diversity.

In my view, it is difficult to see how arguments on species can work independently and without resort to other arguments on which they ultimately rest. They do not stand on the intrinsic value of having species alone but come down to arguments on the sentient well-being of members of the species or of other individuals who suffer as a result of the loss of a species. Loss of a species can be a loss because it involves losing its individual members. It is a loss of individuals rather than the collective entity they make up. Or it is a loss because a particular type of thing is no longer around. This does not make sense as a loss unless it is linked to a lessening of well-being of members of the world as a result. In abstraction from a diminution of well-being the loss of diversity of species remains statistical. It is difficult to see why there should be just more and more categories of things except if linked to the life of members of the species or the well-being of individuals from other species who benefit from the richness of life in a world of natural diversity or from the special value of a species.

The loss of species is bad. But it is so because of the loss of individual members or a diminution of the well-being of members of other species, rather than just the loss of a category itself in abstraction from such other considerations. Species have a value but it is not intrinsic. It is a value for members of the species or other beings in the world who benefit from its existence. Individuals of a species or the individuals of others may have a case on which to call for moral consideration from us. But abstract categories of species cannot make good claims for rights or value in themselves.

Another argument in which value is put on collective entities in the environment is on preserving ecosystems.[14] Leopold (1968:224) argues that 'a thing is right when it tends to preserve the integrity, stability and beauty of the biotic community.' This suggests that value resides in the biotic community and that actions should be judged according to their contribution to the good of the community. The whole itself has an intrinsic value and characteristics worthy of respect and accommodation.

According to this view, our respecting and valuing of nature should be for it as a whole entity rather than, or as well as, for its parts because nature has an identity and functions as a whole. This can go further to a strong fetishizing naturalism. Nature knows best and we should not interfere with it as a system because this goes against what is natural and best for the survival of life. Nature is a whole, we should respect the 'natural' and we should practise non-interference with regard to it.[15]

In my view, there are a number of problems in the arguments tangled up in this 'holist' perspective. First, there is a question mark hanging over the scientific validity of what is claimed. Brennan (1988), by no means an opponent of a more relational and environmental ethics, argues that there is not a factual or scientific basis for the holism that greens aspire to. Greens tend to argue that we should respect ecosystems because we are bound up in them and because it is according to holist systemic principles that nature works. However, on Brennan's analysis it is not clear that ecosystems do actually function according to principles of holism and interdependence. The fact of holism should be analysed rather than assumed. My further discussion of this in chapter 6 bears out Brennan's claim.

Second, there is a problem with the view that we should respect the 'natural'.[16] It is not clear what it is about being natural that means we should respect it. To say we should respect something because it is natural is not enough. This fetishizes 'nature'. It needs to be said what it is about being natural that makes it worthy of respect.

Third, the very dichotomy between the natural and social needs to be challenged. What is it about humans that makes our behaviour not natural and in need of being accommodated to what is? It could be said that humans are just as natural as anything else. We have natural capacities and live within and in relation to nature. What reason is there to define our actions and capacities, development of social organization and technology and our purposive transformation of our surroundings as not natural or not taking place as part of nature? If humans *are* natural then accommodating to nature does not involve changing our patterns of behaviour to fit in with other principles. (On such issues see Dickens 1992.)

Fourth, what nature is is open to question. What goes on in nature is contradictory and often downright undesirable. Nature exhibits both toleration and killing, diversity and extinction, equality and exploitation. There is no apparent general design, guide, intention or rationale in this to show what is the preferred way of nature. It is not clear that there is something which is nature – distinctive or coherent characteristics which are identifiable and can be followed and given respect and value.

There is a fifth problem on interference and non-interference.[17] To defer to nature, not interfere with it and act in accordance with its principles can be a recipe for not doing what seems the best thing in the light of ethical consideration and the perceived best consequences. Further, it can inhibit actions which might seem to be the best for nature itself. Human interference may have played a large part in contributing to environmental problems but it is part of the solution as well. Yet interference in nature to protect it – building dams to protect natural habitats or killing members of species (e.g. locusts or strangling plants) to protect others, for example – is ruled out by deference to nature. We may need greater restraint but on the basis that it is good for the environment rather than because it is 'natural' and not to the exclusion of intervention in 'natural' processes to protect the environment.

Sixth and last, there is a problem with value residing in systems. To say that a system has intrinsic value means that the value is in the system rather than the individuals who make it up. I would argue that there cannot be intrinsic value in an ecosystem. A system's value and claim to respect rests in the value it has for its individual members. This is not to say that value is purely a perception of individuals and not in the objective properties of the system itself. The value may be a result of properties of the system irrespective of whether individuals recognize it or not. My point is that it is a value *for* individuals who make up the system and not of the system itself. The system has no value in itself divorced from the well-being of the individuals it contributes to.

Giving value to systems has dangerous implications. It means we can value systems over individuals and individuals can be sacrificed for the sake of an impersonal structure. Making the ecosystem of intrinsic value creates a conflict between its interests and the interests of the individuals who make it up. Yet it is the latter who matter and the former which should serve them. If the system gains value in itself over and above individuals this can be very dangerous for them.

It ought to be mentioned that I am not arguing for epistemological, ontological or methodological individualisms. It is not my claim that individuals are the source of knowledge or value, or the basic building blocks in natural or social life or the unit on which explanatory analysis should focus. On epistemology, for example, my argument is that value is in objective properties of the environment and not just in the eye of the beholder. But it is a value *for* individuals if not one just dreamt up by them. I am arguing for an ethical individualism and within this for a particular variant of it. My argument in ethical individualism is not for individual liberty (although autonomy is an important *part* of the good of individuals) or for atomistic or egoistic individualism. A scheme within which the well-being of individuals is the end may be collectivist or one in which rules restrict the uninhibited pursuit of self-interests. The well-being of individuals is the end with which my ethical individualism here is concerned.

5 Community Value, rights or obligations may be extended to non-human entities on the basis that they are part of the same community as humans. This is connected to the argument on systems and holism because it suggests that as members of the same whole different entities have obligations to one another. Humans have rights and obligations to non-human entities because they are part of the interdependent whole to which we all belong. Different entities have mutual obligations which come from interdependence, participation and membership in the same community.[18]

I am not going to dwell on whether entities in the environment *are* interdependent or members of the same community (see Brennan 1988). In my view, the argument on community falls down earlier than this – on the idea that ethics should be based on shared community in the first place. Why should we have obligations to someone because they are members of the same community? And why should we not have obligations to someone because they are not? I have already argued, regarding future generations, that we should have obligations to people and other beings who are strangers and not members of our community and with whom we are not in a position of interdependence.

We have obligations to the present-day third world poor because they are needy and we can help them. Even were we not responsible for their circumstances or not dependent on them (neither of which are the case) we would still have obligations to them for these reasons. It would be irresponsible for us not to help suffering beings when we can, regardless of the status of any other connections we may or may not have with them. The same goes for future generations. Because we can both adversely and positively affect their circumstances we are obliged to at least not do the former. This should be incumbent upon us whether or not we are in a relation of mutual dependency or shared community with them.

Shared community and mutual dependence as the basis for obligations depend on ideas of contract and self-interest. We are said to owe obligations to others because of the mutual contract involved in joining a society with them or because we depend on one another. We agree to hold obligations to others because we wish to take part in the community with them, depend on them or want them to do likewise for us. We have obligations to members of our own community rather than to non-community justifications that claimants from outside it could make for our attentions.

My argument, however, is that there are beings in the world who have the capacity to experience well-being and suffering. If we have it in our power to help them without sacrificing our own prospects we have an obligation to do so, as long as they are not needy because of injustices or lack of effort on their part. Obligations extend beyond boundaries of community and such boundaries as the basis of obligations can prevent us from fulfilling obligations to those outside our community to whom we owe them. Community is not only too exclusive in this way but also too inclusive. It incorporates among those to whom we owe obligations people who can make claims on us on the grounds of shared membership of the same community but who have no claims on grounds of needs or well-being.

Intuitions, sentience and relative weight

I have discussed so far a number of different arguments for owing obligations or giving value to non-human parts of the environment.

My own arguments are for obligations to, and value in, sentient individual beings. Let me clarify now on three points which fill out what I have said so far and inform on what I will say in the next and final section of this chapter where I will defend sentience against criticisms of it. (1) I wish to explain why my arguments are based on normative ethical judgements rather than on descriptions or intuitions. (2) I will mention the sort of capacities with which I would argue sentient experience is associated. (3) I will say something about the relative weighting which different species should be given in ascriptions of obligations and value.

I have argued so far that there are two sorts of value – intrinsic and extrinsic. The former is value something has in itself irrespective of its value for others. Extrinsic value is the value something has for other beings in the world.

My argument is that beings who have the capacity to experience a sense of well-being or suffering have intrinsic value in such capacities. Such experience is of value in itself. Beings in the environment who fall within such a category include humans and animals. Others who do not fall in such a category include non-sentient living and non-living things like plants, trees, rocks and sand. These have a value by virtue of their ability to grow and flourish or their existence and presence. However, the value is for sentient beings. It is extrinsic rather than intrinsic. In abstraction from well-being it does not make sense to say that just growing or being is of value in itself.

This goes against my own intuitions and emotional feelings which tell me there *is* something of value in growth and being. However, there are not good grounds for supporting such feelings. It is the job of psychology and sociology to describe what individually or culturally held convictions are and why I might hold them. The job of ethical philosophy must be not to make vivid what our intuitions *are* but to define what our ethical opinions *should be*; otherwise ethics loses its normative edge and distinctiveness from other disciplines. Furthermore it takes on the task of descriptive cultural and psychological analysis in which its imputations are often conjectural and shakily grounded and in which philosophers are poorly trained compared to psychologists and sociologists. In saying this I realize I am going against ethical and political philosophers who do see making vivid our culturally held intuitions as their task, a task in which they too often slip to the 'ought' about obligations from the 'is' of what they are.[19]

So I am arguing for sentient capacities despite my intuitive inclinations. One question which has been left unanswered is the relative weight of ethical priority to be given to different entities on the basis of value in sentient capacities. It is not possible to answer this in detail or with systematic examples in the space here. But I would argue that entities should be given consideration in the degree to which they can experience or contribute to well-being or suffering. This goes against the principle of equality of species favoured by some deep ecologists (see Naess 1973) because it ranks species on grounds of sentience. It also goes against the failure to extend obligations or value to the non-human world because it includes non-human sentient beings, namely animals, in the ethical community.

There are different abilities and expertises through which well-being is experienced. Well-being cannot be divorced from activities or capacities which are not conventionally associated directly with sentient pleasure. Wider activities which have sentient consequences include intellectual activity, artistic creativity, sporting achievement, public participation, relationships, autonomy, control and self-worth. Relative capacities for well-being should be assessed not just according to the narrow range of things which *are* conventionally associated with hedonistic sensory pleasure – eating, drinking, sex, drugs etc. – or with the immediate moment of an activity. Well-being comes through less directly sensual activities in a less immediate and direct and more delayed form more diffused over time than is contained in hedonistic notions of sentient pleasure. Writing this chapter has caused me great pain! But the creativity gives me a sense of achievement which I feel in a sentient way. In addition I know the pleasure I get from writing comes long after I have done it, from having looked into problems that worried me and from having a product under my belt I orient from and identify with for years to come.

Ethical priority should be determined by possession, or capacity to possess, sentient capacities and abilities. On such criteria humans come out high and animals lower down; humans have a greater aptitude for the wider activities associated with sentience mentioned above. As most humans have sentient capacities it is not easy to make weightings within humankind. Within the animal kingdom weighting can be more easily made. The length of life and degree of sophistication of a fly would make it much less able to experience well-being with the longevity and richness that a chimp could. Ethical weighting can be easily made here in favour of the latter. Let me look now at criticisms which might be made of the sentient position I have taken up.

In defence of sentience

I have argued that capacity to sense well-being is the criterion on which moral consideration should be extended. Beings who can do this (humans and animals) have a value in themselves. Beings which cannot (e.g. plants and rocks) have a value but for others who can. All sentient beings should be given moral consideration. Consideration of non-sentient beings depends on their contribution to the sentient well-being of others.

Let me deal with criticisms of this position.[20] These try to demonstrate either (1) that there are sorts of well-being which are undesirable or (2) that we have obligations based on things other than well-being. Criticisms along these lines suggest that well-being is a poor basis for moral worth and that there is more to it than this. In relation to environmental ethics they suggest that beings other than those with the capacity to experience well-being have value in themselves and are worthy of consideration on their own merits. They should be given consideration intrinsically – not just for their contribution to the well-being of animals and humans and not just in cases where they have such implications for these other species. I will look first at undesirable forms of well-being and second at non-well-being obligations.

Undesirable well-being

I can mention four criticisms which suggest that well-being can be undesirable and should not, therefore, be the basis for ethics.

1 Replaceability, multiplication and killing   The first criticism is that basing ethics on well-being justifies practices which are absurd – the replaceability of sentient beings, multiplication to increase the total stock of pleasure and killing to reduce pain. One thing would be that there is nothing wrong, according to sentient criteria, with killing humans or animals as long as they are replaced because killing with replacement does not diminish the total sum of beings capable of experiencing well-being (see Lockwood 1979). Yet, critics argue, this is obviously something we would not wish to justify and our repugnance at it suggests there is something other than just well-being we value – life itself or the capacity to fulfil one's potential. In my view, this criticism does not work, however, because there is a problem with killing-and-replacement on sentient grounds. If the concern for well-being is not just for an abstract total amount of well-being in the

world but for the well-being of real individuals (see Kymlicka
1990:30–5) then killing-and-replacement is not justified on sentient
grounds because it ends the ability of individuals to experience well-
being. The strength of arguments on well-being is that they attach to
the concrete experiences of real individuals rather than abstract principles or values which have no consequence for feeling and experience.
At this level it is immoral to curtail the capacity of individuals to
experience well-being.[21]

Another criticism of sentience might be that a concern with well-
being justifies (1) the killing of all sentient beings so that none would
have to experience pain or (2) massive reproduction and multiplication in order to maximize the numbers capable of experiencing well-
being (Parfit 1984; Attfield 1983:ch. 7). The killing criticism does not
work in my view because it would not only remove capacity for pain
but also capacity for well-being which its valued in well-being arguments. The multiplication criticism does not work for two reasons.
First, multiplication may lead to a diminishing of well-being due to
overcrowding, scarcity, depletion and pollution, rather than an
enhancement of it. But, second, if it could lead to more beings with
the capacity to experience well-being without such negative consequences it is difficult to see what *is* so absurd about it. If sentient
beings can enjoy life it makes sense to have more of them as long as
doing so does not diminish the capacity for well-being of their fellow
beings because of a deterioration in conditions of the sort just mentioned.

2 Artificial pleasures and real pleasures   Another criticism of well-
being arguments is that they justify artificially induced pleasure as
being as good as the real thing. Nozick (1974:42–5) imagines a
machine which injects drugs into people inducing fantastic pleasures. We would not, according to Nozick, want to be plugged into
such a thing because we do not value pleasure above all else. We value
the experiences and development through which it comes. We would
never swap real experiences for artificial replacements. This shows
that it is not just well-being we value but other things such as experiences themselves and authenticity. Well-being as the basis for moral
consideration is, therefore, inadequate.

However, Nozick's criticism is problematic for two reasons. First, it
divorces well-being from the experiences which give rise to it. In my
view, many of us would object to being hooked up to a pleasure
machine because we know that drugs are no substitute for real experiences in terms of the well-being they bring. Drugs do not give the same
experience as writing poetry or playing pool and we would choose the

latter over the former because the good experiences come through the activity itself and are not replaceable. Nozick asks us to imagine the unimaginable and assures us it is because of real experience that we reject the pleasure machine. In fact we may realize well-being would not be the same in the pleasure machine.

A second reason why the pleasure machine idea is problematic is because it may well test the intuitions, emotions and norms of some of us rather than what is preferable normatively. If we do not choose a machine injecting drugs it may be because it goes against our ideas of what a good life is. We may not be tempted by the pleasure machine because we might see such a thing to be empty and false. In other words it may test our cultural values when, as I have argued, ethical decision-making should not be about bringing out what we do believe but, rather, what we should. If we reject the pleasure machine it may be because it is culturally repugnant. This does not necessarily mean that it does not make more normative sense.

The pleasure machine is a disingenuous device. It asks us to prefer the nasty and false over the good and true. Where it tests cultural dispositions this provides no basis for decisions on the different matter of normative ethics. It also falsely divorces well-being from the real experiences in which it is involved. It does not test whether it is well-being or something else which is of value because our choice for real experience is wrapped up in the recognition that it is with this that well-being lies.

3 Indefensible well-being There is a third criticism on undesirable well-being. This is that here are things which contribute to well-being but are wrong. Well-being cannot provide the basis for ethical reasoning because it is compatible with the ethically undesirable. Sadism could be justified on well-being grounds if the pleasure it brings to nine people outweighs the pain caused to a tenth being tortured. The imprisonment of black and gay people may be justified if it makes a racist and homophobic population happier (Kymlicka 1990:26).

However, these examples are problematic because they calculate well-being in abstract aggregates insensitive to the well-being of all individuals. I have argued that well-being arguments go beyond abstracts and ground ethics in the concrete experiences of individuals. In such a formulation the practices of sadism, racism and homophobia are unjustifiable because they cause suffering to sentient individuals, all of whom are entitled to moral consideration on well-being grounds. Sadism could be justified in sentient arguments which deal in total amounts of happiness but not in those concerned for the well-being of all individuals.

4 Self-interests   A fourth set of criticisms of well-being as undesirable focus on self-interest. From one point of view well-being criteria justify the unbridled pursuit of sentient self-interests. This has two related consequences. First, in a hedonistic pleasure-seeking war of all against all there would be a lot of suffering and not much pleasure. Second, the pursuit of sentient self-interests goes against pursuing the well-being of others. A criticism of self-interest from the other point of view is that sentient criteria demand too much selflessness in which we struggle for the well-being of others and neglect our own pleasure and projects. Selfless utilitarianism leaves us with a world of unhappy and unfulfilled altruists (Kymlicka 1990:24–5).

   These criticisms, however, only apply to sentient criteria determining individual choices of action. This use of sentience is undesirable because individuals acting in pursuit of utility may undermine the well-being of all individuals. Selfish action may lead to conflict and selflessness to no happiness at all. The criticisms do not apply to sentient arguments in which sentience is not a criterion for individual decision-making about how to pursue personal ends or those of others. In such arguments it is about deciding which social arrangements are best for the well-being of all sentient creatures, self-interested sentience or outright altruism not necessarily fitting the bill. This seeks a world of happy individuals which may not be best achieved by individuals going around pursuing either self-interest or selflessness.[22]

Non-well-being obligations

I have discussed criticisms which dwell on instances where well-being is undesirable. Let me look now at arguments that there are things other than well-being which should be at the basis of ethical obligations. The environmental implication of such arguments is that entities other than those with sentient capacities, plants and stones for example, should be included in the ethical community as well as animals and humans. I will look at four arguments for non-well-being ideas of what is right or good. These concern: (1) obligations to the dead; (2) secret betrayal; (3) special obligations; and (4) the 'last tree' scenario.

1 Obligations to the dead   I have already discussed the way in which many of us feel obligations to the dead. We think we should be fair or positive about their character after their death. We organize their funerals and distribution of property with attention to what they would have wanted. We like to see their unfinished projects completed or the causes or values they worked for upheld. Yet the dead cannot experience well-being. So if we feel obligations to them there must be some other criteria on which we do so.[23]

I feel such obligations in my heart and try to fulfil them in my life. But there are two problems in using my feeling of obligation as a guide to ethical consideration. The first, as I have argued, is that what we culturally, emotionally or intuitively feel is not necessarily what we *should*. Social reality should not serve as the benchmark for normative ethics and 'obligations to the dead' tests the former rather than the latter.

The second problem is that while I feel obligations to the dead it is difficult to find a justification for doing so. Put in the situation of having to make a choice, obligations to the living seem more important because they have an effect on them. Why should we have an obligation to do things for the dead because it seems right or good when it does no good for their experience or well-being? It is an empty obligation. Why should we fulfil an obligation when it has no consequences for the experiences or good of the person for whom it is done?

This is not to say that on well-being grounds there is no reason for having obligations to the dead. Their well-being when alive is enhanced if they know obligations of this sort are fulfilled and so will be for them. After they are dead there is still some sense in fulfilling such obligations (even though the dead person is not able to experience the benefits) because it shows the living that we fulfil them and contributes to their reassurance that the same will be done for them. The well-being of individuals in society depends on us having obligations and contracts and fulfilling them. We should fulfil obligations to the dead to maintain the trust and stability this engenders and which is essential for the well-being of individuals in society. And fulfilling obligations to the dead contributes to the well-being of those who do so because it gives them satisfaction and helps them avoid the suffering of lack of fulfilment of obligations. In addition I intend to continue to fulfil obligations to the dead (except maybe sometimes where they clash with those to the living) because culturally and psychologically it *feels* the right thing to do despite lack of grounds for it in its implications for the well-being of the dead after they have died.

So the 'obligations to the dead' criticism of an ethics based on well-being is methodologically flawed and disingenuous. It does not show the redundancy of well-being because there are well-being reasons for caring about the dead. It also tests our cultural sensibilities rather than to whom we *should* hold obligations. Disregarding the consequences for the living of holding obligations to the dead and disregarding cultural and psychological attachments to it, there seems little sense in holding an obligation to someone for whose experience and well-being that obligation has no implications. It is an obligation in the abstract with no meaning or experience or consequence when it is carried out for the person for whom it is done.

2 Secret betrayal   Another criticism of sentient reasons for concern about entities draws attention to secret betrayal (Kymlicka 1990:16–17; Hare 1971:131; Raz 1986:300–1). There are two points. (1) Knowledge: most of us, the point goes, would want to know if our partner was betraying us by having an affair behind our backs. We would not want to live in blissful ignorance of it even if knowing about it could not stop it or would cause us great distress. (2) Lack of knowledge: even if we did not know about the betrayal our lives would still be worse because something we would not want to happen would be happening and we would be living a deluded life. We do not want to go on thinking we are good at writing books about ecology or are being loved in an undivided way when we are not. Not knowing the worst keeps us happy but makes our life worse and I do not want to live a lie even if it makes me happier.

These points suggest there are things other than well-being which are important. Some things can make our lives better or worse regardless of their consequences for well-being and even if they have awful sentient consequences. There are two problems I have mentioned in this chapter which apply to the secret betrayal criticism of sentience.

The first is on descriptions of values and normative ethics. What we want – knowledge or truth, for example – is not necessarily good for us or of value. We may want painful knowledge of betrayal rather than blissful ignorance of it but this does not mean it will make our lives better or is of value. Descriptions of our cultural preferences are not a basis for normative ethics.

The second problem is that the argument for living the truth is not strong enough. It does not give reasons for knowledge other than on the grounds that knowledge is good in abstraction from its consequences for the quality of human life. It does not make sense for knowledge to be good independently of its implications for the quality and experience of peoples' lives. Once linked to such factors it can be seen that knowledge, however much we want it, can sometimes not be good or of value because it makes our experiences and well-being worse. Consequentialist arguments about values like knowledge are grounded deeper than deontological arguments that such things are just good because they take these values a step further and explain *why* they are good.

Secret betrayal is actually bad on well-being grounds but because of more indirect consequences than its effect on the betrayed party. It may change the personality of betrayers and make them into the sort of people less reluctant to cause harm with sentient consequences. If we know betrayal goes on we may become anxious it is happening to us. Or in a society where secret betrayal is culturally anathema many of us may be distressed to live with it going on around us. In these respects obligations not to secretly betray are comparable to obligations to the dead. The failure to fulfil such obligations has, as argued above, no sentient implications for the most directly involved person – the deceased or betrayed – but has less direct consequences for others which affect well-being and make the fulfilment of such obligations desirable on sentient grounds.

However, my main concern is with the direct implications of secret betrayal for the betrayed person. This raises whether acts without sentient consequences should be of concern, or whether something (e.g. living the truth) can be good even with adverse sentient effects. In other words it challenges my proposal that well-being is the key criterion for deciding what is of value and concern. I think this proposal stands. To live a lie goes against our intuitions of what makes life good. Many, myself included, find it impossible to want to live such a life. But to make living the truth a criterion which overrides others sets up an abstract value of what is good above the value of human experience and well-being. To do this is not a good way to make human lives good or decide on what is of value or concern because it sets up priorities which work independently of considerations of the quality of life.

3 Special obligations Another criticism of sentient arguments is that we have obligations to others with whom we have special relationships over and above obligations based on well-being. There are cases where value and concern should be invested in the former over the latter (Kymlicka 1990:21–5). We may have special obligations to our children. We are the people who brought them into the world and so it must be we, and not others, who are responsible for their welfare over and above responsibilities to other people on the basis of well-being. We are more responsible for our children than, say, a homeless person on the streets, even though we can make a greater contribution to the well-being of the latter. Or I have special obligations to my parents because they have given me love and financial support. I owe them something over and above what I owe others in the world to whose well-being I could contribute more greatly. Or we have special obligations to people with whom we have set up other sorts of formal or informal contracts in business or love, for example. If someone cleans my windows for £5 then I have an obligation to give that person the £5 rather than send it to a needy person in the third world to whose well-being the money will make a greater contribution.

In other words there are criteria other than contribution to sentient well-being which should determine what our obligations should be and what should be of value and concern to us.

There are, though, problems here related to (1) the foundations of arguments for special obligations in well-being and (2) the lack of power in non-well-being justifications for such arguments. As with obligations to the dead and secret betrayal, the best reasons for honouring special responsibilities are based on well-being. In a society where special responsibilities are held dear it will cause great distress if they are broken. They should be honoured because of the sentient consequences that follow from holding or breaking such relationships for the individuals involved. Relationships entered into, kin or non-kin, chosen or determined, set up mutual affections and expectations, the fulfilment of which creates well-being and the non-fulfilment of which distress. Special relationships and obligations are also important for social stability and harmony and the individual well-being these contribute to. Further, they are directly beneficial for individuals because of the psychological well-being that comes out of being involved in such relationships. This captures why we do and should value special relationships – not because they are good *per se* but because the good in having them is for the quality of our lives and the satisfaction and well-being in them.

This is one reason why special obligations arguments do not undermine the giving of primacy to sentience. The value of special obligations is in well-being and not in some abstract value or contract independent of well-being or suffering in human lives. An implication of this is that non-well-being arguments for special obligations do not hold up. There is no sense in holding to obligations incurred in institutions such as debt and kinship because of some worth in those institutions in their own right independently of human well-being. We should repay debts and give special attention to our kin because it is good for the well-being of people that we do so. The value of debt and kinship is in the well-being these institutions contribute to and not in the institutions themselves without respect for their human implications. In short it does not make sense to fulfil obligations where the pay-off is solely that promises are met or contracts satisfied. Obligations are important where the pay-off is that human well-being is improved.

4 The last tree   The discussions so far have been around whether sentient well-being adequately captures the basis on which we should owe obligations, hold value or be concerned for entities. This has implications for questions in environmental ethics because it determines whether our concern should extend only to sentient creatures (humans and animals) or further. I have argued that such creatures have value and should command concern and obligations because of their sentient capacities. Non-sentient entities have a value but for sentient creatures rather than intrinsically. The general criticisms of sentience so far discussed do not hold up. Let me deal now with a criticism of sentience more overtly linked to environmental issues: whether trees have an intrinsic value or whether value is only in the functions they have for sentient beings (Attfield 1983:155).

Imagine that all humans and animals have been wiped out by nuclear war save one dying human. Suppose also that all trees were destroyed except one which is alive and well and will survive. Would it be wrong for the surviving human to chop down the last tree given that s/he will not survive to benefit from its presence? Most people may say it would be wrong because the tree has a value in itself and not just for humans. The intrinsic value of the trees is in the fact that it has life, or can grow, flourish and develop. If the tree has an intrinsic value in such things then sentience is not the only thing which is of intrinsic value. The capacity for life or development is also of intrinsic value. It is not only sentient beings which have a value in themselves, but also non-sentient living things like trees.

There are problems with this argument. First, our intuitions tell us that we should not cut the tree down and our sensibilities are shocked at the idea that it would be OK to do so. Yet our intuitions and sensibilities should not determine our normative ideas about ethics. The reaction we feel to chopping down the tree is not necessarily the one we should feel.

There is a second point which relates to this issue of intuitions and cultural sensibilities. This is that our response to the 'last tree' scenario could well change if the tree were replaced by, say, nettles or weeds, things which have similar properties of life and capacity for development yet much less of a positive symbolic value. Is it the positive symbolic value in the last tree rather than the argument for non-sentient properties in it which is decisive in affecting our judgement on this issue?

Third, it is not clear whether capacities for non-sentient life and development are of intrinsic value. There is certainly something valuable from a human point of view about life and development. We value such things and gain benefits from the life and development of trees, both practical (in photosynthesis) and aesthetic. Trees bring great joy to human lives. But does the life and development of the tree have any value for the tree? Trees, as far as we know, do not experience life or development. They have capacities of life and development but no sense of them. Life and development happens to them but they have no feeling of it.

Is there a value in life and development alone, independent of the experience or lack of it by sentient beings or trees? It is difficult to see how there can be. The value of life and development is in the benefits and joy of it. Life and development are of value because satisfaction and fulfilment come from them. There is little point in just living or developing in the abstract independently of such consequences. Without them, living and development are empty processes. This is why many of us find it difficult to argue for the continued life of a human who has, say, capacities to live and grow physically but who is a 'vegetable' and has lost functions to think and carry out the processes which bring well-being to life.[24]

Conclusions

I have argued that the extension of value, concern and obligations to existing humans is inadequate. Environmental philosophy shows how our concern needs to be extended more broadly to future generations of humans and present and future generations of animals. These groups have a capacity to experience well-being and suffering which is of value in itself. Capacity to flourish, diversity, species and ecosystems have value, but an extrinsic value for individual sentient beings rather than an intrinsic value in themselves. We should be concerned about these things, but because of the value they have for sentient beings rather than in themselves.

My argument is more environmental than anthropocentric shallow ecology because it sees entities beyond humans – animals – as of intrinsic value and moral concern. It is revolutionary in conventional terms in accepting that beings beyond humans matter morally. However it falls short of deep ecology eco-centrism because it extends intrinsic value only to humans and animals. It does not include all the environment as of intrinsic value. Other living and non-living non-sentient entities in the environment have a value but it is an extrinsic value for humans and animals rather than intrinsic. I argue for a sentient-centric position, one that falls between anthropocentrism and eco-centrism.

This chapter has discussed philosophical issues at the root of concern for the environment. I will look in the next chapter at reasons for the recent spread of environmental concern.

Guide to further reading

Robin Attfield's *The Ethics of Environmental Concern* (1983) is a useful survey of the literature and main issues from a utilitarian perspective similar to mine. The first part of the book is historical. Chapters 6–10 focus more on the philosophical issues I have discussed above. Aldo Leopold's *A Sand County Almanac* (1968) and Arne Naess (see his 1989 *Ecology, Community and Lifestyle*) provide influential classic statements for deep ecology. Naess has also published article-length pieces on deep ecology, for example his 'The Shallow and the Deep, Long-Range Ecology Movement' in *Inquiry* (1973)[16]. Sylvan's article (1984) in *Radical Philosophy* is an important critique of deep ecology. Elliot and Gare (1983) and Mannison et al. (1980) have produced useful collections, both entitled *Environmental Philosophy*. John O'Neill's *Ecology, Politics and Policy* (1993a) is a recent discussion of important issues. His eco-humanist perspective offers an alternative to the views I have supported in this chapter but does not prevent him from being critical of green and liberal arguments where necessary. Andrew Brennan's *Thinking About Nature* (1988) questions the appeal to a scientific basis made by green ethical holists.

4

The Green Movement

I argued in chapter 1 that environmentalism brings insights to the study of society. It shows the need for basic archaeological work on sociology, in particular the bringing of nature into the range of factors relevant to social analysis. I showed in chapter 2, conversely, that sociology can also bring its wisdom to green searches for social and political solutions to environmental problems. I will focus in this chapter on another perspective that sociology can bring to environmentalism. Sociologists can also use their longstanding expertise to explain the rising and waning of environmentalism as a value system and social movement. However, even though this is the sort of thing that sociologists are used to doing, it still requires them to restructure the way they look at the world to get a full and adequate understanding of the rise of environmentalism.

I will first discuss general explanations of social movement activity and, then, more particularly 'new' social movements of which the green movement is one. We will then be able to look at explanations for the rise of the green movement specifically in the 1970s and 1980s.[1]

How do social movements develop?

A social movement can be defined as a collective attempt to further a common interest or goal through collective action outside established institutions. There are three key points to draw out here. First, the movement is *collective*: it involves a collective interest or goal and collective action in pursuit of it. Second, it is based on a shared *interest* or *goal*. Third, it pursues change outside established institutions, so differing from a political party.

Different sorts of general explanation of how collective action or social movements develop emphasize different foci of causality. Sociological explanations often emphasize social or cultural change in society as the basis for movement activity. Political explanations may focus on the character of political institutions or the capacity of social movements to organize politically.

(1) *Structural* theories (shown in column 1 of table 4.1) emphasize the development of collective action or social movements as resulting from changing economic or social structures. On changing economic structure, the shift from pre-industrial to capitalist modes of production can be seen as having led to the growth of the factory system and urbanization and the accentuation of the division between capital and labour, all of which facilitated the formation and organization of the labour movement. The shift from liberal to late capitalism can be seen as precipitating the rise of social movements opposed to bureaucratic expertise and centralized corporate and state power.[2] Similarly, the putative subsequent shift from organized to disorganized capitalism could be seen as leading to the breakdown of traditional class solidarity and a move to more plural and diverse political identifications and foci of conflict.[3] On changing social structure, new social groupings, such as the industrial working class with the rise of capitalism and more recently the unemployed and new middle class, could be seen as susceptible to new ideological orientations and political values and facilitative of social movements.[4] Structural explanations of social movement ideology rather than of the rise of social movements as movements may emphasize it as being geared around opposition to prevailing economic structures or contradictory social groupings.

Table 4.1 *Explanations for social movements*

| | Sociological | | Political | |
	1 *Structural*	2 *Cultural*	3 *Political*	4 *Action*
Focus	Structural bases	Cultural change	Political institutions	Movement activity
Explanation	Changing economic structure New social group/s	Value changes	Access to institutions of interest intermediation	Cohesion, organization, mobilization, leadership of movement
Aims and ideology of movement	Anti-prevailing system Interests of new social group	Cultural change	Political integration or change in political institutions	Movement as end in itself

(2) *Cultural* explanations (shown in column 2 of table 4.1) focus on cultural shifts and value changes in society. A typical example might be the post-materialist thesis discussed later in this chapter. This sees increasing standards of living and material satisfactions as leading to a greater concern with non-material values. The decline of deference and liberation from previous social mores in the 1960s might be seen as other examples favouring the alternative social movements which grew at the time. Davies (1962) emphasizes the significance of a cultural mood of rising expectations. He argues that political change is less likely to be caused by material immiseration, as is often supposed. Poverty and deprivation have more to do with resignation and despair than revolution. Change is more likely to come out of rising expectations fuelled by increasing standards of living. This explanation fits well with the situation of post-war rising standards of living in the developed world. Cultural explanations of social movement ideology, meanwhile, may emphasize opposition to prevailing cultural norms or the promotion of alternative cultural values or lifestyles.

(3) *Political* explanations (shown in column 3 of table 4.1) may see the openness of political institutions as facilitating and encouraging movement activity in society. Alternatively they may see traditional political institutions as failing to incorporate the demands and desires of particular collectivities in society. Collective agents, frustrated by their lack of access to established institutions, then resort to social movement activity outside them. Their aims may be geared around obtaining political representation or integration (see Scott 1990: esp. ch. 6). This may apply to any number of social movements – the labour, women's, peace or green movements, for example. Tilly (1978), for example, has a historically and culturally relative conception of the development of collective action. He stresses the significance of access to institutionalized means of representation and the response of authorities to collective action in determining what direction that action takes, particularly with respect to whether it turns violent or not. Social movements, for him, are a means of mobilizing group resources when the institutionalized means of representation are closed off and groups' demands are politically repressed. Smelser (1963), on the other hand, sees structural conduciveness in the form of open political institutions as a condition for facilitating social movement activity.

(4) *Action* explanations, meanwhile, (shown in column 4 of table 4.1) react against the determinism of other explanations and attempt to restore power to social movements themselves. They stress that the

development of a social movement is at least in part a function of its capacity to organize, mobilize and secure cohesion in pursuit of objectives. Touraine (1981), for example, stresses processes of activism and achievement in the development of social movements. His concept of 'historicity' is intended to encapsulate the centrality of collective actors' development of knowledge of a situation in reshaping their place in it.[5] Touraine takes a special interest in the objectives of social movements and the strategies they develop in fields of action where they are ranged against opposing forces. In other words social movements are not just an effect of structural, cultural or political change but a proactive force in themselves defining and shaping the path of formation they take. Tilly (1978) who, as we saw above, takes a conjectural and contingent view of social movement formation, also stresses the organization of a group, its success in mobilizing resources, be they material or popular support, and its cohesion on common interests, objectives and tactics. In other words, processes of group mobilization are as important as underlying shifts in economic, cultural or political patterns in determining the activity of social movements.

I will use this fourfold typology I have discussed to break up explanations of the rise of environmentalism below, focusing on political, action, cultural and structural explanations in turn. There are, of course, theories which could accommodate a number of these explanations in combination. Smelser (1963), for example, specifies six conditions for the development of collective action. Smelser's theory, set out in figure 4.1, is far from faultless,[6] but it shows how a combination of the sorts of factors mentioned above, rather than any one in isolation, can contribute to the development of social movement activity. In his conditions 1 and 2, for example, Smelser draws attention to political and structural factors in social movement formation. In 3 he highlights cultural

Figure 4.1 *Smelser's six conditions for collective action*

---

1 Structural conduciveness, e.g. political openness
2 Structural strain, e.g. societal conflicts
3 Generalized beliefs, e.g. shared ideas on grievances and action
4 Precipitating factors, e.g. events triggering action
5 Co-ordination of group, e.g. leadership, communication, resources
6 Authorities' social control, e.g. ameliorative or coercive response of authorities

---

and ideological factors and in 5 and 6 action inputs. In 4 he high-lights the role of proximate conjunctural circumstances.

A 'new' social movement?

The categories set out in table 4.1 give us general frames within which the development of social movement activity can be made sense of. There are, however, more particular accounts which try to specify what is new about social movements which have emerged in recent years (since the 1960s in particular) and are seen as novel and different from old social movements. The new social movements are said to include the green, women's, peace and civil rights movements and are contrasted with older social movements such as the labour and trade union or workers' movement.[7]

As can be seen from table 4.2 the main basis on which old and new social movements are often distinguished is that old social movements are seen as being state-oriented and new social movements civil society-oriented. (1) *Location*: old social movements tend to be located in the polity in political parties (Labour and Social Democratic Parties, for instance), whereas the new social movements are autonomous movements outside conventional political institutions. (2) *Aims*: the aims of old social movements are to secure political representation, legislative political reform and rights associated with citizenship in the political community; the new social movements, however, want to defend civil society *against* political power and redefine culture and lifestyle in civil society rather than pursuing legislative change through the state. (3) *Organization*: old

Table 4.2 *New and old social movements*

	Old social movements	New social movements
Location	Polity	Civil society
Ideology and aims	Political integration Economic rights	Autonomy civil society New values/lifestyles
Organization of movement	Formal and hierarchical	Informal network and grass roots
Medium of change	Participation in political institutions	Direct action and cultural politics

social movements adhere to formal and hierarchical modes of internal movement organization whereas the new social movements go for informal or unstructured organization or 'networks' built up from grass-roots participation rather than structures of authority. (4) *Medium of change*: the old social movements are oriented towards political institutions through which change can be achieved. The new social movements go for newer and more innovative forms of direct action and work on redefinitions of meaning and symbolic representation in culture rather than change through the political apparatus.

Is the green movement 'new'? It has many features which fit the 'new' mould. Fierce debates have raged in the movement about the usefulness of participation in the political sphere and the pursuit of change through political institutions.[8] Many greens prefer grass-roots-based decentralized forms of participation or lifestyle politics through green consumerism or communes. Many have argued that political legislation is inadequate without widespread change in our acquisitive value systems and ways of living. This involves changes in modes of consciousness in civil society rather than the passing of new laws through the state. Furthermore, some organizations in the green movement certainly are keen to pursue non-hierarchical forms of political organization in their own movement, playing down the role of leaders with arrangements such as shared spokespeople and the rotation of personnel in office.

There are however also some features of the old social movements in the green movement. Many environmental organizations are concerned to get politicians to do things to remedy degradation. Green parties have sprung up throughout the developed world aimed at getting into political power even if only through coalitional alliances or at non-national levels. While many greens want to pursue radical democratic forms of internal movement organization this has not been a one-way battle. They have come up against so-called 'realists' who see formal leadership structures and hierarchies as the most effective way to pursue political change through conventional institutions. Furthermore, many more 'old-fashioned' environmental organizations adhere to standard conventional 'old' forms of hierarchy and membership participation.

Why does such a contradictory picture emerge? There are a number of points which can be made about the general attempt to apply the new/old dichotomy to social movements and there are some things about the green movement itself which make it difficult to fit it into these parameters. Scott (1990) argues that the old/new dichotomy involves an ahistorical categorization which reifies the initial formation stage when analysing the new social movements, failing to see that old social movements started off from civil society beginnings and evolved into political entities. The current new movements may do the same under pressure from political reality and the necessity of achieving their objectives.[9] Furthermore, the so-called new social movements are not so exclusively civil society contained as suggested by the 'new' category, often being concerned also with legislative reform and political access.

In addition to the formation of green parties and environmental lobbying of politicians in pursuit of legislative change, think also of women's movements, campaigns for abortion rights, sex discrimination legislation, changes in rape laws and fair political representation. Finally, there is much variation among the new social movements between new and old forms of internal organization, and progression among some, green organizations included, towards more formal political structures. In many cases it is only the radicals and fundamentalists within the green movement who fit the 'new' bill well enough. This is not least the case for the diverse green movement. From the National Trust and the Royal Society for the Protection of Birds through Friends of the Earth and Greenpeace to Earth First! there is quite a mix between and within groups which make it difficult to classify the whole movement, let alone single groups within it like Greenpeace, into a new or old dichotomy.

Crook et al. (1992: 151, 162) deal with this question by breaking new social movements into three main components: value content, socio-cultural basis and organizational form. On value content they suggest that appealing to universal values and principles, as the new movements do, is nothing new. Such appeals are typical of modern Enlightenment ideas. On organizational form they suggest that the new social movements may well 'normalize' to more institutionalized and conventional forms in accordance with cycles of social movement formation of the sort highlighted by Scott. But they argue that such movements are 'new' in terms of their socio-cultural bases, breaking radically with old social movements in the shift from class and economic interest to socio-cultural and value bases.

Crook et al. may underestimate the value-content novelty of feminist and green inclusions of the private sphere and non-human interests in political theory. There may be new dimensions to the new social movements in this respect as well as in their socio-cultural bases. But many features of new social movements in general and the green movement in particular are either conventional in internal organization and political in orientation or are becoming more so over time.

Let me turn now to explanations for the recent rise in popularity of environmentalist values and politics. I will look at: (1) political explanations based on institutions of interest intermediation; (2) action explanations based on the role of environmental groups, the media and science in articulating environmental problems as issues; (3) cultural explanations such as the post-materialist thesis; (4) structural explanations based on changes in economic structure and the rise of social groupings such as the 'new middle class'; and finally (5) environmental explanations which focus on objective environmental problems themselves. With the exception of the last, these fit into the categories of general social movement explanation outlined in table 4.1 above.

Political explanations: the failure of political institutions

A first set of explanations for the rise of the environmental movement suggests that environmental demands become channelled into social movement form because of their exclusion from conventional political channels (such as parliament, traditional political parties, corporatist forums or the media). The focus of explanation is on the closure of established political institutions to environmental concerns. Social movements are seen as arising out of groups or demands which have to find alternative channels of expression. These they find in social movement activity in civil society or in organized participation in alternative parties in parliamentary forums. In other words one reason for the rise of environmental movements and parties is the exclusion of environmental issues from conventional politics and their channelling into alternative forms.[10]

Two dimensions to this question can be highlighted here. First, particular *groups* are excluded from political institutions and try to find other channels of expression. Second, this is the case for particular *ideas* or *demands*. I will use this distinction in my discussion below but, in the case of environmentalism, groups which support environmentalist demands and these demands themselves both seem to be excluded.

Scott (1990:143–7) argues that it is significant that environmental movements have become particularly prominent in countries like Sweden, Austria and the former West Germany which have had a strong role for corporatist arrangements of a narrow and exclusive sort. Corporatism involves the formation of a united body, acting as one, out of the bringing together of different individuals or groups. In politics the term usually refers to government by a partnership of governing politicians, business and labour. In such arrangements usually only a selective range of political actors (normally organized labour, government and employers) are included. Environmental concerns tend to be excluded from the deliberations of these actors in such forums. Formal democratic arenas (parliaments and political parties) where environmental concerns might be able to get access are circumvented by corporatist partners who take the major decisions outside them. Environmental social movements and parties are more likely to be formed in circumstances such as these where environmental concerns are excluded from mainstream politics.

Why are environmental issues excluded from corporatist processes and channelled into social movement form? Taking the distinction I made above, the explanation can be broken down into reasons which focus first on the main social groups involved in environmentalist activity and second on the ideas of environmentalism.

First, the main group often said to be most concerned about the environment is the 'new middle class' – white collar professionals who work in the non-productive public sector, in education, health and welfare for example. Members of this group are highly educated but at the poorer and more disenfranchized end of the middle class (Scott 1990:138–9). Corporatist arrangements incorporate a number of groups – the organized working class, private business and government – but noticeably not the new middle class. Feeling excluded from mainstream politics, the new middle class are more likely to channel their energies into social movement activity or alternative parties than corporatist forums or the sort of parties that participate in them. They are particularly frustrated by the coincidence of political exclusion with their relatively high level of cultural and educational assets. Their educational privileges and articulacy clash with their relative economic disadvantage and political exclusion, leading to frustration and ferment channelled through alternatives to main institutions.

The second dimension of the exclusion of enviromental concerns from corporatist arrangements moves on from the social base of environmentalist movements to their ideas. Environmentalist ideas are perhaps most prominent in the emphasis they give to questioning industrialism, economic growth and technocratic scientific rationality. These, however, are the very values corporatist actors are most committed to sustaining and pursuing with ever greater efficiency and success. The industrial working class, private business and government are all committed to economic and industrial growth to provide jobs for workers, business profits and a sound economic base for financing government expenditure and securing electoral success. In other words, not only is the main social group associated with environmentalism excluded from corporatist arrangements but the ideas of environmentalists could hardly be more at odds with the ideologies of the partners involved in such arrangements and so are likely to get short shrift from them (Scott 1990:146).

The rise of the green and other new social movement ideas can also be seen as a political as well as environmental reaction against corporatist-bureaucratic government. In Western Europe corporatist settlements were set up in the twentieth century to incorporate politically capital and labour and to undermine class conflict. However, corporatism has often been a form of elite politics that involves the participation only of the leaders of these classes and the marginalization of other interest groups. New social movements are seen as a response to social and political exclusion. According to corporatist closure theory they are an attempt to gain access for excluded groups and issues but also to propose anti-exclusive and anti-centralist political organization.[11] They propose civil society initiatives, inclusive participation, autonomy, decentralization and universal as against sectional values and try to implement these in their own internal structures. Social movements have served similar functions in Eastern bloc communist regimes where they provided a form through which citizens could oppose centralized regimes.[12]

If the corporatist closure explanation is correct, it may show why environmentalist activity has been less radical and oppositional in the USA and more oriented to mainstream political institutions. USA politics have been less bureaucratic, centralized and corporatist and more focused on processes like lobbying, constitutional interpretation and litigation, which are more open to movements and interest groups. This is not to say that such groups do not require resources to pursue their demands or that such resources are distributed equally (see Dahl 1985). But the political system is sometimes supposed to be more open than in corporatist countries and this may explain the lesser degree of oppositional anti-politics radicalism among the US ecological, civil rights, peace and women's movements (see Crook et al. 1992:137, 159; Lowe and Rudig 1986:528). Corporatist closure may also help to explain why the radical green movement has been less prominent in civil society social movement activity in Britain than elsewhere in Western Europe. Britain has a public inquiry system which can process ecological demands, integrate them into the political system and minimize radicalization of the movement arising out of exclusion and marginalization (see Lowe and Rudig 1986:536).

There are, however, limitations to political explanations for the rise of environmentalist movements based on the closure of established institutions. There are four points: the first relates to forms of political exclusion other than corporatism; the second to the role of institutional openness as well as closure in fostering the growth of environmental movements and parties; the third to the role of corporatist closure in inhibiting rather than fostering movement activity; and the fourth to the inability of political exclusion explanations to explain the rise of environmental concern in the first place.

The first point is that corporatism does not have a monopoly on political exclusion. The first-past-the-post electoral system, for example, under which it is difficult for small parties to get representation in proportion to their support, has excluded the Green Party, and so green issues, from the political agenda in Britain (Dijkink and van der Wusten 1992).

Furthermore, there may be cultural or electoralist as well as institutional reasons for the exclusion of environmental issues from mainstream political concern. Parliaments as well as corporatist forums may exclude such concerns from their agendas. Politicians may, for instance, perceive that environmental issues are not important, are subservient to greater goals such as economic growth or are not electorally viable enough for them to pursue. In other words, if exclusion of environmental issues from the mainstream political agenda is a factor in the rise of environmental movements and parties, this may be due to reasons other than, or in addition to, the presence of corporatist institutions.

A second issue is raised by the question of electoral systems mentioned above. One reason why the green movement may have been less successful politically and culturally in Britain could be due to the nature of the electoral system which excludes small parties and has prevented the Green Party from getting a foothold in political institutions and access to a public profile. In fact it could be argued that political *openness* through proportional representation (PR) rather than, or as well as, corporatist political *closure* has been a factor in the success of the green movement in corporatist countries (Scott 1990:147–8). This would fit with Smelser's (1963) stress on structural conduciveness and political openness as facilitating the formation of collective action. In the former West Germany, for example, the world's most famous green party – Die Grünen – benefited from the party list system in which a party gaining 5% of the vote is entitled to parliamentary representation. Not only does this give small parties in parliament national prominence but they also become eligible for financial support (Yearly 1991:88–9). Political openness, then, could be an explanation for the rise of the green movement in coporatist countries.

A third problem is that it seems plausible to suggest that corporatist closure could lead to the pursuit of environmental objectives through parliamentary channels rather than alternative social movements. Environmental legislation could be passed through parliament using the space left by the hiving off of major decision-making into corporatist forums. Corporatist closure, far from enabling social movement activity, could disarm it by leaving space for mainstream parliamentary participation. Fourth, political exclusion explanations in general do not explain the rise of concern for environmental problems. They only explain why that concern, once it exists, becomes channelled into social movement activity or green parties rather than through established political institutions. Other explanations are needed to explain why environmental concern arises in the first place. These may be provided by action, cultural, structural or environmental explanations of the sort I will discuss in the rest of this chapter.

Action explanations: environmental groups, the media and science

First let me look at action explanations for the rise of environmentalism. These suggest that environmental concern and the green movement are not simply products of political, economic, social or cultural structures but that they are articulated and popularized by social and political actors in the media, science and environmental groups. The emphasis here is on action rather than structure and subjective agency rather than external determination.

1 Environmental groups Some analysts are interested in the political articulation of green issues by pressure groups and political parties and the mobilization of public opinion behind them in pursuit of political change (see Lowe and Goyder 1983; Spretnak and Capra 1986).

Yearly (1991: chs 2 and 3) takes a 'social problems' perspective on the rise of environmentalism, focusing on the definition and articulation of environmental problems by social actors rather than their objective existence as such. The objective existence of environmental problems themselves is not enough to give rise to environmental awareness and concern. Explaining the work of Kituse and Spector (1981) Yearly argues that:

> the mere fact that there were objective circumstances which constituted a potential problem was not enough for a 'social problem' to emerge . . .

> sociologists concerned with social problems should suspend any interest in
> whether the objective circumstances merit the existence of a social
> problem or not . . . they should focus on the social processes involved
> in bringing an issue to public attention as a social problem. (1991:49–50)

And later:

> it might be tempting to argue that the objective problem has finally forced
> its way into the public consciousness. The social problems perspective
> prevents us from falling into that way of rewriting history. (p. 52)

The 'correctness of social problems claims' is, for social problems
analysts, Yearly argues, 'comparatively unimportant' (p. 115).

He argues that the rise in the public prominence of green concerns
in Britain has been the product of the moral entrepreneurship of
organizations like the Royal Society for Nature Conservation, the
Royal Society for the Protection of Birds and Greenpeace. These
define and shape certain environmental phenomena as problems,
using campaigns, the media and politicians and mobilizing sections
of the public behind their social problem claims. Environmental
problems do not become such by virtue simply of their objective
existence; they do not become environmental problems until they
are defined as such. And this definition and its popularization is
engineered and shaped by pressure groups and the environmental
lobby.

Eyerman and Jamison (1991; Jamison et al. 1990) also propose an
action perspective which, while recognizing the role of external
political and historical circumstances, stresses the active role of movement personnel. In particular they emphasize the creative role of ideas
and cognition in social movements – what they call 'cognitive praxis'.
They argue that social movements developed in the latter two of
the three countries they looked at – Sweden, Denmark and the
Netherlands – when three types of knowledge – cosmological, technological and organizational – were combined by environmental
activists.[13] The cosmological dimension involves the translation of
scientific ecology and analyses of natural processes into a social and
political philosophy, as in the burst of political ecology publications
in the late 1960s and early 1970s.[14] The technological dimension
involves ideas about technological processes involved in environmental despoilation and the conceptualization of alternative technologies.
The organizational dimension involves the identification of radical
participatory democracy as a desirable goal. When combined, these
three dimensions made environmentalism into a social movement.
This being so, Eyerman and Jamison emphasize, like Touraine

(1981), action and knowledge and the role of movement actors and intellectuals rather than just the external material structural determination of movement fortunes by economic, social or cultural change.

Yet it is important to note that political activity cannot alone or in all cases account for the rise of environmental concern. Dijkink and van der Wusten (1992), for example, suggest that there is a high level of environmental concern in countries like Spain and Italy without strong environmental groups there. Let me move on to other 'action' explanations.

2 The media   Yearly identifies a key actor in the definition, articulation and popularization of environmental problems as the media. The environmental organizations he looks at, Greenpeace in particular, are shrewd and skilful in their use of the media, designing their campaign activities to be visual, dramatic and easily presentable by the media and especially TV.

Other analysts draw attention to the emphasis on cultural symbols, icons and images, rather than discursive arguments, in new social movement activity. This makes them especially accessible to the media. New social movements, it is argued, are not directly political in the sense of trying especially to obtain administrative or legislative decisions. They are concerned as much to present symbols which challenge dominant cultural codes (Feher and Heller 1983; Melucci 1989). The symbols and language of new social movements are critical, oppositional and adversarial, vague yet simple and compact, visible and didactic. They include signs, badges, banners, chants and utterances calling for 'stops' or 'bans' and warning of danger. Symbols include clothes, taste, behaviour and diet – in short, lifestyle. Demonstrations of meaning are public and visual: marches, rallies, sit-ins, festivals, performances and so on. Furthermore, the presentation of cultural meaning by new social movements is often the substance and end of their activity as much as the form for presenting a case or the means for achieving another end. Social movement activity is about the very living and expression of alternative meaning. All this is unusual, visual and suitable for media, especially television presentation, and access to the media is central to the articulation and publicizing of environmental problems and the mobilization of concern and movement activity (Crook et al. 1992:154–7).

3 Science   Scientists are another group who could be added to environmental groups and the media as central to the turning of objective environmental phenomena into environmental problems and arousing green concern and political activity.

Yearly (1991:ch. 4), however, suggests that science is an unreliable and insufficient friend to the environment.[15] There are a number of reasons for this. (1) Many environmental problems are based in scientific and technological developments, e.g. CFCs, nuclear power, motor vehicles etc. (2) Many scientists actually line up on the side of industry against the environmentalist lobby. On issues such as food safety, toxic waste and nuclear power, scientists are as often to be seen opposed to the green movement as in support of it. Many greens take arguments (1) and (2) further. They argue that science is part of the ideology of industrialism and that modern science has an exploitative view of nature concerned with its instrumental use for human ends and its manipulation, domination and control. Enlightenment rationality, it is argued, needs to be replaced by a new science which is holistic and more sensitive to nature.[16] (3) Scientific knowledge is sometimes incorrect or incomplete. Scientists sometimes have to revoke previous claims or do not have sufficient knowledge to make judgements on all environmental issues because of, say, lack of resources, insufficient information or the complexity or unobservability of ecological phenomena. In these respects, scientists are 'a poor ally to environmentalists' (p. 129). (4) Scientific observations are open to different interpretations and scientific knowledge cannot make epistemological claims of certainty. (5) As well as being unreliable in these senses, science is also insufficient because making judgements about which parts of the environment need protection involves moral rather than scientific issues and deciding on policy must be based on practical and political judgement. Thus science alone is not a sufficient guide to making claims or proposing solutions in the green case.

There are three sets of problems here: first, in relation to science's reliability and sufficiency; second, in relation to its alleged industrialist and exploitative nature; and third, in relation to the idea of an alternative green science.[17] Science is more of a friend to the environment than the points made by Yearly and greens outlined above suggest.

1 Unreliable a friend to the environment as science may have been, it has been as significant a friend to it as an enemy. Scientific discoveries have been basic to the definition of environmental problems as problems and to the revival of environmentalism in the 1960s, 1970s and onwards. The detection of ozone depletion, climate change, acid rain, the effects of exhaust fumes, pesticides and detergent use, to take just some examples, and of the origins of these problems in CFCs, the burning of carbon fuels and so on, have depended on scientific discovery. In relation to points (1) to (4) in

the paragraph above, science is certainly in the very strict sense unreliable. It is partly responsible for some environmental problems, can be made to line up in defence of practices which will perpetuate them, is fallible and falls short of omniscience and cannot make epistemological claims of absolute certainty. Yet, given its role in identifying and solving environmental problems, it is as reliable a friend as the environment is likely to get. Furthermore, while insufficient in the senses Yearly outlines, it is also essential to the resolution of environmental problems.

2   It is right that science has been and is heavily determined by industrialist rationality, particularly by market and commercial priorities. However, the problem here is in the economic and political circumstances within which the priorities of science are decided and not in the necessary nature of scientific procedure itself. Modern science can be put to environmentally friendly uses in the context of different criteria and priorities for its operation. The problem with the domination and exploitation of nature criticism, meanwhile, is that the characteristics of science that critics point to here – measurement, prediction and technical control – *can* be used to dominate or exploit but not necessarily so. In fact, they can be used for quite the opposite – measuring and trying to control pollution in order to protect the environment, for example. Furthermore, measurement and prediction are separate from technical control. The latter involves a technological use to which scientific discovery can be put, given certain economic priorities and political decisions. It is a product of wider socio-economic circumstances and of the technological use of science rather than of science itself.

3   These points suggest that science is not necessarily an enemy of the environment. On the contrary, it is an essential part of solutions to environmental problems. This implies that a different science would be neither necessary nor desirable. In fact ecological and quantum approaches which green science advocates propose as an alternative are problematic. First, they are not holist as such advocates propose. Ecology, for example, studies the interrelations between species and organisms rather than wholes as above and beyond the parts. Second, this is just as well, because if they *were* holist (as opposed to relational) they would have dangerous implications in valuing systems over individuals, as suggested in chapter 3 above. Furthermore, they would be flawed as explanations (see chapter 6 below).

Modern science, in short, like environmental groups and the media, has been and is an important factor in the identification and publicizing of environmental problems and the growth of the green movement. One strength of Yearly's social problems analysis is that he provides a corrective to sociologically determinist explanations which focus on economic and industrial change, changes in occupational structure or value changes in the revival of environmentalism in the 1970s and 1980s. He shows how environmental issues do not merely reflect an objective reality or external social conditions but are shaped into environmental issues by green organizations, the media and science.

However, it is important that a focus on the social definition of environmental problems should complement rather than be counterposed to explanations based on the objective existence of environmental problems and wider economic and social processes involved in their articulation into socially defined issues. There are some problems with the extent to which Yearly takes his social constructionist approach. It is too much, for example, to dismiss the idea that objective problems can force their way into public consciousness. His assertion that the correctness of social problems claims is comparatively unimportant is too strong. Objective environmental problems are what social problems claims appeal and respond to, and environmental explanations are as important as social action approaches in showing reasons for the rise of environmental concern and the green movement. I will return to environmental explanations for the rise of the green movement. But let me look first at cultural and structural explanations.

Cultural explanations: value changes and the post-materialist thesis

There are explanations of the rise of environmentalism based on the role of value changes in capitalist liberal democracies. These link in with economic explanations because they see value change as rooted in economic changes.

The key explanation which focuses on value changes draws on Inglehart's (1971 and 1977) analysis of the rise of post-materialist values since the 1950s and 1960s in the Western world. Inglehart's thesis was proposed in the 1970s following the post-war economic boom, increasing state intervention in the provision of welfare and rising standards of living in the developed world. These developments were coupled with the rise in the late 1960s of social movements concerned with civil rights (especially of women and ethnic minorities) participatory democracy and peace and of the anti-establishment and anti-materialist student and hippy movements.

The post-materialist argument is that with rising standards of living in the developed world many peoples' material wants are being satisfied. Consequently people are becoming more oriented towards less acquisitive and non-material goals to do with factors such as quality of life, intellectual and spiritual development, political rights, participation and the environment (see Cotgrove 1982:chs 2 and 3; Lowe and Rudig 1986:513–18).

There are three critical questions which could be asked about the post-materialist thesis.

1   Is the satisfaction of material needs more likely to lead to the creation of new material needs than to post-materialism? The post-materialist thesis is based on a fixed idea of basic material needs and a hierarchy of 'higher' needs which build on these.[18] This is problematic. What basic needs are may be malleable and open to redefinition. In societies with rising standards of living increasing material satisfactions may lead to a widening range of things regarded as basic material needs rather than a transfer to non-material needs.[19] The evidence of a growing range of consumer goods which are deemed to be 'standard' in developed industrial nations (colour TVs, videos, computers, microwaves etc.) may suggest this to be an equally plausible thesis about the possible consequences of material improvement.

2   Jehlicka (1992:7) casts doubt on the empirical basis of post-materialism. He argues that evidence from a survey of green voters in EC countries shows a diversity of concerns among them, those among the German and, to some extent, Dutch populations being the only ones who really fit the post-materialist mould well (see also Kreuzer 1990). He suggests, significantly, that the only common peculiar green voter concern across the different countries is concern for the environment. This suggests the possibility of an environmental rather than a cultural explanation for the rise of environmentalism. I will come back to this.[20]

3   Another problem is that there may be reasons other than increasing material satisfaction for the rise of post-material values. Inglehart's description of post-materialism as a set of values and concerns could be accepted without accepting post-materialism as an analysis which locates them in material satisfaction (Lowe and Rudig 1986:516–18). Post-materialism could, for example, be the result rather than the cause of the rise of new social movements giving high priority to post-material issues. Or it may be due to an increased profile for environmental issues in the media or education. It could plausibly be the result of a growth in white collar public sector jobs which tend to be concerned with social welfare,

educational improvement, public health and so on, rather than an improvement in the standards of living of people in such professions or others. Or it could be a result of economic, social and political changes in society, associated perhaps with growth and bureaucratization, which lead to an objective escalation of the environmental and political problems post-materialists are concerned with. Post-materialism could be rooted in objective problems in the areas identified in post-material discourse rather than in external economic or social changes. Both the original post-materialist thesis and these other possible explanations suggest, meanwhile, that it is appropriate to see the basis of values in social or environmental processes rather than to see concern or action as deriving simply from values. Rather than analysing the basis for concern or action in values, how values are created and shifted through action in the context of particular interests, structural conditions and power relations needs to be analysed (Lowe and Rudig 1986:537).

Structural explanations: social structure and the 'new middle class'

Two explanations based on changes in social structure are often given for the rise of the green movement. One is that reorganization of the social structure in advanced capitalist countries has loosened traditional class-based political allegiances. These have been replaced by more value-based non-class cleavages and movements. The second is that the rise of environmentalism is a product of the growth of the 'new middle class'.

1 Changing class structure and political allegiances A number of processes are said to have contributed to the decomposition of the class structure. The division between ownership and control in enterprises has split the capitalist class and, together with the growth of the state, led to a large managerial white collar middle class, many of whom work in the public sector. The working class has become more divided by contradictory processes of growing affluence on one hand and unemployment and immiseration on the other. Increasing post-war social mobility, particularly from the working class into the middle class, has diluted class cohesion and identity. All this is said to have shaken up and loosened traditional class identities, consciousness and political alignment. There is a decreasing amount of voting on class lines across the board, whether by working-class people for left-wing parties or middle-class people for the right, a phenomenon described as 'absolute class dealignment' (Heath et al. 1985).

The decline of class economic interest as a basis for political allegiance and loyalty to political parties has led people to owe political allegiance more on value or socio-cultural bases and to movements other than traditional political parties. This favours the new social movements who do not appeal to specific economic interest groups but argue on the basis of universal values and offer an alternative to traditional parties.[21] None of this is to say that class interest is no longer subjectively relevant or should not be an objective factor on which people act. It is merely to say that economic interest and class bases of political allegiance have loosened to the advantage of non-economic non-interest-based and non-class movements like the green movement.

2 The new middle class   One other possible explanation for the rise of environmentalism in the 1970s and 1980s is that it is based on the growing significance of a social class group especially sensitive to post-materialist environmentalist issues – the 'new middle class'. The new middle class is perceived to have arisen out of changes in occupational structure such as the growth, with the division of ownership and control, of managerial occupations and, with the rise of the welfare state and the service sector, of public sector white collar employment. Ecology is widely seen as a predominantly middle-class issue which only the middle classes have the luxury to be concerned with and the green movement is popularly seen as being composed mostly of middle-class activists.[22]

There are four main problems with the class–values link posited here. There may be a link but it is more complicated than it first seems. To get a more accurate picture it is necessary to distinguish first between different types of environmental organization, second between different fractions of the middle class, third to investigate the direction of causality in the class–values link and fourth to look at whether it is in the interest of middle-class people to be environmentally concerned. I will come to reasons *why* middle-class people may be more environmentally concerned when I come to the third and fourth points.

1   The middle class–environmentalism link is complicated when the new environmentalism, symbolized by groups such as Friends of the Earth and Greenpeace, is distinguished from the nature conservationism of groups like the National Trust, the Ramblers' Association and the Royal Society for Nature Conservation (see Cotgrove 1982:ch. 1; Yearly 1991:ch. 2; Lowe and Goyder 1983:pt. 2). 'New'

environmentalists tend, for instance, to favour more radical forms of direct action than nature conservationists and dismiss the possibility of technocratic fixes, believing in the need for fundamental structural change in the economic and social value systems and institutions of the developed countries. Nature conservationists tend to be more moderate and defensive on such issues and focus on reforms within existing structures. This is not a clear-cut distinction as nature conservationists do sometimes use direct action and often are reacting against the broader imperatives of industrialization (Cotgrove 1982:11–12), while new environmentalists on the other hand do put a lot of work into lobbying for legislative and political reforms. However, there is a difference of emphasis and in the sorts of environmentalism that different fractions of the middle class tend to support.

Survey evidence collected by Cotgrove (1982:19–20) shows slightly higher rates of employment for nature conservationists in market than non-market sectors and much higher rates for new environmentalists in non-market than market occupations. Furthermore, focusing on the shared middle-class background of environmentalists of both groups tends to gloss over differences according to age and political ideology between new environmentalism and nature conservationists. New environmentalists are more left-wing and less sympathetic to economic individualist ideas than nature conservationists and tend to be younger.

2   Focusing now on new environmentalism brings us to the second complexity mentioned above: that it is misleading to see environmentalism as a middle-class issue when it tends to be the concern of specific fractions of the middle class with other fractions being among its fiercest critics. Cotgrove's data show that new environmentalists are concentrated in middle-class occupations in the non-market sector, especially in service professions in education, social work and health. Middle-class workers in industry and the market sector are very likely to be opposed to the green movement. Furthermore, the middle-class categorization glosses over differences within that class according to other criteria such as political attitudes. The 'new middle class' radical environmentalists are critical of market values and hierarchical and non-participative structures and are committed to non-material values, on all of which middle-class market sector industrialists hold reverse opinions.

All this suggests that the image of the new environmentalist as a sandal-clad social worker is a more subtle perception of the complex truth than the simplification that all greens are 'middle class'! The above points imply that the non-market occupational location of the environmentally concerned explains their environmental sympathies, and this brings us to the third point noted above on the direction of class–values causality.

3 This is a controversial question among sociologists who have often wished to establish the social bases of values and political behaviour. However, political sociologists have been less confident in recent years in arguing for the class determination of political behaviour because of theoretical critiques (see Hindess 1987) and empirical controversies (Heath et al. 1985) on the issue. Many analysts suggest that value orientations cannot be read off from objective economic interests, that classes do not have clear partisan as opposed to instrumental political commitments or that class is only one among many other significant social factors, such as regional location, according to which political behaviour can be classified.[23]

Cotgrove (1982:93–7) does seem to suggest that, on the environmental question, peoples' values are related to their relationship in their occupation to the marketplace. He argues that new middle-class environmentalists work outside the market sector and have 'an everyday occupational commitment to non-material goals and values'. This 'is an expression of the interests' (p. 95) of people who work outside the dominant institutions of capitalist societies where decisions are made according to economic rather than non-material values. Workers in the productive market sectors, however, have an everyday commitment to market economic values and the non-material values of environmentalism are alien to them.

However, Cotgrove (pp. 44–5) is sceptical about the idea that peoples' occupational role determines their value orientation. On the basis of further survey evidence he proposes that people tend to choose their occupation on the basis of their already existing value commitments rather than vice versa. Post-materialists tend to choose occupations involving working with people, achieving non-material satisfactions, self-expression and intrinsic rewards. Materialists tend to choose jobs offering status, security, money and extrinsic rewards. Values influence choice of occupation rather than the other way round. On the other hand this still leaves open the question of the circumstances in which people gain the values which influence their occupational choice. This could plausibly be related to home background and so leaves room for a class explanation.

4 A fourth problem with explanations of environmentalism as a middle-class movement rests on the motivation often imputed to middle-class people for being environmentally concerned. It is argued that support for new social movements is an attempt by a credentialled yet politically excluded and relatively economically disadvantaged group to achieve political clout (Scott 1990:138–9). Or the

new middle class are seen to have an interest in environmental protection because it involves expanding the state regulatory apparatus in
which they are heavily involved. There will be more jobs for their kind
and they can accumulate greater powers for themselves out of state
intervention to protect the environment. The ecology movement is an
instrument for self-interested state personnel to use to their own
advantage (Whelan 1989).

However, it is difficult to see a basis for economic interest in middle-class concern for the environment. Radical environmentalism
argues for slowing down growth and rates of consumption. A com-
fortable group, yet one which perceives itself to be materially disadvantaged relative to otherwise comparable groups, would not be likely
to perceive cuts in growth as in its interest. This is even more the case
when it is considered that the expansion of the state in the post-war
period has been financed by growth and would suffer from its running
down. Material disadvantage and political exclusion may lead the
middle-class to oppositional, critical and post-material values arising
out of social experience. But such values do not seem to offer much in
their content to the objective interest of this group. Furthermore,
environmental problems have a universal effect and, if anything,
probably affect the working and living conditions of working-class
groups more than the middle class. Class is an economic category
based on shared objective economic interest. Yet middle-class concern for the environment seems to be based more on values and socio-
cultural factors. Without an explanation based on material interests,
middle-class concern for the environment seems less of a class explanation. It may be class-based but does not seem to be class-driven (see
Lowe and Rudig 1986:522–4; Yearly 1991:81–2; Crook et al.
1992:145–6).

So there does appear to be a link between membership of the new
middle-class and concern for the environment but it may be suscept-
ibility to environmental concerns which determines occupational
position rather than vice versa. Occupational position reinforces
already existing value orientations. The growth of new middle-class
occupations may have been important for the consolidation and
strengthening of 1970s and 1980s environmentalism but perhaps
not a key factor in its rise.

This still leaves partially open the question of the social bases of the
revival of environmental concern in the 1970s and 1980s. If the growth
of new middle-class occupations only partially explains this, then
there is space for a post-materialist theory based on the significance
of post-war rising standards of living and a political sociology of the
interest group articulation of green issues. It also leads us to the most

obvious explanation yet that most poorly considered in the sociology of environmentalism: that environmentalism is a response to environmental problems.

Environmental explanations

I have already questioned Yearly's (1991) argument that objective problems are comparatively unimportant to sociological analyses of the rise of environmentalism. Yearly himself recognizes the problems with such a view when he suggests that post-materialist arguments:

> tend to overlook two things: the specifically environmental aspects of green attitudes and the particular events (and their social and political contexts) which prompt people to take an interest in green issues . . . there are specific stimuli to ecological protest.

Among these Yearly (1991:82) lists Chernobyl, food scares and the Exxon Valdez Alaska oil spill as examples. An environmentalist disposition is in part a result of 'particular, personal responses to environmental threats and problems'. There are 'certain types of development which frequently lead to collective responses' (p. 83), the building of nuclear power plants being an example (pp. 82–7).

One problem of theories discussed so far is that they play down or gloss over the 'objective' roots of environmentalism. Environmentalism is a product of the work of green interest groups, the media or scientists, further facilitated by factors such as rising standards of living which may free some people to worry about non-material matters, and the growth of occupational groupings susceptible to environmental concerns. But environmental consciousness is also related to objective problems which are its stated concern and not just to external social causes.

Explanations of environmentalism can be *too* sociological. They explain environmentalism in terms of external social factors, but they too often exclude problems identified in the content of its discourse from having a bearing on the explanation of its rise. In reducing environmentalism to social causes they deny the validity of the content of environmentalist discourse. It is reasonable to suggest that there might have been an escalation of objective problems in industrial societies of the sort identified by greens (resource depletion, traffic fumes, global warming, ozone depletion) which, defined and articulated within a particular political, economic and social milieu, are part of the explanation for the rise of environmental concern.

Environmentalism should be seen not just as a reaction to a set of secondary political, economic and social changes but also to the objective problems to which it actually addresses itself. It is the experience of environmental problems which concern environmentalists and without which it would be difficult for them to define such problems as existing or arouse popular concern over them.

Cotgrove (1982) points out that without alternative value systems capable of interpreting environmental costs as a problem and formulating alternative criteria of evaluation according to environmental rather than economic goals, such problems would never become articulated as such. But equally it is the objective existence of the social and environmental costs that allows such an articulation and underlies the growth of the green movement.

Tester's (1991) analysis of animal rights discourse provides an example of the way in which the objective basis of environmentalism in problems in the environment can be sociologized away by an attempt to explain it in terms of its social causes. Tester's book is novel in the animal rights literature in that it is a historical sociology of animal rights as a discourse rather than an argument within animal rights philosophy itself. In sociology it is novel in paying attention to the non-human world. Its problem is that it does so by focusing on human discourses about that world, denying the content of those discourses and reducing them to their social function.

Tester's argument is that animal rights is all about humans rather than animals. He proposes that animal rights discourses give rights to animals on the basis that they have a *common* sentient or organic structure to humans or are of equal value to us or members of the same community. Yet it sets up humans as the agents of moral concern and animals as the objects of it. In this way animal rights, far from being about animals, functions to establish humans' distance and distinctiveness from them. It is about humans defining themselves as superior and moral beings.

Tester stretches social constructionism too far here, reducing animal rights to human self-concern and morally relativizing it. He argues that the protagonists of animal rights are concerned more with selfhood and human perfectionism than animals. Their theories are about some humans defining themselves as different as moral agents from non-moral humans and from the objects of their concern, animals. Yet in the determination to lay out the *functions* of animal rights for *humans* here Tester sociologizes away the concern for *animals* in its *content*. He denies the stated and objective basis for moral concern.

Furthermore, Tester argues that modern animal rights discourses involve *different* rather than *better* classifications of animals to those previously existing. However, the jump from historical relativity here to epistemological and ethical relativism is too big. Modern classifications of animals can be a historical and social product but still be more sensitive to the objective sentient experiences of animals than previous classifications and so amenable to a superior ethical attitude to them. Tester slips from history to ethics here and once again in locating animal rights in social classifications misses out its basis in the objective experience of animals. Animal rights is certainly a product of how we think about animals but this is in part related to the experience that animals objectively have and not just a product of mental or social constructs. Sociology has the chance in its encounters with the non-human world to be more naturalistic and objectivist and less socially reductionist in its understandings. Tester misses the chance here. I return to his analysis in chapter 6.

One suggestion is that environmental concern is a response to the experience of loss of control over our surroundings as a result of new ecological difficulties which cannot be solved through normal processes of problem solving. There is an objective and natural basis to environmental concern (Lowe and Rudig 1986:517). In a review of the sociological literature on environmentalism, Lowe and Rudig are worried about the tendency of sociological explanations to divorce environmental concern from ecological problems (p. 518). Environmental concern is too often seen as resulting from a shift in values related to social rather than environmental causes, as a social symptom or pathology rather than a response to the problems it identifies itself. For Lowe and Rudig 'the relation between environmental problems and environmental attitudes is . . . one of the major research topics which has not been adequately addressed.' They argue for more studies of local responses to problems. Social scientists show 'an ignorance of, or an unwillingness to consider the role of environmental problems and the particular way in which they have been perceived and politicised in different countries' (p. 536).

Sociological analysis should incorporate natural environmental factors in order to get a full and complete understanding of the rise of the green movement:

> the stimuli for environmental action and their causes should be analysed. There would be no environmental problems and no green parties without the existence of environmental problems. This rather trivial point seems to have been forgotten in the literature. (p. 536)

Beck (1992) and Giddens (1990 and 1991) talk about modern societies as characterized by global risks and ecological degradation. We rely on science to understand environmental problems yet are increasingly sceptical about it and see it as part of the problem. The enormity of the risk and its inaccessibility to general understanding lead to anxiety and insecurity. Ecological anxiety is, in short, linked through the mediation of science to objective global risks and environmental problems themselves.

Jehlicka (1992) cites attitude surveys which suggest that it is general concern rather than nimby (not in my back yard) self-interest which is at the root of environmental anxiety (see Rudig et al. 1991). But he agrees that environmentalism is as much a response to environmental problems as a social pathology. He cites variability in explanations for green concern in different countries noting that concern for the environment is the only common denominator. Beyond Germany, post-materialist values are less prevalent and environmental concern more of a response to ecological conditions (1992:7). He suggests that the British are less concerned about global environmental problems because acid rain and river pollution are less prevalent in Britain than elsewhere. Countries in Western Europe where air pollution, acidification, deforestation, soil erosion and river pollution are most serious – southern Germany, Belgium, Luxembourg, the Netherlands, northern France and Switzerland – are where mature (globally concerned rather than self-interested) environmental concern is most developed (pp. 11. 18). Environmentalism is more moderate and absorbed into mainstream politics in areas like Britain and Scandinavia where, among other things, environmental deterioration is less marked. In the Czech Republic, he argues, environmental problems and votes for the green party are linked. The most environmentally affected areas record the highest votes for the greens (pp. 15–16; Jehlicka and Kostelecky 1991).

All of this suggests that even in a traditional area of sociological analysis – the study of the bases of political values and movements – a full and complete understanding requires the inclusion of natural environmental factors and society–nature interactions within the sociological rubric.

Explaining the green movement

Some of the discussion so far has suggested that there are locally or nationally specific explanations for differences in the preponderance of green values and politics.[24] The degree of environmental concern, support for green parties and green party success varies. This is not surprising as there is variation in many of the conditions which lie at the basis of environmental concern and green politics: political closure or opennness, environmental group activism and the existence of environmental problems themselves, for example. Assuming a comparative framework, there are a number of possible explanations for environmental concern and political activity. The first four correspond respectively to the political, action, cultural and structural frames for the general analysis of social movement formation which I outlined in table 4.1 The last adds a fifth category of explanation based on objective environmental problems themselves.

1 Openness or closure of political institutions Political institutions which are more open to environmental lobbying may incorporate environmental concern into mainstream politics and disarm green social movement activity. Corporatist closure, on the other hand, may exclude environmental concern and so contribute to its channelling into radical and oppositional social movement action. Some forms of electoral system – PR party lists, for example – make it easier for green parties to get elected and gain prominence and develop. Others – first-past-the-post for instance – are obstructive to green party success. These factors, however, explain the political direction green concern takes. They do not completely explain why it arises in the first place. For this other explanations need to be included.

2 Environmental groups, media and science The role of environmental groups mobilizing resources and pursuing political change and publicity effectively is important to the acceptance of environmental degradation as a problem on the public agenda. Their adaptability to the media and the interest of the media in the environment as newsworthy as well as the work of scientists in identifying environmental problems, their causes and solutions are also important.

3 Values The preponderance of value dispositions favourable to environmental concern and of economic and social circumstances favourable to such values helps the green case. However, these values are not produced in a vacuum but are located in material social actions and experiences which support and give rise to them. Such material bases might be social and environmental.

4 The new middle class The availability of groups in society with a material existence conducive to concern for post-material and environmental concerns provides a social basis for such concerns. The existence of such groups may not produce environmental concern but can provide a home for it.

5 *Environmental explanations*   Another material basis for environmental concern is in environmental problems themselves. Environmental concern may vary according to the experience of
environmental problems and no full and complete explanation of
the rise of green values and politics can be adequate without an
account of the environmental problems they identify in the content
of their discourse. Sociology needs to break with anti-naturalism and
include natural environmental factors and society–nature interactions
if it is to give an adequate account of the rise of environmentalism.
Social constructionism, which reduces environmental problems to
social symptoms, misses the chance to do this.

How do these categories interact to explain the development of green
movements? An explanation of the development of environmentalism
needs to go back to material experience. It is on the basis of experience
of environmental problems that a concern about them is developed.
For it to be developed and popularized requires the identification of
such problems (by science) and the successful and effective mobilization of resources (by environmental groups) in pursuit of environmental concern. Such groups and values form and develop within a
particular social, economic, political and cultural context. The availability of social groups with a material existence conducive to environmental concern and of propitious economic conditions and value
concerns affect the degree of receptivity to green values. Environmental concerns also develop within the context of sets of power relations.
The closure or openness of political parties and institutions, for
example, may affect the direction in which environmental concern is
channelled politically.
  I have looked in the previous chapter and this one at the philosophical bases of environmentalism and reasons for its rise in popularity. I will look in the next couple of chapters at the implications of
environmentalism for traditional political and social theory.

Guide to further reading

Lowe and Rudig are leading environmental sociologists and their
trend report on 'Political Ecology and the Social Sciences' (1986)
provides a useful review of the literature. They are critical of post-
materialist explanations and stress the importance of political, comparative and environmental factors. Stephen Cotgrove's *Catastrophe
or Cornucopia* (1982) covers many explanations including post-
materialism and the middle-class issue. Chapters 2, 3 and 4 of Yearly's

The Green Case (1991) take a social problems approach to the role of green groups and the media in popularizing environmentalism but question the role of science. Eyerman and Jamison provide an 'action' explanation in their *Social Movements: A Cognitive Approach* (1991). This book arose out of the Jamison et al. comparative study *The Making of the New Environmental Consciousness* (1990). Chapter 5 of Crook et al.'s *Postmodernization* (1992) accessibly and succinctly analyses the rise of social movements and new politics from a point of view influenced by postmodern ideas about shifts in the structures of late capitalist societies. Alan Scott's *Ideology and the New Social Movements* (1990) provides a 'political' explanation which plays down the newness of the new social movements and tends to give succour to 'realists' rather than 'fundamentalists' in the green movement.

5

Ecology and Political Theory

Chapter 6 is concerned with explanatory social theory; this one is about the encounter of ecology with normative political theory.[1] Radical greens claim that ecology constitutes a new perspective in political theory which leaves behind the older longstanding traditions.[2] They argue that there is a green view of society and politics and that specific social and political arrangements can be argued for on green grounds. Just as there are conservative, liberal and socialist political theories and forms of social and political organization, so there is a green political theory and green forms of social and political organization.

The main issue in the encounter of ecology with political theory is whether ecology does undermine traditional political theories and constitutes a new theory itself. In the light of the rise of ecology are traditional political theories put into question or how should they be altered? Does ecology constitute a new paradigm through which environmental, social and political issues can be answered on green grounds? These are important questions because they determine which theoretical perspectives can help with fundamental environmental, social and political concerns. There are two issues: (1) the implications of ecology for traditional political theory and (2) the possibility of a green political theory.

1 Ecology as revolutionary for political theory Ecologists do bring new insights to political theory. They bring in nature in two mould-breaking ways. First, they show that there are natural limits to social and political life. The latter has to be evaluated in terms of natural limits and not just on social desirability. Second, they argue that there is an intrinsic value in non-humans, who should be considered in moral evaluations.[3] These points require political theory to include natural limits and non-humans. They are revolutionary for political theory in the same way that the feminist insistence on including the personal in political thinking is, because they imply the need for bringing in previously excluded issues of concern.

2 A green political theory?   There are two main problems with the case that ecologists make for green political theory. First, it is true that some sorts of social and political arrangements are more conducive to ecological ends than others and so could be seen as green. However, these are fewer in number than many greens argue. Greens put down too broad a range of values as being green. Many of the values they propose – equality and diversity, for example – are not definitively green. Ecological stipulations do not necessarily imply egalitarian or pluralist arrangements. Some – decentralism and non-interference, for instance – are problematic on green grounds.[4] Second, there are a wide range of problems – for example on justice, equality and liberty – which environmental criteria are not equipped to solve. On such issues older political theories are more helpful.

In short, ecology does bring mould-breaking insights to political theory. But the capacity for ecology to support a political theory can be exaggerated. With radical greens I agree that ecology is revolutionary for political theory. Against them I do not think traditional political theory is redundant or that ecology can support a new political theory. Against sceptics, however, I think that some principles and social and political arrangements (e.g. centralized co-ordination and selective growth) are more adequate on green grounds than others and that ecology can, therefore, support a limited range of political theory principles.[5] Let me explain some of these points, looking at ecology in relation to traditions in political theory such as conservatism, liberalism, authoritarianism and fascism, socialism and feminism.[6]

Conservatism

Conservatism is a political philosophy which is averse to progressive change, oriented to the preservation of institutions and values and committed to tradition and authority. It is concerned with conservation of the best of the past and of hierarchy and the *status quo*. It should not be confused with the politics of, say, the British Conservative Party which, as well as containing conservative strands, also contains strong elements of radical *laissez-faire* liberal politics. It should also not be equated with the right in general. While in the West conservatives are often right wing, conservatism in the former Soviet Union, for example, is a label attached to Communists, with right-wing free marketeers who espouse liberal economics seen as the radical progressives.

Some greens urge humans to be more humble and accommodating before nature, adapting to its laws and rhythms and putting less emphasis on exercising control over their environment and manipulating it to their own advantage. They are often sceptical and critical of Enlightenment ideas about the capacity of human rationality and the commitment to progress and innovation. This gives ecology a distinctively conservative edge, emphasizing conservation and adaptation to the existing order rather than intervention and change. Many greens hark back to the golden days of a pre-industrial past and use organic metaphors in ways also typical of conservative thought.

Naess (1989:ch. 1), for instance, argues that our ignorance about the long-term consequences of our actions for the ecosystem means that the burden of proof should rest with interventionists rather than ecologists. In the absence of convincing evidence that our encroachments on the environment are not likely to be detrimental we should opt for a conservative stance of non-interference, accommodation and restraint. Naess echoes the holist and non-interventionist sentiments and conclusions of others like Lovelock (1979) when he argues that the awesome complexity and ability of nature to achieve balance and optimal conditions for sustaining life are sufficiently beyond our comprehension – yet to our benefit – that we are better advised to adapt to it rather than disturb it.

However, there is much in green thought which is distinctly radical and non-conservative (see Eckersley 1992:21–2 and Wells 1978). Many greens call for quite radical changes in economic priorities, political structures, social lifestyles and cultural value systems. There are also strong elements of democracy and egalitarianism in radical green thinking which are at odds with conservative emphases on authority and hierarchy. In addition, ecology brings new insights with its emphasis on natural limits and the moral standing of non-humans. Ecology does have strong conservative elements. But there are ways in which ecology is opposed to many traditional conservative tenets and brings new issues and concerns to political theory that are not accounted for in conservatism.

Liberalism

Liberalism is a political philosophy committed to the rights and liberty of the individual. It contrasts with socialism or conservatism which are seen by liberals as being too tied to ideas about the obligations of individuals to the collective and the state rather than their freedom from such institutions. As with conservatism, it should not be equated with the politics of Liberal parties which, while often embedded in the liberal tradition, are also wedded to interventionist social democratic values which go against the liberal grain.

The inclusion of nature in the ethical community can be seen as an extension of liberalism in an ecological direction because it speaks in a typically liberal language of rights and obligations. What greens can say is that they are taking the liberal language of rights to its logical conclusions (see Callicott 1980 and Nash 1985 and 1989). Rights have been extended from propertied men to slaves, the propertyless and women and through the legal, political and social spheres of society. It is the next logical step for them to be extended to future as well as present generations and to animals and other living and non-living organisms (animals, plants and maybe even rocks, stones and sand). Humans, by virtue of our relationship to nature in a wider community, have ethical obligations to it.[7] Ecologists discuss their concerns with concepts and preoccupations of longstanding concern from liberal political theory. Influential classic liberals have, in fact, explicitly preached environmentalist virtues. John Stuart Mill (1979) was an early advocate of the stationary state economy and Jeremy Bentham (1960) of the extension of rights to animals as sentient beings.

However, there is a lot in liberal political theory that runs counter to radical ecology. Individualism, the pursuit of private gain, limited government and market freedom are contradicted by radical ecology commitments to the resolution of environmental problems as a collective good and to intervention and restrictions on economic and personal freedoms to deal with them. Liberal political economy is seen to underpin the commitment to economic expansion and accumulation and to the identification of wealth and material advancement with progress and improvement.[8] Furthermore, the commitment to institutions of liberal democracy does not seem to fit well with strands in radical ecology which stress either decentralized participatory democracy or centralized authoritarian survivalism.[9]

So while ecology could be seen as an extension of liberalism, there are other senses in which the two are contrary to one another. There are elements of liberalism in ecological political theory but ecology goes against liberalism as well as drawing on it. In this case ecology challenges traditional political theory. But, by drawing on it, it does not undermine it and shows that green political theory does not stand alone as a new political theory which breaks with the old traditions to support itself on environmental arguments alone.

Authoritarianism and fascism

Ecology is often seen as conflicting with liberalism where it requires coercive solutions to environmental problems. It not only goes against liberalism in attributing environmental problems to market freedoms and the pursuit of private gain but also in suggesting that liberal principles may need to be overridden to prevent environmental degradation and the loss of human freedoms in the future as a result of worsening natural necessities. Ecology is seen by many critics as an illiberal political theory which draws on authoritarian and even fascist doctrines.[10]

Critics suggest that green demands require excessive restrictions on human freedom. Sustainability, according to greens, requires governments to impose stiff restrictions on levels of consumption, family size and individuals' freedom to pursue their preferred lifestyle. These sorts of restrictions strike at the heart of liberal concerns. They suggest centrally imposed, co-ordinated rationing and intrusions into the most private aspects of our lives.

Writers like Heilbroner (1974), Ophuls (1977) and Hardin (1977) who propose centralized or coercive solutions fear genuinely for human survival.[11] Fired by notions such as the Club of Rome's 'exponential growth' they feel a need for urgently effective solutions. Given conditions in which individuals are motivated by self-interest and the maximization of private gain, strong centralized state action is needed to enforce behaviour necessary for common survival. Individuals are too self-interested to pursue this by themselves. Even if human nature is transformable, the requirement for immediate action does not allow us to wait. Radical action is needed in the meantime and, in the absence of individuals' willingness to take it, has to be enacted by the state. A more liberal scenario would be preferable but pressing necessities require immediate state action to ensure survival and protect human freedom from worse future impositions on it due to disintegrating ecological necessities.[12]

Some of the 'coercive' perspectives touch on arguments to do with population control and deal with distributions between developed and less developed countries and issues to do with immigration and race. It is in areas like this that coercive solutions are sometimes seen to be also fascist. Let me illustrate arguments put forward by some allegedly authoritarian or fascist environmentalists by looking at the proposals of ecologists like Hardin and others.

Hardin expresses many of the themes to do with private self-interest and commonly agreed coercion now to avoid worse ecological impositions in the future. He looks at population control and distributions between developed and less developed countries. His allegory on the 'tragedy of the commons' is a classic in the ecological literature (Hardin 1977).

Hardin argues that the 'tragedy of the commons' happens when herdsmen (*sic*) using common pasture decide individually to add animals to their herds to maximize their own gain. Each herdsman calculates that he will reap the full gains from grazing an extra animal because it will all be his but will be able to spread the consequences of the overgrazing caused by this because it affects property which is communal. On balance it is worth it for the individual. The tragedy is when all the herdsmen start to do the same thing and get locked into a spiral where each looks to their own individual interest and disregards the interests of society. The commons are, of course, subject to natural limits which do not allow them to carry the escalating level of use and they become overgrazed and eventually ruined because of the free pursuit of self-interest on common property. 'Freedom in a commons', Hardin argues, 'brings ruin to all' (1977:20) and this, of course, is an analogy for the planet-wide situation.[13] This is where the population question comes in because Hardin argues that the commons are safe while the population of herdsmen and cattle are kept down by war, disease and so on. But it is when population growth begins to exceed the carrying capacity of the land that the problems start.[14]

Hardin's metaphor could be used to come to different political conclusions and is very relevant to whether liberal or socialist perspectives are more adequate to a green perspective in political theory. From the left it could be a condemnation of private ownership, market freedom and self-interested economic rationality. If the herd as well as the land was owned commonly then the communal impact of overgrazing would receive greater attention. From the right it could be an argument for private ownership of the land as well the cattle so that private decisions would have a private rather than a common impact and people would be personally liable for their decisions. This would inhibit them from pursuing environmentally damaging practices if they were to bear the full brunt of its effects and would provide a self-interest motivation for protecting the environment.

Hardin himself advocates various solutions – private property and pollution and population controls – which involve impinging on peoples' freedoms. Mutual coercion, mutually imposed, is how he envisages it. But Hardin argues that these restrictions prevent us from imposing common ruin on ourselves and safeguard our future freedom to pursue our goals. Furthermore, coercion rather than exhortation is necessary because appeals to act conscientiously do not recognize the self-interest maximizing orientation of individuals and their ability to remain stubbornly unshaken by common interests in a context where greatest value is placed on liberal individual freedoms.

Hardin's argument is powerfully evocative and many greens are convinced of the need for some measure of coercion, if only to a degree comparable to the coercions in law we already accept and in pursuit of longer-term freedoms. This is not least the case on the question of population control that most concerns Hardin. Irvine and Ponton (1988:18–23), for example, argue that:

> Nature would eventually solve the problem of human numbers but in ways unacceptable to civilised thinking. The only alternative, therefore, is human self-restraint . . . Freedom is divisible . . . If we want to keep the rest of our freedoms, we must restrict the freedom to breed . . . There could be payments for periods of non-pregnancy and non-birth . . . tax benefits for families with fewer than two children; sterilisation bonuses; withdrawal of maternity and similar benefits after a second child; larger pensions for people with fewer than two children; free, easily available family planning; more funds for research into means of contraception, especially for men; an end to infertility research and treatment; a more realistic approach to abortion; the banning of surrogate motherhood and similar practices . . . In terms of foreign aid, the cruel truth is that help given to regimes actually opposed to population policies is counter-productive and should cease. They are the true enemies of life and do not merit support. So too are those religions which do not actively support birth control.

Proposals such as those for the ending of fertility research and surrogate motherhood raise an issue central to many environmental proposals but often overlooked: equality (for exceptions see J. Young (1989) and Jacobs (1991)). These proposals place the burden of population control disproportionately on one group: infertile women. Apart from this fact and the stridency of the final remarks quoted, though, what is most shocking and unsettling for many of us about what Irvine and Ponton advocate is in a cruel illiberal irony. This is that to rescue one thing we categorize as 'nature' – the external environment – they propose manipulation of another activity we feel should be immune to interference because it is regarded as natural and private – having children.

In another controversial allegory in which he proposes this time a 'lifeboat ethic', Hardin shows how environmentalism can be turned into authoritarian or fascist proposals. He conjures up a lifeboat carrying ten people on a sea full of others drowning. The boat only has supplies for the ten. Hardin argues that to let any extra people on board would lead to starvation and the death of them all because of insufficient supplies to go round. This is easily translated into arguments against food aid to the third world on the grounds that the earth cannot supply enough for everyone and that third world peoples will have to go without, not least because they are the ones supposedly responsible for 'overbreeding'. This is echoed in the quote from Irvine and Ponton above but is fiercely attacked by environmentalists like Trainer (1985) and Caldwell (1977). They argue that both environmental and third world problems have more to do with first world over-consumption than third world over-population. Either way it shows that environmentalist concerns with issues such as population growth and scarcity are easy prey for translation into the reinforcement of stereotypes and discrimination on the grounds of race (Pepper 1984:204–14).

Critiques of aid link in with solutions to population control proposed by some greens which draw on Gaia-influenced ecological ideas about the self-balancing capacity of the earth to stabilize and provide the optimal conditions for life. Aid, it is argued, removes natural checks on population growth by improving health and mortality and fertility rates. A report by the Environmental Fund (which includes environmentalists like Paul Ehrlich and Garrett Hardin) argues that: 'improving the nutrition of poor women increases their fertility . . . simply sending food assistance to hungry nations, or even helping them grow more food isn't enough. It simply makes the problem worse' (Environmental Fund 1977, quoted in Pepper 1984:210). Similar Malthusian reasoning is expressed in the journal of the green group Earth First!: 'If radical environmentalists were to invent a disease to bring human population back to sanity, it would probably be something like AIDS . . . the possible benefits of this to the environment are staggering' (quoted in Dobson 1990:64).

Hardin's views go on to advocacy of triage (criteria for selecting which third world countries should be eligible for aid and which not) and eugenics (improvement of the human species by encouraging breeding among its more intelligent members and sterilization of the unintelligent and irresponsible (Pepper 1984:211–12)). Such discussions are based on Hardin's arguments about ecological scarcity and over-population and it can be seen here how ecological thinking can have clear commonalities with fascist political theory.

Other supposedly quite moderate liberal greens propose tight immigration restrictions to protect communities from population growth (Porritt 1986:191; Goldsmith 1988:203). This is a recipe for parochial self-protection, implying that communities should separate themselves off to look after their own interests and leave others to it. It would be made worse in the autarkic self-sufficient communities advocated by many greens. Furthermore, it does not tackle the problem which is to do with overall population levels rather than their distribution between territories. Immigration controls do not solve the over-population problem but merely displace it onto someone else. They do not relate to over-population but provide a breeding ground for xenophobia and racism.

The emphasis of many greens on self-restraint, self-policing and re-education through the state or decentralized community, and the ultimate fallback of coercion and law should moral pressure fail, all smack of the totalitarian (see Goldsmith et al. 1972:14). And there is in some ecological writing a 'romantic quasi-mystical sentimentality' (Pepper 1984:207) and a metaphysical spiritual power given to the wilderness and 'Mother Earth' (see Lovelock 1979). This is reminiscent of non-rational semi-religious notions of race and destiny in Nazi philosophy. Like fascists, many greens are preoccupied with organic and holistic notions, naturalness and the natural rightness of hierarchy and the survival of the fittest (Pepper 1984:206).

All of this is of concern to critics of fascism and authoritarianism. In considerations of population, immigration and the third world and in the concepts and rhetoric of some green thinking there are racist and fascist potentialities. In proposals for restrictions on population, consumption and lifestyle a significant loss of human freedom seems to be implied.[15]

Ophuls (1973, 1977) is a survivalist advocate of coercive solutions who tries to deal with liberal criticisms of such a position. He argues that some rights would have to be given up in a sustainable society, especially rights to use private property as capital. But he suggests that restrictions on such economic rights do not imply restrictions on political rights or liberal constitutionalism. Restraints on consumption and lifestyle can be self-imposed. In fact, it is the absence of greater ecological consciousness and lifestyles rather than its imposition which is likely to lead to tyranny. Escalating resource depletion, population growth and pollution will, in line with the expectations of the limits to growth thesis, necessitate eventual recourse to even greater totalitarian and authoritarian measures by political authorities if these problems are left untouched by early action and are allowed to reach crisis point. Alternatively, nature will exert its own tyranny when extreme lack of resources and pollution place restrictions on human lifestyles. The choice is not between restrictions on one hand or freedom on the other. It is between freedom of lifestyle now or freedom from external necessity in the future and between restrictions imposed by political choice in the present or involuntarily later. Ophuls also argues that the decentralized self-reliant local communities envisaged by greens would involve less centralized power and intervention rather than more. Furthermore, greens tend to favour a freedom of local communities to adopt whatever social and political systems they prefer, with a resulting free diversity of forms rather than their imposition from above.

Some of Ophuls's arguments are powerful, particularly that failure voluntarily to change our own behaviour now stores up the possibility of greater authoritarian action in the future. But his hopes for self-imposed changes are optimistic and understate the degree of centrally imposed restrictions that are necessary. Furthermore, small-scale autarkic local communities can be authoritarian in the degree of close community control they are able to impose, whether through coercion or simply the pressure of social norms. Larger, less easily monitored and controlled communities can be less effective in this respect. And a liberal tolerance of diverse forms of political organiza-tion in different communities may be illiberal because of the author-itarian regimes it could allow to exist.

So the strength of Ophuls's arguments is mixed. But the key point is that centrally imposed curtailments on peoples' freedoms now are likely to be less authoritarian than those that would be required at a later stage and so can obviate more authoritarian solutions in the future. Impositions on our freedom to pursue the lifestyle of our choice now will be nothing compared to threats to our ways of living, health and even survival if we do not make them. Greens can argue that restrictions on our freedom to pursue whatever lifestyle we choose are inevitable and that if we do not impose them politically ourselves they will be imposed in a more ferocious manner by nature. Libertarians are sensitive to the oppression of the state but at the expense of a sensitivity to possible threats to freedom from non-state sources (such as economic power or ecological necessity) and to the capacity of state to be a friend as well as sometimes an enemy of freedom (in this case intervening to pre-empt environmen-tal crises). They are also reluctant to consider that restrictions cannot only be mutually imposed but also mutually agreed through normal channels of democratic accountability. State action can be combined with liberal and democratic institutions.[16]

So environmentalist concern can involve appeals to authoritarian or fascist ideas. On authoritarianism, however, many environmentalist proposals do not involve a qualitative shift from democratically agreed coercions we already agree to accept mutually in liberal soci-eties. Furthermore, coercive action now is intended to pre-empt greater restrictions on freedom in the future whether imposed by political authority or natural necessity. Mutual impositions can also be sub-ject to mutual agreement through normal channels of democratic accountability and liberal restraints. On fascism, environmentalist ideas can be compared in some cases to elements in fascist ideology. However, fascism is possible in, rather than necessary to, environmentalism. Many values in environmentalist thinking – the valuing of diversity and equality of species, for example – also go against the sort of totalitarian and racist aspirations of fascist ideology.

Marxism and socialism

Many ecologists argue that ecology is neither right nor left. Capitalism and socialism are seen as equally unecological because both accept the logic of industrial growth. Green thinking rejects that logic and goes beyond both. Porritt and Winner (1988:256), for instance, say that there is a 'super-ideology' which unites capitalism and socialism in a common pursuit of economic and industrial growth (see also Porritt 1986:44). Socialists as much as capitalists, it is argued, are committed to growth and the development of productive forces. Ecological problems in Eastern bloc state socialism have been worse than in Western capitalism, Chernobyl being the most prominent instance. Western parliamentary socialism on the other hand has envisaged growth as creating the wealth needed to finance the relief of poverty, egalitarian distribution and the welfare state.

However, there are questions on which ecology does not break so decisively with socialism. Socialists have been keen to reinvigorate their own embattled ideology by aligning it with ecology whose fortunes are seen to be more on the rise than on the wane. But the reason for seeing some common ground between ecology and socialism cannot be reduced just to socialist expediency.

Socialist writers have attempted to explore the relationship between socialism and ecology with varying degrees of receptivity or hostility to green thinking.[17] I will look in this section at the relation of ecology to Marxist and socialist perspectives in political theory. Does ecology challenge such perspectives or require them to be adapted? How much can it draw on them to further its own analysis? Does it completely undermine them and establish itself as a new and distinctive doctrine which can break with traditional political perspectives?

I will look first at positive things which could be said about Marxism and socialism in relation to ecology before turning, in a fourth section, to a more critical assessment of their adequacy on environmental grounds. There are three main ways in which Marxism and socialism could be looked at positively in relation to ecological thought. (1) Marx had interesting things to say about the relations between humans and nature which could be useful to a green political theory. (2) Socialist political economy is a useful contributor to the analysis of capitalist and market structures that contribute to environmental problems and of institutions of socialist economic organization that could facilitate their resolution. (3) There is a decentralized communitarian tradition in non-Marxist socialist thought which is comparable to some strands in radical ecological thinking.

1 Marx on humans and human nature   A number of writers suggest that there are elements in the social theory of the early Marx which contribute to green political theory and an environmental theorization of the relations between society and nature. On this account, far from being undermined or surpassed by green political theory Marxism is a key contributor to it.[18]

Dickens (1992) and Lee (1980) argue that Marx has (1) a dialectical understanding of the relations between society and nature; (2) a notion of human realization which stresses relations with nature; and (3) an analysis of capitalism which criticizes peoples' alienation from nature. All this points to the beginnings of an ecological perspective in Marx which can be used in green political theory.

Marx argues in his early writings that peoples' being is not simply psychologically internal but is constituted in their relationships with the wider social and natural world. People work on and transform their environments and the environment they are in affects what they become. More practically, people depend on nature for their material existence. Nature is 'man's inorganic body'. Marx felt that the powers and needs of humans, for intellectual, spiritual and aesthetic fulfilment, perception, interpretation, exploration and appropriation, are realized through interaction with their environment, social and natural. Without such interaction these powers are left unrealized or distorted. This is a dialectical conception which goes beyond unecological frameworks in which humans and nature are divorced or opposites. Marx argues that among the forms of alienation suffered by people under capitalism one involves alienation from nature. Under capitalism nature is transformed into something 'other' to be exploited and valued for its utility and exchange value or as a property, possession or commodity. Overcoming alienation involves restoring our relationship to nature and rediscovering it as something of value in itself.

All this sounds promising for ecological analysis. It gives a useful picture of peoples' interconnections with nature and an antidote to the idea that we can alter and transform it without this having implications for us. In the picture of human realization through interaction with nature there is a reason for humans to look after and protect the natural world. These observations suggest that, far from being made redundant by ecological political theory or transcended by it, Marxism may provide a basis for a more ecological social and political theory.

2 Socialist political economy   Socialist political economy suggests that environmental problems under capitalism are caused by its competitive and expansionary dynamic. Market rationality, the imperative to accumulate and the unbridled pursuit of profit produce externalities such as depletion and pollution. These do not matter in capitalist calculations which are focused on what comes up on the balance sheet. In the effort to compete and accumulate, natural resources are over-exploited and polluting side-effects created. Market rationality is driven by short-term interests in profit which triumph over consideration of the consequences for resources or pollution in the distant future. Furthermore, environmental problems are not driven just by forces of production – industry and technology – but are also related to asymmetrical relations of production. Behind environmental problems are material interests and power relations. Capitalist owners are keen to pursue their material interests and, because they own the means of production, are dominant in power relations and able to do so. It is not just environmentally damaging technology which is at fault but also material interests in wealth accumulation and power structures deriving from ownership which allow technology to be used in pursuit of such ends.

Socialist political economy suggests the need for the dilution of the profit motive and market rationality in economic decision-making in pursuit of broader and more long-term social and environmental objectives. Such a change requires a shift in relations of production in which at present those with a material interest in accumulation have disproportionate power deriving from ownership. Long-term co-ordination in the common interest, as opposed to competitive self-interest in pursuit of private gain, would require collective ownership.[19]

I argued in chapter 2 that states acting on behalf of the general interest through legislation and enforcement provide a more realistic prospect for environmental change than decentralization. I also argued that it is problematic to see market rationality or capitalist self-interests as coinciding with a general interest in environmental protection. Ecological imperatives imply the priority of general interests, intervention and planning over self-interests, *laissez-faire* and market capitalism. Such priorities find support in socialist political economy. My discussion in this chapter has also suggested that collective ownership of the means of production is more adequate to solving environmental problems than private capitalist ownership.

3 Decentralist socialism   Socialism has, throughout its history, been a rich and diverse tradition but one in which its decentralist and liberal variants have been squashed by reformist statism in the form of social democracy in the West and revolutionary statism in Eastern bloc Marxism-Leninism. Decentralist versions of socialism, personified by writers like William Morris, G. D. H. Cole, J. S. Mill, Proudhon, Robert Owen and the French utopian socialists, have been the subject of rescue and revival attempts in recent times by liberal and pluralist socialists.[20] The significant point is that the autarkic, decentralized, simple, self-sufficient commune envisaged by many greens (and discussed in chapters 2 and 7) is similar to that advocated by these socialists. What is more, some of them, Morris and Mill for example, were well aware of and concerned about environmental problems and the possible consequences for the environment of unsustainable forms of growth. Mill, ahead of his time also on socialism and feminism, even wrote, as I have mentioned, on the steady-state economy.[21]

So in Marx's theorization of nature, socialist political economy and decentralist socialism there is a grounding for ecological theory in socialist thought. There are questions of political values on which ecological imperatives do not specify an answer and this is another area in which traditional political theories like socialism remain relevant. Ecology by itself does not make a whole politics or social programme. Questions of justice and authority, for example, cannot always be answered by environmental requirements. Ecology needs political theory as well as vice versa because 'we are social/political animals as well as denizens of an organic biosphere' (Ryle 1988:20). Ecological imperatives require some forms of social and political response but cannot alone determine them across the board, and structures of a sustainable society have to be judged in terms of traditional as well as ecological perspectives. This is another respect in which socialism might be required by green political theory rather than being made redundant by it.

4 Ecological problems with socialism   Let me look now at the extent to which ecology challenges socialist theory or requires it to adapt. I have already discussed the merits and limitations of decentralization in chapter 2 and will return to them in chapter 7. There are two further problems I will focus on here: (1) the usefulness of Marx for a theory of the environment; (2) the incorporation of natural limits and non-humans into socialist thought.

Marx's discussions of the environment are more ambivalent and complex than positive views of his ecological merits suggest. There are two problems: first, Marx's theory involves too heavy an emphasis on the human transformation of nature, and, second, it is concerned with humans at the expense of non-humans.

On the first, nature is seen as a medium for labour. Humans appropriate nature through labour and technological advancement. Through the transformation of nature human essence is realized. The relationship between humans and nature is certainly dialectical and double-sided with nature playing its part in transforming humans. But part of the dialectical process is also the humanization of nature by people. Human freedom is seen in overcoming the constraints of nature. Marx's philosophy of history and social transformation and his theory of human nature recognize a dialectical relationship between humans and nature but one in which humans realize and transform themselves and their successive historical forms of social organization in the transformation and exploitation of nature through labour and the development of productive forces.[22]

Second, Marx's conceptualization of the human–nature relationship is based on human betterment and not the well-being of non-human entities or of nature itself. The significance of the human–nature relationship is that it is through this relationship that humans realize their essence. The theorization of nature as our inorganic body is not set up to provide a basis for care for nature but to show how transformation of it is part of the furtherance of human development. There is nothing here about the betterment or well-being of non-human entities. In fact animal activities are downgraded to being lowly or basic compared to human activities which are higher and more lofty and sophisticated. Common sentient being as a basis for comparing ethical treatment is not even considered.[23]

The usefulness of Marx's dialectical conception is compromised and complicated by the view of the transformation of nature given in it and its orientation to the betterment of humans to the exclusion of concern for non-humans. The contradictions with ecological concerns complicate the usefulness of Marx's framework for a theory of environmental protection as much as they contribute to it. Given that the strength of Marx's approach is in its dialectical framework it may be better to pursue such a framework through other sources or original work on dialectics rather than in the texts of the early Marx which are too complicated and contradictory on ecological concerns.[24]

The second area in which socialist theory could be criticized on ecological grounds is for ignoring, first, natural limits and, second, obligations to the non-human world. The first of these does not stand up. Much socialist political economy *is* concerned with productivity, growth and the development of productive forces and their use to escape scarcity and create wealth in order to tackle poverty. It often focuses on restructuring relations of production leaving the commitment to developing the forces of production unquestioned. However, more and more socialists now question these assumptions. Growth and technological advance are seen to be subject to natural limits and susceptible to environmental side-effects. Socialist political economy is now often centrally concerned with the environmental externalities associated with market rationality and capitalist relations of production. Proposals for alternative forms of economy are based on adaptation to physical finitude and restraint in the development of productive forces and environmental exploitation. Eco-socialists recognize that a change in ownership of the means of production alone will not resolve environmental problems as these also require changes in the productivist outlook and restrictions on expansion in the forces of production. Many, furthermore, propose widening agency from the productivist industrial working class to social movements outside the labour movement.[25]

While socialists have shown a capacity to re-orient to concerns to do with natural limits and the problems of growth they have done so because of their anthropocentric concern for the well-being of humans. Socialists have been conscious of the implications of physical finitude and environmental externalities for humans. But they have been less concerned for non-humans and have drawn back from a genuinely environmental ethic. On 'the critique of the cornucopian and anthropocentric assumptions of modern political thought', Eckersley argues, eco-socialism 'has challenged the former but made no substantive inroads into the latter' (Eckersley 1992:120).

There is some truth in this but even here changes in eco-socialism are occurring. Benton (1993), for example, attempts a socialist theory of animal rights which goes beyond both cornucopian and anthropocentric assumptions but within a distinctively socialist perspective. Eco-socialism is sensitive to natural limits and weaker on obligations to non-humans. But on both it shows a capacity to revise its assumptions, even on the latter, where it has been slower, yet on which it can alter its conception of the relation of humans to animals on the basis of a socialist theory of equality and rights. Eckersley (1992:131) considers that while eco-socialism does not go beyond the human community this is not necessary to its outlook and can be remedied within a socialist framework.

Let me summarize on socialism. While Marx is well worth returning to for a political economy of capitalism I am not convinced of his usefulness for the interpretation of environment–society relations. Otherwise, though, green political theory does not make socialism redundant. Socialism is challenged by the need to incorporate natural limits and non-humans into its political thinking and these are adaptations socialists can and are making. Green political theory can also take a lot from socialist political economy. Furthermore, socialism is necessary to resolve non-environmental problems to do with issues such as authority, freedom and justice. Socialism is, in short, reconstructing itself in the light of green challenges and is of use to ecology. Ecology does not render it redundant. In fact it may find in it a good basis for eco-socialist alliances, theoretical and political.

Ecology and feminism

Another area in which ecologists are influenced by and find common areas of interest with traditions in political theory is in their relationship with feminism. In recent years some feminists have shifted from the main thrust of traditional feminism. They have moved away from an egalitarian and rights based emphasis on achieving equality in a man's world to a 'difference' concern with re-emphasizing the virtues of the specifically feminine. For its advocates this means breaking with the terms of reference and undesirable values and characteristics endemic in patriarchal institutions. To its critics it means returning to a celebration of all those submissive and privatized conceptions of femininity which have been at the very basis of womens' oppression.[26] This difference of emphasis and direction has laid out preoccupations and concerns which have defined the studies of some ecological thinkers. Many ecologists have been drawn to the insights and concepts of feminism in their analysis of the relationship between humankind and nature.[27]

Some eco-feminists argue that ecological sustainability requires placing greater value on balance and interrelationships, on biological and natural processes beyond human rationality and control and on attitudes of caring, nurturing and humility. All of these correspond to personality traits and values traditionally associated with femininity. Eco-feminists conclude that women, or at least feminine values, have a special place in change towards greater ecological sustainability.

Women are traditionally thought to have a greater sense of the worth of relationships and, as childbearers, to be closer to the rhythms of biological and natural processes. In their traditional domestic and maternal roles they are in day-to-day touch with tender, caring and nurturing concerns. Femininity is more conducive to ecological sustainability than the individualism, mechanistic instrumental rationality and dominating exploitative rationality of patriarchal masculinity.

Many feminists reject this approach for the manner in which it reproduces stereotypes of traditional femininity which have been at the root of women's oppression. It ties women to the servicing and care of men and children, equates womanhood with a dangerous and mysterious biological emotional irrationality to be controlled and mastered, and it subordinates women to roles of humility and submissiveness.

There are a couple of clarifications worth making about eco-feminism at this point, first on biology, second on men. First of all, eco-feminists do not necessarily seem to be saying that feminine values are biologically inherent to women and therefore fixed, immutable and confined to them. Femininity could be a socially constructed role which women are expected to live up to. In fact, that eco-feminists aspire to femininity becoming more generalized throughout the population as a whole suggests that they do not assume femininity is biologically determined and fixed. The biology and nature eco-feminists talk about is not the biology of genetic inheritance but of biological processes like childbearing, lactation, ovulation and menstruation. They do not generally endorse the psychology of genetically inherited personality traits or intelligence but are suggesting, rightly or wrongly, that by having special experience of childbearing women are closer to natural and biological processes of reproduction. This does not mean that men cannot have a 'feminine' sensibility but that the sexual division of labour combines with biological experience to make it more likely among women.

The second clarification to make is that eco-feminists, for good or ill, are not generally separatist, anti-men or anti-masculinity. On separatism they propose not that femininity should be expressed by women in a world of their own away from men but that the shared world of women and men should be more feminized. On men and masculinity, they seek a balance between masculinity and femininity in which men and women each share characteristics of both. They reject traits associated with masculinity such as aggressive individualism and domination but would find it difficult to reject the idea that women and men should not take from masculinity the values of being strong, assertive and making demands. In the sense of both the clarifications I have mentioned eco-feminists appear to be different from some 'difference' feminists who sometimes have a biologist or separatist ring to their arguments.

So eco-feminists argue that the 'feminine' stress on relationships and caring and women's closeness to biological and natural processes of childbearing and birth make them better equipped for the relational ecological sensitivity necessary for greater sustainability. The greater generalization of feminine traits and values among the entire population, female and male, can foster a more ecological society.

Some eco-feminists argue, in a way that Bookchin (1980) does on hierarchy in human society in general, that there is a connection between the exploitation of women and the exploitation of nature. This may be because exploitative relationships in parallel spheres take place through similar hierarchical and dominating structures or, more strongly, because women and nature are actually connected in the same process of exploitation. On the weaker argument women and nature are simply both victims in different spheres of a society based on hierarchy and domination. More strongly, it can be argued that there is some greater connection in that structures of hierarchy and domination are sustained by the same patriarchal Enlightenment rationality which emphasizes 'masculine' values of mastery and rational control (Shiva 1988). Stronger still is the argument that women and nature share common characteristics or are constituted similarly in patriarchal myths and discourse (see Merchant 1990). Both nature and women are seen as having similar negative characteristics: irrational, unpredictable, biological, mysterious and in need of control. Women and nature are not merely separate phenomena subordinate in parallel dualisms. They are subject to the same mechanistic patriarchal domination and constituted identically by it. Their exploitation is identical, and ecological and women's liberation are linked. This common identity of womanhood and nature could imply political alliances between the women's and green movements. Both, from this view, could benefit from the articulation of relational concerns and a greater value being placed on caring, nurturing and humility.

I have argued that eco-feminism does not necessarily see femininity as biologically determined nor, for good or ill, is it separatist or anti-men. It does provide a corrective to the devaluation of feminine values and traditionally female activities in patriarchal and some feminist discourses. There are two problems in eco-feminist thinking I can mention here. The first concerns the problem of identifying feminine traits and the second the tactical advisability of focusing on revaluing femininity.

A first criticism is that it is difficult to identify what feminine traits are when women often exhibit masculine traits and men feminine ones. To put it another way, it is difficult to find a consistent set of traits which women share and makes them distinct from men. The problem with this criticism goes back to the clarification made earlier on biology. It operates on the level of biological sex rather than social gender. Feminine personality traits are those socially associated with the social construction of femininity. They are not traits biologically inherent to women or that women always express and men do not. Feminine traits are not any less feminine if men sometimes exhibit them. This merely demonstrates that men may sometimes be feminine, and the traits remain those socially associated with femininity and particularly expected of women. It is not that women exhibit consistent traits that make them feminine but that they are traits conventionally defined as feminine and expected of women. Most of us are fairly clear about what the core traits of femininity are on this understanding.

There is a more tactical or strategic question which many feminists, with some justification, point to. This is that the activities and traits ecological and difference feminists seek to see more positively valued – care, nurturing, humility etc. – are those which have been at the root of women's oppression for centuries, confining women to servicing and subservient roles in the private sphere. Re-emphasizing such traits is likely to get us back to a situation from which feminists have spent a lot of time trying to extricate women.

This is a strong criticism but there is an answer. Feminists can escape the reproduction of women's oppression yet still positively value feminine traits by focusing less on women's aptitude for them and more on the virtues of men expressing them. The focus can be on deconstructing masculinity and feminizing men rather than on women celebrating and expressing femininity. The latter strategy, pursued in a patriarchal society, is likely to reproduce and strengthen women's subordinate position. The former offers the possibility of promoting feminine values without merely reproducing women's confinement to traditional feminine roles.

This does not preclude women celebrating feminine values or taking strength, assertiveness and self-worth from traditional masculinity. But it does imply a tactical shift of emphasis towards changing men which can avoid a return to female submissiveness. This engages with a stumbling block facing the women's movement. Problems in the past have often been based around mobilizing women into making demands and progress outside traditional feminine spheres. An increasing problem is men's refusal to be moved from their traditional masculine sphere towards more feminine values and into traditionally feminine areas of work, such as domestic work and childcare in the private sphere and traditionally female occupations and concerns in the public. Women seeking equality in paid employment or public involvement have found that they carry a double burden because they have to combine their public roles with continuing responsibilities in the domestic sphere. These are as great as before because of the lack of movement by men towards playing a role there.

Whatever its difficulties, eco-feminism recognizes that traditionally feminine personality characteristics and activities have been devalued. This has been to the detriment both of women who have performed their tasks too single-handedly and subject to low esteem and of men who have not helped or benefited from 'feminine' work (childcare in particular). Traditional egalitarian and rights-based feminism might have been an unwitting accomplice in devaluing desirable values and characteristics and rejecting potentially rewarding and fulfilling human activities as oppressive.[28] Feminine values and activities, some feminists argue now, need to be more positively evaluated in future, for the benefit of women and men. Childcare and domestic work becomes impoverished when it is devalued and disproportionately loaded onto women. However, given more value and more equally shared, such tasks can be a source of fulfilment for women and men alike; similarly with feminine personality traits of tenderness, caring, nurturing and concern for relationships. The absence of such traits from public life hinders ecological progress and the amelioration of conflict and inequity. In private life their greater concentration on one side of the sex divide hinders liberation and fulfilment for both men and women.

Feminism is another example of a tradition which ecology draws on rather than renders redundant. Ecology does not break off as a new paradigm with the ability to deal with environmental and social issues on green grounds alone. Just as it draws on ideas to do with obligations and rights from conservatism and liberalism and on socialist political economy, so feminist thinking is a resource for ecology rather than a tradition it transcends.

Ecology: new political theory or no political theory?

Andrew Dobson argues, when discussing O'Riordan's (1981:303–7) typology of global, centralized-authoritarian, authoritarian-commune and anarchist versions of environmentalism, that:

not all of these presentations can accurately be described as corresponding to the political ideology of ecologism . . . the closest approximation . . . to the centre of gravity of a Green sustainable society is the last one: the so-called 'anarchist solution' . . . the Green sustainable society . . . will not be reached by transnational global co-operation, it will not principally be organised through the institutions of the nation-state, and it is not authoritarian . . . it would therefore be quite wrong to see ecologism as an ideology (like nationalism?) that can be either right or left-wing . . . its political prescriptions are fundamentally left-liberal, and if a text, a speech or an interview on the politics of the environment sounds different from that then it is not Green but something else. (Dobson 1990:83–5)

Ryle on the other hand argues that:

'Ecology' . . . does not in itself determine in a positive sense the future development of social and economic reality. A society adapted to ecological constraints . . . could take widely varying forms. This is . . . implicit in the fact that very diverse 'sustainable societies' have been projected by different thinkers.

One can imagine an authoritarian capitalist or post-capitalist society . . . in which those at the top enjoyed ecologically profligate lifestyles . . . protected by armed guards from the mass of the people, who would endure an impoverished and 'sustainable' material standard of living . . . One can imagine a 'barrack socialism' in which an ecologically well-informed, bureaucratic elite directed the economy in accordance with environmental and resource constraints . . . Ecological limits may limit political choices but they do not determine them. The green movement may attempt to assess every option against ecological criteria, and may claim that all its proposals are compatible with sustainability; but we should not make the mistake of thinking that no other proposals, and no other outcomes, could be compatible. We should not assume that 'ecology' can satisfactorily define the new politics we are trying to develop. (Ryle 1988:7–8)

Dobson is arguing that there can be a green political theory and that it is left-liberal anarchism. Ryle argues, however, that there cannot be a green political theory because ecological imperatives are open to different sorts of social and political arrangements. I would argue against Dobson that there cannot be a green political theory because while ecology implies some forms of social and political arrangements rather than others it also draws on older traditions to work out which are preferable on these grounds and to answer non-environmental questions to do with issues such as justice and liberty. Where different sorts of social and political arrangements are compatible with green objectives, traditional non-ecological criteria are needed to decide which are preferable. Ecology can be part of a political theory but does not provide the basis for such a theory in itself.[29]

However, ecology is not completely open. I have argued that interventionism and central co-ordination are implied by ecological imperatives rather than markets, capitalism or decentralization. Environmental demands do imply some sorts of social and political arrangements rather than others. Nevertheless, Ryle is right to say that many questions cannot be answered by ecology and, this being so, that a political theory cannot be constructed on green criteria alone.

Traditional political theories are challenged by ecology. Ecology requires that they are adapted to take into account natural limits and non-humans. It has further implications for political theory in that some social and political arrangements are implied rather than others by environmental requirements. However, ecology cannot provide a new paradigm through which a political theory can be constructed on green grounds. Dealing with environmental issues involves drawing on old conservative, liberal, socialist and feminist analyses. Furthermore, there are non-environmentalist issues to which green criteria do not determine answers and which have to be answered by these old traditions. Ecology has to combine with other perspectives to put together a theory and politics on preferable regimes of economic, social and political organization.

Environmentalisms

Before the next chapter let me summarize the different sorts of environmentalist argument I have identified. In chapters 1 and 2 I suggested that one issue on which different environmentalist arguments can be identified is to do with solutions to environmental problems (see table 5.1).

Many greens propose technocratic solutions based on the development of environmentally friendly technologies. These might be

Table 5.1 *Solutions to environmental problems: technical or structural*

Type of environmentalism	Solution
technocratic environmentalist	technical
structural environmentalist	structural

'cleaner' or less polluting or can harness renewable (e.g. wind, solar power, tides) rather than non-renewable energy sources (e.g. coal, gas, oil). Other greens propose that underlying structural factors to do with social value systems and lifestyles are the basic problem to which technical solutions cannot be found. Ecological degradation will continue until we halt growth and wind down consumption and population levels.

In chapter 2 in particular I suggested another distinction within green arguments between those that rely strictly on environmental considerations for certain courses of action and those that rest their case also on independent social arguments for the intrinsic desirability of such courses (e.g. frugality, self-sufficiency) (see table 5.2).

Table 5.2   *The sustainable society: reasons for proposing it*

Type of environmentalism	Arguments
environmental	environmental
social	environmental and social

The latter category of arguments can lead to conclusions which coincide and support more specifically green arguments, but they are not themselves strictly green in content. I have suggested that environmental arguments should be distinguished from social arguments put forward by greens. Some green proposals (e.g. for lower levels of consumption and lower population levels) can be justified by recourse to environmental arguments alone. Others (e.g. the argument for decentralized self-sufficient communes) are not such clear-cut candidates for environmental justifications. Consequently green arguments for them rest more heavily on social arguments about intrinsic rewards and desirability which are not specifically green and should not be portrayed as such.

In chapter 3 I also distinguished between different green arguments on reasons why we should care about the environment (see table 5.3). Shallow ecologists argue for care for the environment on the grounds of its utility for human beings. In this sense it is humans and not the environment itself that they are really concerned about and this is what prompts some to regard people in this category as not really environmentalist at all. Deep ecologists argue that we should care about the environment because of its intrinsic value and entitlement to the same sorts of rights traditionally extended to human beings. These ecologists argue we should care about the environment for its

Table 5.3	*Environmental ethics: reasons for caring about the environment*

Types of environmentalism	Reasons for caring
Deep ecologist (eco-centric)	Intrinsic value of all environmental entities
Sentient ecologist (sentient-centric)	Intrinsic value of sentient beings. Extrinsic value of non-sentient things
Shallow ecologist (anthropocentric)	Intrinsic value of humans. Extrinsic value of non-humans

own sake and irrespective of its usefulness for humans. Sentience advocates argue we should take special care to protect and respect all creatures who have the capacity to enjoy life and should also protect parts of the environment which have value for such creatures.

On the basis of sentient arguments such theorists extend obligations to animals as well as humans. On the basis of intrinsic value arguments deep ecologists extend them to more of the environment: sentient and non-sentient living entities (i.e. plants as well as animals) and in some cases non-living organisms as well (e.g. earth, water, rocks etc.). How far the extension of rights goes depends on the characteristics according to which entities in the environment are seen to have intrinsic value. If merely being part of the community is what counts, then all things might be seen to have value and command respect. If capacity to flourish is what gives them intrinsic value then respect may extend to plants (and in differing quantities to different species of animal and plant according to their varying capacity to flourish) but not to non-living organisms like rocks.

The arguments I have advanced through this book in relation to these various distinctions are deeper than light-green proposals in that I reject technical fixes (while recognizing green technological advances as *part* of the solution) and purely human-centred concerns. However, they do not go as far as deep ecology. While they advocate structural change and non-anthropocentrism they extend the ethical remit to sentient creatures only, and not to non-sentient and non-living aspects of the natural environment on an intrinsic value basis. My arguments also go against green political theory. This is because I have argued that ecology can contribute to political theory but cannot make a political theory itself. It revolutionizes traditional political theory by bringing in natural limits and non-humans but also needs it to help solve environmental problems and deal with non-environmental issues to do with social and political organization. In so far as green political theory does have definite political implications, I am not convinced that they are of the decentralized sort that many green political theorists propose. This chapter has dealt with the relation of ecology to traditions in normative political theory. Let me now turn to ecological concerns in explanatory social theory.

Guide to further reading

Robyn Eckersley's *Environmentalism and Political Theory* (1992) is a likeable and open-minded discussion of the ecological credentials of different political theories. Garrett Hardin's 'The Tragedy of the Commons' (1977) is a classic and very important discussion which raises issues in liberal and socialist political philosophy in relation to ecological questions. Martin Ryle's brief and readable *Ecology and Socialism* (1988) is the best place to start an investigation of the relationship between the two traditions. A view by an influential figure on the new left is given in Raymond Williams's 'Socialism and Ecology' (1989) in his *Resources of Hope*. Joe Weston's collection *Red and Green* (1986) and Enzensburger's 'A Critique of Political Ecology' (1974) (in *New Left Review* 84 and his *Dreamers of the Absolute*) give traditional socialist views on the green movement. Rudolf Bahro's books *Socialism and Survival* (1982) and *From Red to Green* (1984) trace, as the title of the second suggests, the shift of one prominent writer from Marxism to the green movement. Peter Dickens (1992) in chapter 3 of *Society and Nature* and Ted Benton in chapter 2 of *Natural Relations* (1993) discuss the ecological credentials of the early Marx. *The Ecologist* 22, 1, 1992 is a special issue on ecology and feminism which goes through many of the debates raised in the meeting of these two perspectives. Val Plumwood's 'Ecofeminism: An Overview and Discussion of Positions and Arguments' (1986) is a useful supplement to the *Australian Journal of Philosophy* 64. Dobson's *The Green Reader* (1991) includes extracts from an ecofeminist point of view by Shiva, Plant and Merchant which give a flavour of the perspective.

Rethinking Relations between Society and Nature

I wish to return in this chapter to a main theme of the book: how sociology can respond to the significance of the environment and make a more ecological analysis of society and its relationship with nature. I have argued that the sociology of the environment is undeveloped. This is worrying when you think of the connections that exist between social life and ecosystems. But it is a perhaps unsurprising result of the political and disciplinary resistance of sociologists to incorporating nature within the sociological remit.

I will look in this chapter at ways in which a conceptual framework might be set up with which sociologists can theorize how the relationship between society and the natural environment works. This can be applied and used in sociological investigations in a way which will make them more adequate as full and realistic understandings of the range of factors involved in society–environment interactions and of the nature of their interaction.

I will look in turn at three ways of conceptualizing the relationship between society and nature: (1) Dunlap and Catton's 'ecological complex'; (2) 'social constructionism'; and (3) 'realism'. The 'ecological complex', which I will consider first, was set up in the 1970s by the American environmental sociologists Riley Dunlap and Will Catton and is a conceptual map that includes the environment in the range of factors relevant to a full and realistic understanding of social development. I will then move on to two ways of analysing society–nature relations which have more specific things to say not just about the range of factors involved but also about the *way* they interact and their relative weighting and causality. I will look first at the 'social constructionism' of sociologists of environmentalism like Keith Tester (1991). This emphasizes the 'social', with the natural environment seen as being constituted and understood through social practices. I will then look at the 'realist' approach of people like Ted Benton (1993) and Peter Dickens (1992). This puts more emphasis on the 'natural'. It sees nature as having independent objective properties and causal powers, albeit mediated by their interaction with social processes.

Dunlap and Catton: the 'ecological complex'

There was an attempt in the late 1970s to lay out an analytical framework which could form the basis for an environmental sociology. Rural sociologists Riley Dunlap and Will Catton Jr published a number of articles attempting to establish a framework for environmental sociological analysis.[1] The opening set up by Dunlap and Catton has been built upon in some recent attempts to theorize society–nature relations (see Benton 1991 and Dickens 1992).

Dunlap and Catton's outline of the attempt by human ecologists to bring wider ecological factors into sociology provides an insight into the barriers sociologists have to break through to introduce environmental considerations into sociology and provide a more realistic and complete picture of the range of factors relevant to the structuring and dynamic of social life. In addition, without being perfect or complete, it provides an illuminating, interesting and useful starting point for thinkers wishing to mould a more environmental consciousness in sociology.

Human ecology: a brief 'glasnost'

Dunlap and Catton take up from where they regard the 'human ecology' approach in American sociology left off. This approach was founded at the University of Chicago in the 1920s under Robert E. Park. For Dunlap and Catton the disciplinary prejudices of sociology inhibit it from reaching a 'realistic' appraisal of the contemporary human condition' (1978a:57). Sociology focuses on social explanations for social life but shuns wider ecological factors as irrelevant. Yet human ecology, they believe, made some attempts to break out of those prejudices and establish a more inclusive realistic appraisal. It signalled the start of a short-lived 'glasnost' in sociology, trying to incorporate an understanding of the influence of the physical environment (notably the spatial organization of the urban built environment) on social life. However, it did not last.

> At first, human ecology appeared to be a major departure from the
> trained inability or unwillingness of sociologists to see the significance

of environment–society interactions. Later, however, it was substantially drawn back into the larger discipline's habit of disregarding non-social variables, though it had laid foundations upon which modern environmental sociology can build. (1978a:59)

These are foundations on which Dunlap and Catton go on to elaborate and expand. The human ecologists, however, were unable to break out from the traditional taboos and prejudices of sociology. Sociological dogma brought a halt to the project and human ecology retreated from the position from which Dunlap and Catton had wished to advance it.

Anti-ecological sociologists revived the notion that the explanation of social life can go no further than reference to other factors of social life in which there is no place for the wider environment. Dunlap and Catton saw this as a 'backing away from their [human ecologists'] realistic approach to influences of a physical world upon human society' (1978a:59). Dunlap and Catton quote Quinn's insistence that human ecology 'studies the relations of man to man, and never the direct relations of man to environment' (p. 59). 'Environment' for sociologists remained a signifier for the social milieu (in socialization studies) or, at the most, the built enviroment (in urban sociology) but was denuded of its natural connotations.

Developing the 'ecological complex'

While sociologists are not enviromentally oblivious, much sociology seems to be so. Sociologists seem more concerned by environmental problems privately than in their professional work. This puts sociology behind other social sciences – geography, economics, philosophy and politics, for instance – on environmental consciousness (see Newby 1991). These have less anti-naturalist baggage to ditch, are perhaps less restrained by politically charged debates around 'nature' within their subject and maybe feel less need to justify the distinctive role of their discipline. Subsequently they have incorporated environmental considerations into their investigations much more readily than sociology has.

Yet Dunlap and Catton quote Klausner and Burch as arguing that 'Physical environment problems are symptomatic of our social organization for use of physical resources. A reorganization of society in this respect is a basic part of the solution.' Investigation is needed 'to identify some of the social origins of environmental problems and to speculate as to how these problems in turn generate certain kinds of special consequences' (1978a:60).

Dunlap and Catton's concern is that sociologists should tackle the sort of problems that Klausner and Burch identify. They argue for an environmental sociology based on the 'acceptance of "environmental" variables as meaningful for sociological investigation . . . a concern with understanding societal–environmental interactions – i.e. how human behaviour affects the environment and how the environment in turn influences human behaviour' (p. 61). To achieve this they take up the ecological framework that was developed in the human ecologists' brief 'glasnost' and attempt to develop it further into territory previously taboo to sociologists.

They propose an ecological analytical framework based on the sociological human ecologist Otis Dudley Duncan's concept of the 'ecological complex' (Duncan 1959 and 1961). They argue that this concept takes us beyond an exclusive focus on social organization to the incorporation of the physical and human-made environment within the sociological remit. Amended and expanded upon, it can be taken further to include the natural enviroment in the range of factors relevant for sociological analysis.

There are four categories in Duncan's ecological complex: population, organization, technology and environment (see figure 6.1). Dunlap and Catton argue that the ecological complex, however, is used unsatisfactorily in sociological practice. Sociologists tend to focus on the 'organization' variable in its cause or effect relations with other single elements. And in their concept of environment they concentrate on the human-made environment. Environmental sociologists, however, would focus on the environment variable and re-orient it to include the natural environment.

Furthermore, for sociological rather than environmental reasons, Dunlap and Catton propose disaggregating out the oversimplified 'organization' variable into cultural, social and personality factors. This leaves us with a complex oriented around investigating the mutual interaction between the physical environment on one hand

Figure 6.1 *The basic ecological complex: four factors*

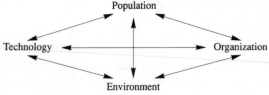

Adapted from Dunlap and Catton (1978a)

and aspects of the social complex on the other: population, technology, culture, social systems and personality.

Having disaggregated the social factors in the ecological complex, Dunlap and Catton do the same for the concept of 'environment'. There are distinctions between the social environment (social relations), the built or human-made environment (e.g. houses, towns, roads) and the natural environment (the earth, seas, mineral deposits, air etc.). Dunlap and Catton add a fourth category – 'modified' environments – aspects of the natural environment modified by human action (polluted air or altered landscapes, for example). The social environment is, of course, the traditional object of sociological concern. The built or human-made environment was introduced as a relevant subject area by urban sociologists and human ecologists. Dunlap and Catton suggest that a few sociologists have been willing to look at the social impact of the modified environment. The natural environment, meanwhile, has been most shunned as irrelevant to sociological analysis. Sociologists studying human social life in the context of the ecological complex would have to look at all the aspects of the 'environment' in their interaction with the other factors of population, technology, culture, economic and social system and personality both in their influence on these other factors and in the effect the latter have on the different aspects of the environment (see figure 6.2). All these factors together form a dynamic, processual, flowing complex. The factors constantly interact dialectically back and forth upon each other – environment influencing technology, technology in turn influencing environment and factors such as culture and social structure and being influenced by them and so on – the whole complex and its parts constantly shifting and changing in character. The environment's interactions with the other factors and the whole meanwhile remains the focus of the environmental sociologist's attention, although this would not be the primary focus in other subsections of sociology or sociology in general.

Let me illustrate the usefulness of the complex by looking at three areas of analysis where it could be helpful: analyses of causes and effects of societal development, of causes of environmental problems and of environmental effects on society.

1 Causes and effects of societal development   If you think about industrialization and the complex interrelation of factors such as cultural change (e.g. entrepreneurial and consumerist values), changing social structure (e.g. the role of the industrial bourgeoisie and working class), technological developments (e.g. mechanization and computerization), population change and migration (urbanization and

Figure 6.2   *The ecological complex: extended version*

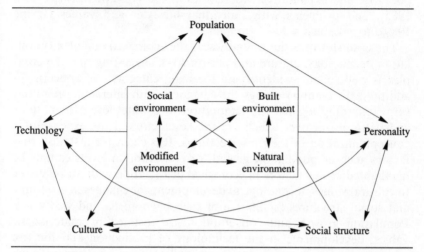

de-urbanization) and environmental change (e.g. resource depletion and pollution) involved in this process you can see what a powerful instrument this complex can be. It can make sure you give a full account of all the dimensions involved and draw your attention to the need to explain the relations between them. Using the complex forces you to give full consideration to each factor and its relations with all the other factors in explaining societal development.

One problem is that sociologists are sometimes tempted into counterposing single factors against others in monocausal analyses. Was industrialization the product of cultural change (e.g. Weber's Protestant ethic) *or* the development of productive forces or the rise of new classes (in Marxism), for instance. Another is that the environmental variable in the complex has rarely been included in sociological analyses, whether as cause or effect or both.[2] The complex provides an antidote to monocausal and environmentally insensitive analyses because it brings in many possible causal factors, including that of the environment itself.

2 Causes of environmental problems   Similarly, you can see the possible value of using the complex when looking at ecological problems. Environmentalists have highlighted numerous causal factors in environmental crises: population growth overburdening the earth's carrying capacity (Ehrlich 1970), the use of environmentally

damaging technology (Commoner 1972), the development of anthropocentric and exploitative rationalities in the Western world (Capra
1985), and problems with individual lifestyles and values (Irvine
1989), to take just a few examples.

These all slot into the categories of the ecological complex (population, technology, culture and personality), suggesting that the complex is well suited to identifying the main categories of concern. In
addition, the complex brings the categories into interacting relationships, guarding against the temptation to counterpose explanations
and battle it out over which are the key factors at the expense of a
conceptualization of their interrelations. It is clear, for instance, that
factors such as population growth or consumption levels cannot be
highlighted as key factors in ecological degradation without reference
to cultural values, technological developments or changes in economic
and social structures facilitative of such phenomena and vice versa.
Population growth and consumption are fostered by materialistic
values, developments in the technology of production and the rise
of entrepreneurial social groupings willing to push forward such
developments within a capitalist market context. Capitalism, the
industrial bourgeoisie and the development of productive forces,
meanwhile, rely on levels of population and consumption to provide
the markets which underpin their development.

This is not to say that hierarchies of importance and primacy
cannot and should not be sought out in the investigation of significant factors in ecological crises. The complex merely prevents a slide
from such an approach into monocausal and atomistic explanations.

3 Environmental effects on society   The complex also comes in
useful in analysing not only the effect of changes in the range of
social factors on the natural environment but also vice versa.
Changes in the natural environment, whether to a greater or lesser
extent a consequence of the actions of humans, have effects on social
life. Resource depletion, pollution or ozone depletion, for instance,
have immediate or foreseeable long-term effects on the use of technology, population and consumption levels and value orientations, for
example. It is conceivable that such environmental changes may lead
to the use of new, less damaging energy technologies, reductions in
population and consumption and less materialistic values, all because
of the earth and atmosphere's declining natural capacity to supply and
absorb at current levels of growth.

Dunlap and Catton make a call to arms on the need for a more
broadly ecological sociology within which their analytical framework

would be a major methodological tool. It is worth concluding my discussion of them by quoting from it.

> Modern people . . . have become so accustomed to living in a world of humanity's own making, and so aware of technological power over the physical environment that it is easy to forget that . . . we continue to be involved in and dependent upon ecosystems, and that we remain creatures that are subject to the forces of nature at all times (even though we have acquired the power to manipulate some of these forces somewhat sometimes).
> . . . limits to our freedom tend to be conceived wholly as arising from the antagonism of other people . . . but there are also limits which arise from the characteristics of physical environments and from the nature of ecosystems.
> The framework we have presented calls attention to the need for sociological research . . . transcending the obsolescent boundaries of traditional sociology . . . once it is acknowledged that human societies remain forever ecosystem-dependent, then projections of future environmental circumstances become important factors to be taken into account when considering the future of human populations . . .
> . . . Environmental sociologists, mindful of the interdependence of population, technology, and social, cultural, and personality systems, all adapting to environmental circumstances and producing environmental impacts, should play a major role in research on the feasibility of various adjustments required for the achievement of a 'steady state' . . . the necessary research will only be done by minds that have freed themselves from the obsolescent world view and disciplinary traditions [of traditional sociology]. (*1978a*)

Social constructionism

One limitation of Dunlap and Catton's ecological complex is that while it gives a map of the range of factors to be included in any full analysis of social processes it does not give us a conceptual feel for the way in which different factors interact and affect each other. There is no concept of the status of the different factors in their interactions or the nature of the effect they have on one another. The relative efficacy, causal powers or hierarchies of importance of different factors are left untheorized. In this section and the next I will look at two approaches which try to fill this gap. 'Social constructionism' puts the weight on the social and is sceptical about objective properties and causal powers in nature in its analysis of the relationship between society and nature. 'Realism' conceptualizes the relationship between society and nature with the latter as having socially mediated but independent properties and effects.

I discussed Keith Tester's (1991) historical sociology of animal rights in chapter 4. I looked there at its usefulness as a sociological explanation for environmentalism. Some of the claims in it also have implications for understanding the status of society and nature as entities and the character, balance and effects of the relationship between them. Tester writes about animals and human discourses on them but his conclusions are based on assumptions about the relationship between human societies and the non-human world. He focuses on animals specifically but what he says can be generalized to a theoretical conceptualization of the relations between society and nature at large.

Tester is keen to deny that, in the relationship between human societies and nature, the 'natural' has independent objective properties or causal powers. His argument is that nature is socially constructed and does not have a being independent of its social construction. The status of nature in the nature–society relationship is less that of an objective independent entity with powers in its own right and more of an entity which is a product of the social world.

This argument can be interpreted along three dimensions: ethical, epistemological and ontological. Ethics refers to normative moral evaluations about what is right or good. Epistemology is about the nature of our knowledge of the world. Ontology is about the nature of the being of things in the world. Ethically, the implication of Tester's views are that rights are not objective in animals but are subjective and ascribed by society. Epistemologically, he argues that what we know about nature does not spring up out of nature itself but is a product of the social interpretations ascribed to it. Ontologically, the implication is that animals do not have a nature or being which resides objectively in them but only one which we attribute to them.

Let me expand on these in turn. There are three points on ethics worth drawing out from Tester's considerations that animal rights are: (1) about humans rather than animals; (2) social rather than objective; and (3) relative rather than absolute. (1) Tester's argument is that the ascription of rights to animals has less to do with the objective status of animals or care for them and is more about the attempt by humans to set themselves off from animals as moral agents. In other words, animal rights derives from the social function it serves humanity. (2) Furthermore, rights are not an objective reality which exist out in the world in animals. They are the product of human discourses. Animals only have rights when we give them to them. (3) As the rights of animals are historical and social products rather than deriving from some objective reality there is no independent standard according to which they can be said to be better in any one historical period or society than another. 'Animal rights . . . is not a morality founded upon the reality of animals, it is a morality about what it is to be an individual human who lives a social life' (Tester 1991:16). Elsewhere, he observes that 'Animal rights . . . comes from the appearance of a historically new set of foundations for the ordered understanding of animals and not from any more objective knowledge of them at all . . . our understanding and classi-fication of animals is different, not . . . better' (p. 78).

There are a lot of problems here. I have already discussed the first point about ethics mentioned above in chapter 4. The basic problem is that in attempting to lay out the social functions of animal rights for humans Tester sociologizes away the concern for animals in its con-tent. It is not clear why the content of animals rights discourse which expresses concern for animals should be invalid and overriden by its putative social function for humans as being of greater explanatory validity.

Tester's second point on ethics is that rights are ascribed, not inherent or related to the objective reality of animals. It is certainly true that rights come on the scene in discourses on rights. In this sense their articulation is social. But I would argue that if animals have rights they have them even when we do not ascribe them. This is because one reason they have rights is the nature of their objective being. Animals have rights by virtue of being feeling, sentient or flourishing beings. It is because they feel pain or have the capacity to feel pleasure or flourish that we ascribe to them rights not to suffer and to survive and fulfil such capacities. Their rights are intrinsically bound up in such properties and while articulated socially they are not so in abstraction from them. Without such properties it would not make sense for animals to have rights. In other words, in relation to Tester's second point about ethics being social and not objective, their rights are socially ascribed but in relation to objective properties of being an animal. And even though rights are ascribed they still exist prior to, after, or in the absence of their ascription because they are wrapped up in objective properties which endure beyond social ascrip-tions.

If a reason why animals have rights is that they are feeling sentient or flourishing beings then they have them as long as they feel or are sentient even if society does not recognize this. Hence, in relation to the third point on ethics above, their rights are universal rather than relative. Different ethics on animals are not all equally valid depending on the historical period or society in which they arise and do not cease in a context in which they are not socially realized. There is an objective standard on which rights are ascribed which makes conceptualizations which tap into that standard better than others that do not and which makes rights continue even in situations where the objective reality still stands but rights are not socially recognized. Rights may not become attributed or socially meaningful until they arise in discourse. But they are related to objective properties in animals which make them worthy of rights and if the philosophical case for rights is based on such objective properties then it stands as long as such properties exist even when sociologically unrealized.

Tester makes a sociological explanation of the articulation of animal rights. But he is wrong to slip to implications about their universal philosophical validity from whether they are sociologically articulated or not. The general upshot of this is that on ethics a conceptualization of the relationship between society and nature which is overly social constructionist will not do. It has to recognize independent objective properties in nature in its relationship with society.

Let me move on to epistemology. Epistemology, remember, is about the nature of our knowledge about the world. Again here Tester leans towards social constructionism. He says that our knowledge of the non-human world derives from the social categories we impose on it rather than a recognition of the objective properties of that world itself. Objectively, the world outside is a blank paper open to different social interpretations rather than a predefined thing which comes up before us in our field of vision when we go out looking for it.

For instance, Tester criticizes the 'naturalism' of animal rights theories which try to 'distinguish being from the knowledge of being' (p. 31). He argues that 'any reliance upon naturalistic foundations cannot explain the social interpretation of animals and, more broadly speaking, the external world' (p. 48) and that, 'all the writers who pretend to tell, or try to discover, the real truth of animals and humans are writing in bad faith . . . The supposed real truths display an astonishing tendency to turn out to be little more than social inventions' (p. 48). 'Statements about what is true are social artifacts rather than an approximation to a real nature' (p. 33) and 'animals are indeed a blank paper which can be inscribed with any message' (p. 46).

This is too strong. While it recognizes social mediation it puts too much emphasis on the power of the social. How we understand and classify the non-human world partly depends on the systems of social classification we have to hand. However, these attach to properties in the real world and cannot classify it any old way. They are, in part, constrained by independent objective realities which cannot be stretched to fit any categories, and the nature of which constrain what discourse can say about them.

Tester uses fish, for example, to illustrate his arguments at several points in his book (e.g. p. 46). For him fish could be classified along with other sorts of animals if we used taxonomies which categorized animals according to criteria other than those that we use at present. However, the problem here is that fish cannot be categorized any old way because they have objective properties which cannot be fitted into any category. They cannot be categorized as feathered because they do not have feathers. And they can only be categorized as scaly because they have scales.

Our categorization of fish as scaly creatures depends on having social categories of scaliness but also the material objective reality of their being entities with scales. We can only categorize them as scaly because they have scales and we could not categorize them as not scaly because they do have scales. There is a being which is objective and independent of our knowledge of being which, along with social discursive classification, is part of the story of our knowledge of fish. In other words, knowledge of being is partly in the store of classifications and perceptions we use to make sense of the world. But it is partly also a product of independent objective properties to which such categories may or may not approximate.

On epistemology our knowledge of nature is, in sum, partly a social construction but is also dependent on objective properties of nature itself. Social constructionism is inadequate for conceptualizing the society–nature relationship if it is insensitive to the objectivity of the latter in this relationship and a conceptual scheme which rectifies this imbalance is needed for an adequate theorizing of the relations between society and nature.

The third and final dimension of the social constructionist perspective on society–nature relations is the ontological. The social constructionist perspective here is really in what it says about epistemology. Entities in the natural environment do not have an objective ontology. The being of nature is not something in nature but is something we attribute to it. To attempt to theorize objective properties of nature in the society–nature relationship is to attribute to nature properties which are not there but are ascriptions of society. In other words, ontology in the sense of objective being is thrown out altogether and collapsed into epistemology. Being is said to be something which is not objective and ontological but epistemological and a property of knowledge rather than nature.

The problems with this are the same as those with epistemology. The very idea of 'being' and the qualities of being we ascribe to entities are a product of social perceptions. However, they only work in so far they approximate to objective properties which are real. To say the being of humans is that we are straight-standing, relatively hairless, social, creative and intelligent is an attribution by discourses which have concepts for being and for these things and can set them up as attributes against their opposites. But these attributions only work if they say something about real empirical characteristics and that they are conceptualized in discourse does not mean that they do not also happen objectively and so are in a real sense part of our being.

Tester says less about ontology than epistemology and ethics and what he thinks is less well defined here. As it happens, some comments he makes suggest that he thinks there is being independent of knowledge of it. When he says, for example, that the 'knowledge of being . . . shapes action more than being itself' and that 'natural dimensions of being human are fairly trivial' (p. 32) there is some conception of being separate from knowledge of it and of natural dimensions to that being.

The problem now, though, is that this more moderate and realistic social constructionist perspective assigns overly minimal empirical causal powers to nature as 'trivial'. Natural being is said to be relatively insignificant. Applied to nature generally, this is an implausible understatement. The ethical and epistemological points above on the lack of objective grounds for rights and knowledge of nature also leave aside and ignore too much the real empirical causal powers of nature that exist even if the epistemological and ethical points were correct. A perspective that stresses the social and underplays the natural on ethical and epistemological dimensions is inadequate if it does not see how big nature is in its empirical ontological powers. Supposing that there are no objective grounds for rights in nature and that knowledge of nature is social rather than objective, a social constructionist perspective is still inadequate if it does not conceptualize the causal determinant power that natural effects like resources, waste-absorbent and food-production capacities and climatic and atmospheric effects have, even if on ethics and epistemology social constructionism were to hold up.

Social constructionists can say that such causal powers are only significant in a context of human actions or needs (like resource use, pollution, sensitivity to climate and atmospheric effects) that make them so. This is true, but limited. Even if such natural causal powers only make sense in the context of human social needs they are still of massive objective causal importance in such a context and a conceptualization of the relationship between society and nature has to incorporate these natural powers. A perspective that focuses on social construction in ethics and epistemology is inadequate to an understanding of the causal powers of nature in the society–nature interaction.

Realism

There is another perspective which does not give up a hold on understanding nature as socially mediated but also sees it as having real independent objective causal powers of its own. Realist social thinkers on environmental issues like Dickens (1992) and Benton (1989) are sociologists and are not ignorant of the role of social consciousness and action in the constitution of the natural world in the ethical, epistemological and ontological senses I hav discussed. But they draw on the 'critical realism' of writers like Sayer (1984), Bhaskar (1989 and 1991) and, further back, Marx (1975) in order to combine an awareness of social mediation with an awareness also of independent natural powers (see also Outhwaite 1987).

There are four points in Dickens (1992) which are particularly relevant here. (1) *Dialectics and realism*: Dickens argues for a dialectical and realist approach to conceptualizing the relationships between society and nature which sees them as mutually constitutive but with independent objective potentialities. (2) *Stratified knowledge*: He argues for stratified knowledge of entities in the world which sees them as having properties at different levels of abstraction and specificity. He conceptualizes there being objective generative potentials in entities at the most abstract level with socially mediated conjunctural effects at the more specific. (3) *A unified science*: He argues for greater unification between the natural and social sciences which recognizes the interconnection between the natural and social within a dialectical realist scheme. (4) *The early Marx*: He sees the early work of Marx as offering sketches of what such a scheme could be, and finds Marx's investigations along these lines preferable either to outright social constructionists who fetishize the social or to environmentalists who do the same for the natural. Many of Dickens's remarks are addressed to nature in the sense of human nature. I will examine them here as they engage with, or are relevant to, questions of nature as the natural environment.

1 Dialectics and realism   Dickens argues that the relations between an organism and its environment need to be seen as dialectical or mutually dependent and constitutive. Organisms have potentialities and act, but how or whether they realize their potentialities or act is conditioned by the context in which they find themselves. The environment, however, is also affected by the action of the organism. This action is conditioned by the environmental context and so on. The implications of this for the society–nature relationship should be clear. Society and nature are not completely independent atoms. Nor is the relationship between them one way. Their fortunes are locked together in a mutually constitutive dialectical relationship.

For Dickens the conceptual problem at the moment is that sociology either ignores the society–nature dialectic or sees it in a one-way social constructionist way, with social processes as constitutive of the environment and too little attention paid to natural causality. Environmentalists, conversely, are too focused on a one-way determination of nature upon society. Either way there needs to be more of a meeting of minds and a more dialectical conception of society–nature relations. For Dickens a good place to look for such a conception is in Marx's theorizations in his early 'Economic and Philosophical Manuscripts' (Marx 1975).

Yet for Dickens it is not enough for this conception to be dialectical. It must also be realist. This involves an idea of there being real independent generative structures which underlie manifest phenomena. Both organisms and the environment have latent potentialities, powers or capacities which are objective and independent of social processes and can be realized. Yet whether or how they are realized depends on existing circumstances. They do not just spring out from their latent potential but are mediated through contingent relations and processes.

The realism in Dickens (1992), then, posits independent properties of things. But it is not a socially ignorant realism. It sees that those properties come through the social mediation of contingent circumstances. The implication for the society–natural environment relation is that nature has natural capacities, powers and properties. It is the realization of these through contingent social circumstances which shapes what the natural environment becomes and how, therefore, as an entity dialectically related to society, it affects the latter. Nature has real independent properties, socially mediated. The resources and processes of the natural world are enabling, constraining and have the potential to be manifest and effective, given human practices and interactions with nature which can make them so.

2 Stratified knowledge   All this implies a stratified idea of forces in operation in the relationship between organism and environment, or society and nature. Dickens argues that the central significance of realism is its stratification of information and theory. Three general levels of theory can be defined going from the abstract to the concrete in the realist stratification of knowledge.

(1) At the most abstract level are conceptions of underlying generative structures and the potentialities and powers of objects. These

may include concepts of human nature or natural being or transhistorical claims. (2) Then there is knowledge of more contingent factors. These are factors which are not structurally essential in the sense of (1). They are specific to given historical and social circumstances. (3) There are then empirical phenomena in conjunctures which arise out of the combination of objective powers with contingent factors and can be observed at a given time and place. These involve the abstract tendencies of (1) as they emerge through specific conditions of (2). Tendencies are objective, but the form they take depends on existing conditions they encounter in a historically and socially specific situation (see Sayer 1984).

Figure 6.3 *Stratification of knowledge in realist philosophy of social science*

(1)	*Abstract level*	Objective powers of objects
(2)	*Contingent level*	Contextually specific factors
(3)	*Conjunctural level*	Observable phenomena

Dickens explains:

> causation . . . is seen . . . as 'the necessary-ways-of-acting of an object which exists in virtue of its nature' . . . organisms are seen as having necessary latent or potential ways of acting but the actual concrete results of those general relations and ways of acting critically depend on contingent circumstances. (1992:178)

The implication for the society–nature relationship is that nature is not only constituted by society as in social constructionism. It has independent powers of its own but how these manifest themselves, or whether they do, is mediated through society. Realism puts a stress on objective causal powers in nature of a sort denied by strong social constructionism. But it is not sociologically naive as Dickens suggests environmentalism often is. It recognizes that the form these powers take is socially mediated.

3 A unified science Dickens argues that a conceptualization based on knowledge at different levels implies the need for a unified science combining such levels. Biological and physical sciences are concerned with theories of life at the level of abstract objective powers in natural objects. Social theory is focused on contingent factors and conjunctures and is dismissive of abstract natural objectivity. What is needed is a unified science which brings the different levels of knowledge together in interaction. Social theory needs to be combined with natural sciences to see how society is embedded in nature. But natural science needs to be combined with social theory to understand the conjunctural forms it takes through historically and socially specific contingent relations.

Realism which stratifies different sorts of knowledge highlights the need to combine different disciplinary perspectives responsible for each type of knowledge respectively. Furthermore, it does so without a simple *ad hoc* eclecticism which just jumbles all relevant factors up together. It systematically orders the different levels of knowledge into layers of causal effectivity and then conceptualizes the nature of the relationships between them.

4 The early Marx   There are realist theorists who argue that the conceptual apparatus of the early Marx offers ways of thinking through the relationship between society and nature in a dialectical and realist way with a stratified concept of knowledge amenable to a unified science. Some like Benton (1989 and 1993) have more of a qualified attitude to Marx than others like Dickens (1992), but they share a commitment to seeking a realist approach to understanding the society–nature relationship through his writings, particularly his early 'Economic and Philosophical Manuscripts' (Marx 1975).

Marx used a dialectical method. He treated objects not as atomized and separate but as parts of sets of relations in which they are both constitutive and constituted moments. This ontology transfers into a method in which objects are analysed relationally rather than atomistically. According to Dickens, Marx's dialectical conception is also realist. Marx analyses the objective latent potential in objects (humans or nature, for example) and whether or how these are realized in concrete conjunctures according to contingent historically and socially specific circumstances.

Within this scheme Marx operates with a stratified concept of knowledge. He recognizes different levels of abstraction at which phenomena can be examined, whether at the level of objective potentials, or contingent circumstances or conjunctural empirical realities. Within such a stratification Marx provides the basis for a unified approach, positing natural, physical and biological potentialities to be conceptualized in conjunction with an analysis of economic, social and political contingencies through which these are realized and take form. This unified approach, it is argued by his contemporary admirers, could form the basis of a more unified and less disciplinarily exclusive approach.

Marx said some specific things about the relationship between human society and the natural environment which fit into this scheme and are relevant to my concern here with theorizing the relations between the two. In brief, Marx's conceptualization was that humans are so dependent on nature that nature can be seen as their 'inorganic body' (Dickens 1992:ch. 3), as part of them. Humans live from nature and nature becomes part of human-being. This guards against any dualist distinction of nature and society and necessitates a unified approach which includes both in an understanding of the dynamics and processes in either one.

As I argued in chapter 5, there are some limitations to the adequacy of Marx's work for a more realist environmentally sensitive perspective on theorizing relations between society and nature. First, while Marx posits objective natural properties in entities he puts heavy emphasis on humans' active appropriation of nature. Epistemologically and ontologically this is problematic because it de-emphasizes the realist emphasis on causal powers in nature. Ethically it seems to maintain an anthropocentric attitude to nature which sees it as just a tool for the satisfaction of human needs. The extension of moral concern to non-humans does not really come into it (Benton 1993:ch. 2; Dickens 1992:85–8).

Second, where he does give them their due, Marx does not say much on physical, natural and biological potentialities. There is not a good enough notion in Marx of what sort of causal powers nature actually has, both with reference to human nature and even more so the natural environment. There is something from which a stratified unified conceptualization of the society–nature relation can be built. But this really only lays out a conceptual structure. There is not enough about what the content of that relationship is. Furthermore, what *is* said by Marx, both on the nature of human nature (as active, creative, social and so on) and the properties of natural environmental forces, needs to be systematically assessed and tested before it is accepted as truth.

Yet Dickens argues that Marx is better than social constructionism not only in ways I have already suggested a realism sensitive to natural causal power is. He suggests that a Marxian realism is also better than environmentalist systems perspectives. These go the opposite way to social constructionism and give too much power to nature in theorizing the society–nature relationship.

According to environmentalist systems perspectives, life is bound up in the essential interrelations and interdependence of all phenomena in the world. Different entities belong to wider wholes which reproduce themselves in a state of balance, self-adjustment and self-regulation.[3] I have discussed problems with the ethical holist valuing of species and ecosystems in chapter 3. There are also problems with ontological naturalist holism. For Dickens, the first problem with this is its ignorance of the role of social relations and its fetishization and reification of the natural. It sees systems of life governed by natural self-regulating systems. But nature, he argues, is partly socially constructed, and environmentalism fetishizes and takes too far the causal powers of nature. Nature has independent objective causal powers but they do not form a governing system. They are realized and take form through specific contingent sets of social relations.

Second, different entities in the system are not just bound up in systems of interdependence. They are related in specific relations of causality which broad-brush systemic views cannot identify. Seeing entities as merely the products of systemic wholes fails to account for the relations, relative weighting and causal hierarchies between entities in the whole system. Seeing parts as products of the whole fails to analyse the role of relations between the parts in constituting the whole. An analysis of the mechanism of relations and interdependence between parts is needed. But ecological relationism should not be allowed to slip into the holism some greens propose, which sees the whole as more than, and constitutive of, the sum of the parts.

In short, while social constructionism lacks any notion of the independent causal powers of nature, environmentalist systems approaches fetishize such powers and fail to conceptualize the role of contingent social circumstances and the specific mechanisms by which natural causal powers are filtered and formed through them. A dialectical and realist approach, however, conceptualizes different strata of knowledge and the relationships between the entities in them. It theorizes nature as having causal powers and society as providing contingent circumstances through which they are realized. A sociologically sensitive naturalistic realism thus offers an alternative preferable to both strong social constructionism and fetishized naturalism in green thinking as a way of conceptualizing how the relations between society and nature work.

I have argued in this chapter that for sociology to be more sensitive to environmental problems and fuller and more realistic in its understanding of the causes and effects of societal processes it needs to be more widely ecological and to include the natural environment within the boundaries of the things it studies. This involves basic archaeological restructuring to rid sociology of longstanding disciplinary prejudices about studying nature and to bring nature back in.

However, expanding the range of factors involved in society–nature relations is not enough. Social constructionists like Yearly (1991) and Tester (1991) bring in the non-human world but, to differing extents, continue to examine them in the terms of conventional sociological explanations as the product of social processes. What is needed as well as a more inclusive understanding of the range of factors involved in society–nature interactions is a conception of the nature of the interaction between factors, what the weight and balance of causality is between them. Archaeological restructuring involves not only greater inclusivity but also more explanatory power being given to the role of nature within the wider range of factors shown to be involved.

Social constructionism, realism and environmentalism all provide a conception not only of the factors involved but of the nature and mechanisms of the relationships between them. Social constructionism fetishizes the social, seeing the non-human world as a product of social conceptions of it. Environmentalist holist perspectives, however, see society and nature too much as a product of overarching determinant ecosystem powers. While the former fetishizes the social the latter fetishizes the natural. I have argued for realism as a perspective which, unlike social constructionism, recognizes causal powers in nature but, unlike environmentalism, sees nature as mediated through social processes.

Guide to further reading

Dunlap and Catton (1978a) provide an outline of the range of factors involved in society–nature relations in their contribution to O'Riordan and d'Arge's *Progression in Resource Management and Environmental Planning*. In the *Annals of the International Institute of Sociology*, 3, 1993 they provide an update on the environmental sociology literature and on the lack of, and need for, a more ecological sociology. Keith Tester (1991) gives an example of a social constructionist perspective on relations between the human and non-human world in his *Animals and Society*. Yearly's 'social problems' approach advocated in chapter 2 of *The Green Case* (1991) is a more moderate version of such an approach, dropped in other parts of the same book. Peter Dickens's *Society and Nature: Towards a Green Social Theory* (1992) is the most developed attempt so far to move in the direction suggested by the subtitle of the book. He proposes a dialectical, realist unified science drawing on the work of the early Marx. Ted Benton's 'Biology and Social Science: Why the Return of the Repressed Should be Given a (Cautious) Welcome' (1991) is an important more general discussion of the need for more inclusion of non-social factors in the analysis of social processes. James Lovelock's *Gaia* (1979) is a controversial and well-known example of a green holist perspective on society–nature relations.

The Future of
Environmentalism

As I have explained, most political ecologists reject the idea that
ecological problems can be solved by technical fixes or reforms
within existing economic and social systems. It is the fundamental
values and practices of industrial societies that are at the basis of
environmental problems. Change to greater sustainability is more
than a technical question. It is a social and political issue about
different values and styles of life. What are the means appropriate
to moving towards these? Agency and transition are the concern of
this chapter.

Greens propose different strategies and agents of change. Strategies
advocated include education, parliamentary and party politics, lifestyle politics (such as green consumerism or ecological communes)
and sabotage. Amongst agents of change proposed by greens are
the new middle class, the working class, the unemployed, new social
movements or universal agency. I wish to argue that greens are best
advised aiming for political parties as agents of change and that they
need to pursue political change in alliances with social democratic or
socialist movements. This can be combined with non-parliamentary
pressure group activity and lifestyle politics and appealing to all social
agents who can be mobilized.

Education

Many greens emphasize ideas and call for changes in values and
consciousness. The limits to growth thesis implies the need for significant cut-backs in rates of consumption in the developed world to
minimize resource extraction and pollution. This requires a turn
away from materialistic and acquisitive values towards forms of

consciousness based on non-material fulfilment through labour or intellectual or spiritual activities.

Because of this, greens emphasize the importance of educating people in alternative and more ecological forms of consciousness in the transition to a sustainable society.[1] The question is through what forms green education can take place.

Some propose changes in education in its narrowest sense, in school curriculums and higher education syllabuses, for instance, incorporating ecological perspectives across the board and not just in what is conventionally recognized as scientific ecology (see Leopold 1968:223).

Others justify their orientation to legislative action on the grounds that parliaments offer forums in which green issues can be brought to people's attention. Pursuing education here may involve making compromises over what it is possible to say without alienating the public – stressing utilitarian and anthropocentric over non-human intrinsic value reasons for caring about the environment, and initially encouraging green consumption rather than exhorting people to live more frugally. The idea is that once these ideas become accepted greens can move on to more radical ideas to which people might then be responsive (Porritt 1986).

The problem with green education proposals is that they divorce ideas from material experience. People do not come to accept green demands unless they gel with material experience which gives meaning to or confirms what greens say. This was my argument in chapter 4. The rise of the green movement has to be explained in terms of the coinciding of environmental issues with experience of environmental problems or with economic, social or cultural bases for the acceptance of green concern (e.g. material satisfaction, non-market occupational orientations, post-materialism). Some greens do stress education through experience rather than through the didactic exhortations of teachers or politicians. Their emphasis is on the educational value of encouraging green lifestyles, and they advocate green consumerism or living in green communes to give two examples. Green education, from such perspectives, is wrapped up in other political strategies. I will look at these and other options in the rest of this chapter.

Green consumerism

I have discussed green consumerism in chapter 2 and will not dwell on it here. I will however briefly summarize positive and negative arguments around green consumerism specifically as a political strategy. There are four positive arguments. (1) Green consumerism draws people's attention to the role of consumption in ecological problems and encourages producers to switch to less environmentally damaging practices. (2) It can indicate to politicians as well as producers that popular concern about the environment exists. Purchasing patterns show that there is an environmentally concerned constituency and brings this to the attention of politicians. Political parties perceive an electoral incentive to react to consumer demand. (3) For individuals who feel alienated from conventional political structures and power relations green consumerism is something they can do in their own everyday lives outside such spheres. (4) Green consumerism serves mobilization, motivational and educational functions. It is a way in for many people which can lead to further involvement in green politics. It gives them something to do and maintains their motivation for environmental protection. It may lead to a more generalized and deeper understanding of ecological problems.

However, the idea of ecological objectives being realized through environmentally selective consumerism has been criticized (see Irvine 1989). (1) The natural limits thesis suggests that reduced levels rather than different sorts of consumption are necessary for sustainability. (2) Green consumerism reinforces the illusion that environmental problems can be solved within existing materialistic lifestyles and consumption patterns and without changes in value systems. (3) It relies on accurate and accessible information on environmental friendliness, something that capitalists, who have control not only over the means of production but also the provision of information, are unreliable in providing. (4) Green consumerism is expensive and only an option for the better-off. It excludes the poorer from environmental activism.

In practice it is not clear that politicians or capitalists are responding on a sufficient scale to green consumerism. Capitalists and mainstream political parties in the Western world remain committed to economic growth over environmental priorities. This is reinforced by the fact that electors vote more for parties they perceive to be best equipped to deliver economic prosperity than they do for environmental friendliness. Greens may be better off intervening directly in political processes and capitalist priorities through state intervention. This brings me to green participation in parliamentary and party politics.

Parliamentary and party politics

Many greens advocate participation in electoral politics whether through green movement pressure on established parties, green activism in mainstream political parties, the participation of green parties themselves or some combination of these. Some greens think they can bring their ideas to a wider audience through involvement in electoral politics. By establishing green issues on the political agenda and as electorally significant greens can pressurize mainstream parties to respond to public environmental demands. Or environmentalists can attempt to win power themselves through green parties winning elections or, more realistically, through forming coalitions or alliances with other parties to push through ecologically concerned legislation. There have been fierce debates in the movement over whether greens should get involved in party politics and, if so, whether green parties should adopt traditional hierarchical structures or get into coalitions with other parties. Arguments over these issues have rocked and bitterly divided the German green party, Die Grünen, into opposed camps of so-called 'realists' and 'fundamentalists'.[2]

The involvement of greens in party politics, even if only through external pressure groups lobbying the traditional parties, can reap legislative and publicity benefits. However, party politics also has drawbacks from which greens are not immune. As well as encouraging social movement activity green political involvement can disarm it by prompting people to abdicate to political parties and leaders to produce green change. Party politics attracts and forms careerists, the personally ambitious and those hungry for power and publicity for their own sake. Even those who do not start off with these ambitions and manage to stave them off in office find it difficult to maintain their adherence to the principles they went into politics to pursue because of their subjection to other pressures, in part electoral, in part a product of operating within economic and political constraints.

Rudolf Bahro is a one-time Marxist who was imprisoned and then deported from the communist German Democratic Republic following the publication of his allegedly heretical book *The Alternative in Eastern Europe* (Bahro 1978). In West Gemany he became involved in Die Grünen, later leaving to argue for a greater emphasis on communes and spiritual change in the transition to a green society. The much-quoted speech explaining his resignation from Die Grünen at the 1985 party congress is worth quoting not only for its drama but also for the end-note he makes. This is relevant to any assessment of the role and limits of parliamentary party activity in pursuing

ecological objectives. Bahro is speaking after the party has failed to
support a total ban on animal experiments.

> What people are trying to do here is to save a party – no matter what kind
> of party, and no matter for what purpose. The main thing is for it to get re-
> elected to parliament in 1987. It has no basic ecological position . . . There
> is not a single issue where the greens are taking seriously the purpose for
> which they ostensibly entered the political scene . . . this experience is the
> end of traditional political existence for me altogether. At last I have
> understood that a party is a counterproductive tool, that the given political
> space is a trap into which life energy disappears, indeed, where it is rede-
> dicated to the spiral of death. This is not a general but a quite concrete type
> of despair. It is directed not at the original project which is today called
> 'fundamental' but at the party. I've finished with it now . . . I am not
> becoming unpolitical. I am not saying goodbye to the intellectual pro-
> cess. I want to contribute to creating a new place and a new practice.
> Clearly we have to take a longer run-up. We must risk some cold water
> if we want to assemble the necessary substance for our withdrawal from the
> industrial system, first of all within ourselves. (Bahro 1986:210–11)

Whether Bahro's statement constitutes a fair assessment of the state
of Die Grünen at the time or not, there are two interesting points in it
which draw attention to the limitations of party politics. First, at the
beginning of the quotation and for most of the rest of it Bahro draws
attention to the inherent problem of being involved in democratic
party politics. This is that the pressures of electoralism and the need
to get the party re-elected to parliament tend to assume an importance
which overrides the reasons for forming the party in the first place.
Policy becomes subordinate to electoral success rather than prior to it.
Electoral survival becomes almost all-consuming – 'a trap into which
life energy disappears' – at the expense of political progress.

Second, Bahro proposes an alternative to party politics in his final
remarks. He suggests that the entry of greens into party politics was
pursued because it promised an inviting short cut to resolving ecological problems. He now feels that this was a mistaken, even 'counterproductive', choice. The alternative he proposes involves a longer and
harder transition and is based, he implies, on a change in values
'within ourselves'.

Green communes

I will return to parliamentary and party politics shortly. However,
Bahro's closing remarks signal his switch of strategy from party
politics to spiritual renewal. Many greens argue that you cannot

legislate for ecological change because it is something that necessitates a new value system and new forms of behaviour. To curb growth, depletion and pollution people will have to accept lower levels of consumption and material standards of living and place greater value on work and spiritual and intellectual fulfilment over acquisitive materialism. For this reason some greens suggest that ecological change can be achieved in spite of the politicians. If people behave differently and aspire to different values ecological balance and sustainability can be achieved regardless of what politicians do.

The question is how such a shift in value systems can be achieved. I have already suggested that formal education, parliamentary activity and green consumerism are channels through which a greater ecological consciousness can be promoted. But other greens like Bahro (1986) point to the role of green communes which can provide experimental forms in which a greater ecological sensitivity is promulgated.[3] This is done through example, lived experience of ecologically sensitive lifestyles and the proliferation of green communes from below. The idea is that rather than pressurizing and agitating for re-education and legislative change greens can just get out and get on with being ecological, leading by example from below.

Bahro sees communes as a goal and the form of social organization most appropriate to a sustainable society, in ways I have discussed in chapter 2. He preaches the virtues of self-reliance and small-scale communal living as an ideal form for the practising of more frugal lifestyles and the cultural shift needed to go along with them. He argues that the commune level of organization is more appropriate to human scale, being greater than the stifling confines of the family but smaller than the alienation of giantism, more psychologically rewarding and conducive to the formation of fulfilling social relationships and more appropriate for participatory democracy and the control of social power.

Most of all, Bahro feels monastic communes offer the ideal social location for the cultural development of alternative non-economic and ecological ways of thinking and acting. This is where his advocacy straddles an admiration for communes as an ideal social goal with his view of them as a transitional mechanism. He argues that fundamental historical change has always been based on changes in culture and religious consciousness. He sees such changes being initiated here and now by the withdrawal of people from dominant psychological structures to free autonomous spaces where they can develop new values and modes of thinking. In 'liberated zones' people would be able to achieve ecological and cultural renewal away from the corruption of industrialist rationality. They could provide leadership and guidance out of ecological crisis for the rest of society.

There are many criticisms which can be made of decentralized communes as ultimate goals for a sustainable society. Some of these I discussed in chapter 2. Small communities can exert oppressive control over their members, something which is less possible in more anonymous larger communities. Perhaps the political participation of all members is not something all of them would want. Isolated communities may become parochial or antagonistic. Solving environmental problems requires co-ordinated not atomized actions. How would vital products (e.g. medical technology) which require the pooling of resources and skills be produced?[4]

My main concern here, though, is with the viability of green communes as a transitional mechanism. The virtue of the commune proposal as a transitional form is that it might offer a forum through which alternative forms of consciousness and behaviour can be developed, experimented with and held up to provide lessons and examples on the merits and problems of sustainable living. The problem is that it is not clear how ecological modes of thought developed in communes will be expanded into a more generalized consciousness. The argument that it can is based too heavily on a reliance on the power of example. It assumes that a possible form of human nature – green and communal – is a necessary or likely one (see Eckersley 1992:170–3). As Dobson (1990:149) puts it, 'community strategies rely entirely on their seductive capacity. The problem is that people refuse to be seduced.'

Sabotage

Another strategy for green change is carefully calculated sabotage of wilderness encroaching projects. 'Monkeywrenching' (named after the technique for putting machinery out of action) is an example of this strategy.[5] The calculation underlying sabotage is that it can have an economic impact on the profit margins of companies involved in 'developing' wilderness areas. Sabotage forces them to pay out on security and repairs, halts production and creates difficulties with attracting investment and reasonable insurance deals. This may make companies think twice about pursuing development projects. Specific forms of sabotage include spiking roads, flattening vehicle tyres, putting sugar in fuel tanks, unscrewing vehicle bolts and spiking trees with nails so that saw blades used to cut them are damaged (Goodin 1992:134).

Monkeywrenching is not a call for mindless and blanket sabotage. It has a rationale, principles and ground rules (see Dobson 1991: 225–8). It is intended to be defensive rather than a proactive or revolutionary strategy. It is aimed at resisting corporate incursions into areas of wilderness by disabling machinery and tools rather than attacking humans or forcing social change. Monkeywrenchers advocate nonviolence and avoidance of harm to people. They demand care to identify the real culprits rather than indiscriminate vandalism and they aim to stay within the boundaries of maintaining public sympathy for the environmental movement.

However, monkeywrenching is almost impossible to carry out within these constraints. It is difficult to restrict its effects to corporate bosses. Workers are at risk both physically and economically from the strategy's potential economic effects. However carefully and cautiously done it is dangerous. Injuries and accidents can and have happened as a result of monkeywrencher activities (Dobson 1990:64; Goodin 1992:135). There are problems with the legitimacy of sabotage. One guideline might be whether practitioners of monkeywrenching would see it as legitimate for similar strategies to be used against them. Sabotage can get out of hand. To work it has to be supported by an attitude of militant conviction which can gain a momentum of its own and exceed rational thinking, leading to worse and counterproductive consequences often less and less carried out with the original aims in mind. Militancy and sabotage can result in more of the same. It can start a spiral of destruction and reaction on the borderlines of violence which once established is mutually reinforcing and difficult to break out of. Finally, because of its destructive and dangerous nature, it is difficult to carry out within the bounds of keeping public opinion with the environmental cause.

Agency

So far I have focused on strategies for transition to greater sustainability. Greens are also concerned to identify specific social constituencies in society likely to support change towards more ecological forms: 'agents' on whom greens can focus their appeals and try to mobilize as the driving force for change.[6] A number of different possibilities for green agency have been canvassed in environmentalist circles: the new middle class, the working class, the unemployed, new social movements, even everyone!

1 The new middle class   The new middle class seem a likely prospect for reasons discussed in chapter 4. Empirically they make up a significant proportion of supporters of radical environmentalism as do the young and well-educated. The new middle class have higher standards of living and so might be more susceptible to post-materialist values. They tend to work in nonmarket occupations where they have a daily commitment to the non-economic values of ideologies like environmentalism.

However, high standards of living may be just as likely to lead to the acquisition of new needs as to a turn to post-materialist goals. Studies in the past have shown that middle-class people tend to be more incorporated into existing economic and political structures than other groups (Mann 1966). Because of their relatively higher standards of living than working-class people they have more to lose from a transition to a frugal sustainable society. Furthermore, when it comes to direct experience of the effect of environmental pollution on their lives the new middle class tend to live in areas and work in jobs which are 'cleaner' than those experienced by working-class people.

So there have to be ambiguities and qualifications in any advocacy of the new middle class as an agent for green change. Nevertheless the empirical evidence I referred to in chapter 4 does seem to suggest they provide a strong constituency sympathetic to green aims.

2 The working class   On the above evidence working-class people might seem a good choice for ecological agency. Anecdotal evidence suggests that there is a greater level of working-class participation in the green movement than is popularly perceived. Working-class people tend to live in urban areas and are more likely to work in jobs where they suffer the effects of pollution. Furthermore, they have lower rates of consumption than middle-class people. It is theoretically plausible to say that they might find it less of a wrench to adopt non-materialist values and more frugal lifestyles. In addition, the attitudinal evidence referred to above that suggests middle-class people are more incorporated into existing economic and political structures also suggests that working-class people are less so. Some empirical evidence suggests that working-class people state a willingness to spend a proportion of their income on environmental quality greater than that the rich say they would (Goodin 1992:175). Furthermore, if class is looked at from a global perspective it could be argued that there is an international division of labour between the capitalist developed world and a third world proletariat. The proletariat of less developed countries who suffer the effects of exported pollution from the north and of multinational operations in their own countries have a special interest in ecological sustainability. In many cases they have access to resources, bio-diversity for example, which give them clout in international power relations.

But there are reasons why the working class would not seem to be an obvious choice of agency over other groups. Precisely because working-class people are excluded from higher material levels of consumption they could be less, rather than more, likely to let go of materialistic expectations. Exclusion from material acquisition may lead to greater acquisitive aspirations. Furthermore, the working-class does not come through in the studies referred to in chapter 4 as empirically a main agency for green change.

3 The unemployed Another group which greens like Dobson (1990:162–9) and Gorz (1982 and 1985) identify as a prime candidate for green agency is the unemployed, what Gorz calls a 'non-class of non-workers'. This group are supposed to be susceptible to sympathy for the green cause because they do not have a material stake in production and consumption. They are excluded from both sectors and, because of natural limits to growth, are unlikely to regain access to them. They feel segregated from the society of industrial production, are unlikely to see their future with it and are particularly open to persuasion on the virtues of a society not based on accumulation or material values.

It is true that there is a section of the unemployed in some European countries who are committed to alternative lifestyles and comprise a visible section of the green movement. But these are only a section of the unemployed. The problem with Gorz's analysis is that the exclusion of the unemployed from production and consumption is just as likely to make them more committed than anyone else to accumulation. Material values may well be uppermost in their minds. Their segregated experience may accentuate their desire to become part of the industrial system rather than make them feel alienated from it. Furthermore, the unemployed in Western industrial societies are a politically marginalized, poorly organized and relatively powerless group who, regrettable as it may be, seem unlikely contenders for the vanguard of a future society.

4 New social movements Other new social movements are sometimes seen as possible partners for greens in pursuit of greater ecological sustainability. The women's and peace movements seem especially likely candidates as feminists and peace activists have been closely associated with green politics, both ideologically and in practice. The Greenham Common women's peace camp in Britain, for example, combined aspects of feminist, peace and anti-nuclear environmentalist ideologies. And the other new movements share ecologists' concerns with nonmaterial values, decentralization, human realization and political participation, for example.

But again there are problems. These do not undermine the idea of the other new social movements being partners for the greens. But they do call into question their special suitability as agents of green change. The main problem is that the women's and peace movements are concerned with women's liberation and peace. These objectives are intertwined with environmental concerns. But the environment is not their main concern. Other new social movements may be good partners for the green movement but would not seem the best suited for green agency when they have their own causes in which green issues are important but not primary. Looking at new social movements suggests to me that the best agents for green change are activists in the green movement itself.

5 Universal agency   Many greens argue that the key thing which distinguishes ecology is that it represents the interests of everyone rather than specific classes or groups. Ecological degradation does not discriminate by class or gender but affects all of us so that the whole species can be called on to back ecological politics in their own interests (see Bahro 1982).

There are problems here. First of all, it is not clear that ecological problems do affect everyone equally. It is naive to think that an appeal to everyone will fall on uniformly receptive ears or that universal agency is a likely prospect. The discussion above suggested that working- and middle-class people are affected differently. I argued in chapter 1 that less developed countries are particularly subjected to environmental problems created in the developed world and affected by the activities of multinational firms within their own borders. Capitalists and industrialists positively benefit from ecological problems. Their resource-depleting and polluting activities are in their economic interest. They can be expected to be an obstacle to green change rather than part of a universal agency. There is a danger in focusing on agents of green change in such a way that hurdles to it are overlooked. The case of capitalists is a sobering reminder that obstacles are at least as important to green change as agents for pushing it through.

Another difficulty is that some environmental problems – resource depletion, ozone depletion and the greenhouse effect, for example – affect future more than present generations. On these questions ecological change is less in anyone alive's strong interest and greens are more likely to mobilize no one than everyone. On the other hand this assumes a self-interested rationality in political participation. People get involved in political movements for non-instrumental and affective reasons as well as self-interest. On this account concern for future generations is a basis on which many of us could be mobilized.

6 Political agency and socialist politics What are my views on the possibilities discussed so far? The discussions in previous chapters and this one suggest two things. First, agents for green change should be political rather than specifically social. Second, political agents for green change should link up with social democratic or socialist movements. I would argue that green agency and transition should combine different groups and strategies. Within such a framework it should focus primarily on political agency and alliances with socialist movements. Let me expand on these points.

First, the issue of political rather than social agency. There are problems with all the social agents I have looked at. There seems to be a possible basis in each of them for support for the green movement. On the other hand there are reasons in relation to all why their support may be ambiguous or qualified. Green concerns are, in fact, of broad (if uneven and not universal) relevance and should be articulated to groups across the board.

Another problem here is that looking for a social agent runs the risk of distorting ecological concerns by tailoring them to a particular group, compromising and diluting the content of ecological ideology. Identifying with specific groups and mobilizing them on the basis that ecology coincides with their interests runs the risk of turning the ecology movement into an expression of their perceived self-interest, rather than a movement concerned with ecology. Furthermore, it may alienate and neglect other groups in the politics of transition and the formulation of ecological ideas and programmes. It can put off and disenfranchise social constituencies in the politics of support, agency and transition and lead to a class-biased ideology and programme in the politics of power. An issue of sociological interest – social agency – should not become the basis of political strategy.

One obvious possibility which reflections on agency overlook is that the green movement itself and the supporters and activists of which it is composed, rather than external social groups, could be the main agent for change. Green ideas can be articulated by the green movement to mobilize all who are willing behind them, rather than green ideas being geared to appealing to group interests. Like Goodin (1992:174) I would prefer to see green agency 'as being very largely a question of political argument rather than social structural determinism. Ideas as well as interests are capable of moving people to political action.' People should be mobilized behind green ideas on the basis of the strength of the ideas rather than on the basis of the interest of their social constituency in green change. This is not to deny the importance of material experience in political mobilization. I discussed this in chapter 4 and touch on it below. But it does go against basing politics on specific group interests.

The action-orientation as well as the basis of green politics suggests a political angle on agency. I argued in chapter 2 that green change requires centrally engineered global co-ordination. This necessitates direct intervention in the political process by greens. It suggests that, whether through pressure group or party activity, green agency should be oriented towards the political process and getting political actors to pursue environmental objectives. Green agency, in short, should be based on green political actors – pressure groups, the green movement and green parties – and be oriented to politicians whom greens must press to push through political change.

So I emphasize political over social agency. The other issue I highlighted above was that of green change coming through involvement with socialist or social democratic (S/SD) programmes. I argued in chapter 5 that greens cannot alone make a political theory or social programme. Greens have to ally with other political ideologies and movements which can help explain the origins and solutions to environmental problems and supply ideas about non-environmental problems. I suggested in chapters 2 and 5 that capitalism and *laissez-faire* are inadequate on these grounds. Greens, however, can find a basis for explaining environmental problems in socialist political economy. This suggests that they should ally with proponents of socialist or social democratic programmes in pursuit of green change. These programmes are best suited to the achievement of green change.

The need for political alliances is further accentuated by the pragmatic problem of getting into power. Green parties do not win enough seats to gain parliamentary majorities and form governments. They have to ally with bigger parties to get power. Other bigger parties often have an interest in forming alliances with small parties like the greens to help them form parliamentary majorities and get into government.

There are four ways in which greens can engineer an involvement in S/SD programmes: (1) pressure group activity; (2) coalitions with S/SD parties; (3) participation in S/SD parties; (4) the formation of new red/green parties.

The first involves green movement pressure group activity, based in civil society but focused on lobbying for legislative change and persuading politicians to pursue green objectives in public policy-making and international agreements. Social movement activity which restricts itself to lifestyle and cultural politics in civil society, while important, excludes seeking change in the political process and getting politicians to pursue global co-ordination to deal with ecological problems. Politically as well as civil-society-oriented social movement activity is necessary. The problem is that politicians can ignore or marginalize it, especially if electoral appeal relies on economic growth priorities which clash with ecological demands.

If green objectives require involvement in S/SD programmes a second possibility is green parties forming alliances with traditional S/SD parties. Green 'fundamentalists' like Bahro (1986) and Kelly (1984) complain that entering into coalitions makes greens dilute their ideology too much. On the other hand, in my view, it does link ecology in with S/SD programmes and pushes it into the political process. If ecology is diluted by coalitions then at least it has some sort of political impact. Staying out of possibilities for getting into the political process can ensure original ecological objectives are retained uncompromised but without them having any political effectivity.[7]

A third possibility is green activists participating directly in traditional S/SD parties. This may be more suitable in countries and regions where green parties do not have sufficient support to get into parliament or are not numerically strong enough to look like a possible coalition partner. One problem is that S/SD parties are heavily committed to economic growth and, while they are environmentally concerned, they do not build ecological objectives into the basic foundations of their programmes across the board. Often environmental policy is a separate sub-set of their programmes. If an S/SD party requires coalition with a green party for its majority it might be persuaded to shift a bit on such positions. But in the case of participation in the S/SD party this does not apply. As long as electoral success relies on the priority of economic prosperity it is difficult to see this pattern being broken. S/SD parties may suck up green issues, compromising and diluting them within the framework of their pursuit of economic growth.

A fourth possibility is the formation of new red/green parties. It would be possible to ensure from the start that these do not start off with anti-ecological objectives. Green criteria could be built into the formulation of red/green programmes from the beginning. In different countries the prospects for the formation and electoral success of such parties will vary, depending on factors such as political culture and electoral system. But where circumstances within existing S/SD and green parties are favourable to the formation of a red-green party and where the electoral system would allow one to get a foothold in parliament this may be another way of pursuing ecological involvements in tandem with S/SD politics.

I have argued that greens should avoid affiliations to specific social groups and mobilize as many of them as possible. They should focus on the green movement for agency. Political, parliamentary and party activity, for all their problems, are, alongside lifestyle politics, central to strategies for transition to greater sustainability. Greens also need to ally with S/SD politics to secure environmental objectives. I have suggested four ways in which they can do this. Which are more suitable will depend in part on political and cultural circumstances.

The success of the green movement is also tied to material experience. The definition and publicizing of ecological problems by environmental groups, the media and science are essential to green change. But how environmental concerns are received depends in part on economic circumstances and the existence of facilitative value systems and social groups with a material experience which makes them susceptible to such concerns and values. In addition it depends on experience of environmental problems themselves.

Ecology and society

This book has been about the relationship between ecology and society. I have looked at what ecology brings to social thinking and what social analysis brings to ecology. Radical ecology revolutionizes traditional social and political thinking. But it also requires it.

1 Radical ecology   I have not found it possible to accept radical ecology consistently. I accept green proposals on the need for fundamental economic, social and cultural change to achieve sustainability (although with qualifications about blanket prescriptions for no-growth). I agree that social and political thinking needs to incorporate natural limits and the moral standing of non-humans. On the other hand I do not accept radical green positions on the valuing of holistic or non-sentient entities in the environment or radical green advocacies of decentralized communes. I do not agree that radical ecology breaks with traditional political theory. It fundamentally affects but also needs it.

2 Social and political thinking   On social and political thinking my conclusions vary. I think it needs to restructure its basic assumptions by incorporating natural limits and non-humans. That the natural environment needs to come more into sociological concerns is something I have pursued throughout the book. Societies are affected by and have effects on the environment which bounce back on society. Non-humans as well as humans matter morally. Trying to explain society–nature relations purely in terms of social categories without recognition of the independent objectivity of nature fails. Ethically, epistemologically and ontologically the independent objective properties of nature are important. There is a need for an overall conceptual framework which recognizes this. In sociology such a framework requires fundamental changes in the boundaries and foundations of the discipline across the board.

On the other hand traditional social and political thinking is essential to resolving ecological problems. Social processes are at the basis of environmental problems. Resolving such problems requires social as well as technical change and the expertise of social as well as natural scientists and technologists. Social analysis of the conditions for the growth of the green movement and political analyses of opportunities for its future political development are important to its fortunes. Traditional political theory is necessary to explain environmental problems and non-environmental issues which still have to be tackled alongside sustainability. Within traditional political theory I reject capitalist and *laissez-faire* solutions to ecological problems and find myself coming more and more back to socialist political economy. I think state intervention, global co-ordination and political action by the green movement are necessary for resolving such problems.

Ecology, in short, revolutionizes thinking about the social and political world but also needs it. Both are important to green change. An alliance of the green movement with social democratic and socialist movements, pushing for political globally co-ordinated solutions is the basis on which such change can be achieved.

Guide to further reading

Andrew Dobson argues for going beyond conventional politics and for the unemployed as a green agent in chapter 4 of *Green Political Thought* (1990). In his *The Green Reader* (1991) there is a section of extracts from green writings on 'green political strategies'. Rudolf Bahro discusses green strategy from a fundamentalist point of view in *Building the Green Movement* (1986). Robert Goodin in chapters 3–5 of *Green Political Theory* (1992) and Alan Scott in chapters 4, 5 and 6 of *Ideology and the New Social Movements* (1990) provide more 'realist' analyses. Goodin is a critic of decentralist and lifestyle politics and argues for change through global and political institutions and for political alliances. Scott argues that the green movement will inevitably accommodate to conventional political approaches.

Acknowledgements

I am grateful to Peter Dickens, John O'Neill, Neil Stammers, Linda Merricks, Darrow Schecter and Matt Gandy for their much appreciated and very useful advice on the book. My thanks to David Held and Jennifer Speake at Polity Press for their conscientious help. Also to the students who took my course 'Ecology and Society' in 1991 and 1992 for their valued and enjoyable company and ideas. I owe thanks to Sussex University for a term's research leave to work on this book. And finally thanks to Christina, Brian, Katie and Jake – for just being there.

Notes

Introduction

1 For an excellent discussion of the main global environmental problems, which is accessible, gives the important technical details and sets them in their political and economic context, see Yearly (1991:ch. 1). The main strengths of Yearly's book on the sociology of environmentalism are in its discussions of the objective reality of environmental problems and of political and economic relations involved in development and environmental degradation in developing countries. I draw on Yearly's work on these issues in this introduction and chapter 1. I am less convinced by his 'social problems' analysis of the development of green concern and by his downplaying of the role of science in solving environmental problems. Yearly adopts a too strongly social constructionist perspective which I criticize in chapters 4 and 6. See also note 8 below.

2 For exceptions see Saunders (1990:ch. 2), Benton (1991) and Dickens (1992). These are recent examples of sociologists who take biology more seriously. It is possible to distinguish between internal and external nature. Internal nature involves factors internal to human nature or biology which go across cultures and historical periods even if culturally and socially manifested differently in different places or times. Relevant attributes here might include sexual desire, hunger, embodiment, sentience, reproduction, emotion and death. The concern of this book, however, is with external nature – features of the external natural environment. These may be socially mediated in varying degrees but also contain properties deriving from their external natural objectivity.

3 See, for example, Porritt (1986), Dobson (1990), Atkinson (1991) and Merchant (1992) for advocacies of many of the main planks of radical ecology.

4 See the references listed under note 3 above for good introductions to radical ecology by proponents. Much that comes out of the green literature is insufficiently substantial or critical. For more critical and sophisticated discussions of radical ecology from positions sympathetic to it, see Goodin (1992), Eckersley (1992) and O'Neill (1993a).

5 For more recent work in rural sociology and the sociology of the environment see Catton and Dunlap (1980), Dunlap (1980), Dunlap and Catton (1978a, 1978b, 1983), Newby (1980), Cotgrove (1982), Bradley and Lowe

(1984), Lowe and Rudig (1986), Buttel (1987), Jones (1987), Field and Burch (1988), Freudenburg and Gramling (1989), Yearly (1991), Catton (1992), Beck (1992), Dickens (1992), Benton (1993), Dunlap and Catton (1993).

6   See Yearly (1991:6 and 49–50) for a sociologist of the environment who is unhappy about lack of objectivity. I do not share Yearly's desire to stay objective on environmental demands. Sociology is in a prime position to analyse which environmental claims are more valid than others and should attempt to do so when it can.

7   For Marxist critiques along these lines see Weston (1986) and Enzensburger (1974).

8   As will become clear in chapters 4 and 6, some sociologists argue for basic restructuring to bring nature within the sociological remit (e.g. Benton 1991, Dickens 1992, Dunlap and Catton 1993). Others, however, (e.g. Yearly 1991 and Tester 1991) are happy to use traditional sociological approaches – social problems theory, social movements theory, the sociology of science and historical sociology – without basic reconstruction. This derives from their social constructionist approach which I criticize in the two chapters mentioned.

Chapter 1

1   For general references on these issues see Kumar (1978) and Lee and Newby (1983). On the link between patterns of residence and migration and the development of industrial capitalism see Harvey (1985). Classic studies of the effects of industrialization on social relations include Tönnies (1963), Durkheim (1933) and Simmel (1950). Thompson (1983) and Grint (1991) provide overviews of some of the main issues in the sociology of work. The development of modern forms of political system is discussed in Held et al. (1983) and the links between the needs of industrial capitalism and the family and education are explored in Barrett (1980) and Bowles and Gintis (1976).

2   On the shift to late capitalism see Badham (1984:pt 3). On disorganized capitalism see Lash and Urry (1987), Offe (1985b), and Crook et al. (1992). The chief proponents of convergence theory are Kerr et al. (1960). Bell (1973) and Touraine (1971) provide different perspectives on post-industrialism. See Hirst and Zeitlin (1990) on post-Fordism.

3   For a critical view on dominant ideology see Abercrombie et al. (1980). On state legitimation and contradictory demands on the state see Habermas (1975) and Offe (1984).

4   On the sexual division of labour, family and education see Barrett (1980) and Bowles and Gintis (1976). An influential study of ideological reproduction is Althusser (1984).

5   On the effects of industrial development on work and occupational structure see, again, introductions to the sociology of work by Thompson (1983) and Grint (1991).

6   Although see my discussions of Marx in chapters 5 and 6. Marx clearly had something to say on human–nature relations although I would argue it is too little and too contradictory to constitute a prime resource for ecological social theory. Dickens (1992), however, takes a more favourable view than me.

7   On the meaning of ecology see Owen (1980) and also Brennan (1988).
8   I discuss human ecology and wider ecological conceptual frameworks for an ecological sociology more fully in chapter 6.
9   Marx's view of the factors driving historical development is proposed forcefully in Marx and Engels (1969). Weber's theory on the role of religious ideas is put forward in Weber (1930). On choice and openness in historical development see Piore and Sabel (1984).
10 These issues are outlined in the introduction above and in Yearly (1991:ch. 1).
11 See also the like-minded United States Council on Environmental Quality (1980) 'Global 2000' report to the President. Critical assessments of this report are discussed in Simon and Kahn (1984). Mesarovic and Pestel (1975) and Meadows et al. (1992) have produced sequels to the *Limits to Growth* report.
12 I discuss ethical holism in chapter 3 and explanatory holism in chapter 6. Both, as I shall explain, are flawed. I am in favour of relational analyses of interdependence but I think holism takes it too far.
13 The merits and limits of decentralized self-sufficiency are discussed further in chapter 2.
14 See Cole et al. (1973), Maddox (1972), O'Riordan (1981:section 2.2), Allaby and Bunyard (1980:180–200). Kahn et al. (1976) propose a more optimistic view of the future. There is an overview of the debate in Gribbin (1979:ch. 1). See also note 11 above.
15 See Cole et al. (1973:10–12, 109–10, 117–19, 153–4, ch. 14).
16 See the World Commission on Environment and Development (WCED) (1987).

Chapter 2

1   See, for instance, Trainer (1985), Ophuls (1977), Irvine (1989).
2   On which see Hardin (1977), Ehrlich (1970) and Irvine and Ponton (1988:ch. 5).
3   Qualifications should be placed on the case for reductions in growth. As discussed in the last chapter some parts of the world have good claims for increasing growth in the context of globally slowed growth. Furthermore, growth in some goods and services (e.g. in health and education) is less environmentally problematic than in others (e.g. parts of manufacturing industry). Advocacies of lower growth should discriminate according to its composition, distribution and extent.
4   For a study of the importance of material possessions in the formation of personal identity see Dittmar (1992).
5   Gorz (1982 and 1985) proposes a more hi-tech work-free utopia.
6   See Sale (1980 and 1985), Goldsmith et al. (1972) and Schumacher (1973).
7   See Goldsmith et al. (1972). Paehlke (1989:156–7 and 244–50), however, argues that it is more efficient to provide energy and absorb the ecological effects of human populations if they are co-located in urban centres rather than spread over a large distance.
8   See also Callenbach's novel on 'ecotopia' (1978) and Tokar (1987).

9 See also Die Grünen (1983:preface) and Bookchin's (1990) 'social ecology' where great weight is put on non-environmental proposals to do with decentralization, grassroots democracy and party structure as part of the green programme.

10 For criticisms along these lines see Frankel (1987) and Goodin (1992:chs 1, 4 and 5). Ryle (1988) and Eckersley (1992) also make relevant critical points.

11 See Heilbroner (1974), Ophuls (1973 and 1977), Eckersley (1992:173–6) and Ward and Dubos (1972).

12 See Goodin (1992:88) for a similar argument. Goodin suggests that decentralization, grassroots democracy and internal party structure as main planks of green programmes are not really strictly environmental at all.

13 Goodin (1992:119–21) suggests that the content or attitude of a society is more important with regard to its environmental friendliness than its structure. Eckersley (1992:173) argues that the 'general ecoanarchist approach of "leave it all to the locals who are affected" makes sense only when the locals possess an appropriate social and ecological consciousness.'

14 This is a problem revealed in the famous 'prisoner's dilemma' and also in Hardin's 'Tragedy of the Commons' (1977). I will discuss this further in chapter 5.

15 For a discussion of international regimes in relation to the environment see Young (1989). The issue of liberal fears of centralized solutions to environmental problems is discussed further in chapter 5.

16 See Whelan (1989) and Lal (1990) for views favouring capitalist and market solutions to environmental problems. For further references to proposals from this perspective see n. 18 below.

17 There have been some controversies over whether Body Shop products are or are not tested on animals, although the Body Shop has successfully challenged allegations against it on this issue in the courts.

18 In addition to Pearce and his colleagues, other environmental economists who discuss 'internalizing' external costs such as those of pollution include Fisher (1981:ch. 6), Freeman et al. (1973), Kneese et al. (1970), Kneese and Schultze (1975), Kemball-Cook et al. (1991).

19 See O'Neill (1993a), Eckersley (1992) and Brennan (1988). I return to the relation between humanism and eco-centrism in chapter 3.

20 See Yearly (1991:ch. 3) for examples of unreliable product information on environmental friendliness.

21 I have discussed these inadequacies in the liberal theory of freedom in more detail in Martell (1993) and I will return to this issue in chapter 5.

22 For some of the more radical advocacies of alternative green technology see Lovins (1977), Illich (1973), Dickson (1974), Schumacher (1973) and Boyle and Harper (1976). Some of these suggest socio-economic as well as technical changes.

23 Gorz (1982 and 1985) is an example of a hi-tech post-industrialist. See the discussions in Frankel (1987).

Chapter 3

1 For general references on green philosophy see Dobson (1990:ch. 2) and Dobson (1991:233–68). These are good initial introductions if a bit

partisan. Also see Attfield (1983: especially part 2) – a good introductory overview of the literature and main issues from a sentient or utilitarian perspective not dissimilar to that proposed in this chapter. See also Taylor (1986) for a biocentric perspective and the collections edited by Elliot and Gare (1983) and Mannison et al. (1980). O'Neill (1993a) and Brennan (1988) provide discussions from eco-humanist perspectives. A recent discussion is by Goodin (1992:ch. 2).

2   Singer (1976), for instance, focuses on sentient arguments whereas Regan (1988) does not.

3   For discussions of 'shallow' and 'deep' ecology see Dobson (1990:ch. 2), Dobson (1991:233–68), Naess (1973, 1984 and 1989), Sylvan (1984), Devall and Sessions (1985), Fox (1984).

4   See Brennan (1988), O'Neill (1993a) and Hill (1983). Benton (1993:ch. 2) is less convinced of the possibilities for ecological sensitivity in humanism and Ehrenfeld (1978) even less so.

5   For discussions of issues on future generations see the collections edited by Sikora and Barry (1978) and Partridge (1981). Also see Barry (1977), Raz (1986), Goodin (1992:65–73), Attfield (1983:chs 6 and 7), O'Neill (1993b) Routley and Routley (1978).

6   See Routley and Routley (1978) for a discussion of nuclear power in relation to obligations to future generations. On risk in modern societies see Beck (1992).

7   For influential classic statements by deep ecologists on intrinsic value in nature see Naess (1973) and Leopold (1968). Also see the discussion of value in the environment in Goodin (1992:ch. 2).

8   Griffin (1986) discusses issues such as these using the term 'well-being'. I will return in more depth to sentience and the literature on this issue later in the chapter.

9   For recent discussions of animal rights see Tester (1991), Benton (1993) and Garner (1993). For influential 'classic' statements see Bentham (1960), Salt (1980), Singer (1976), Clark (1977), Regan (1988) and Midgeley (1983). Also the collections edited by Singer (1985), Regan and Singer (1976) and Miller and Williams (1983). Different theorists argue for obligations to animals on different grounds and, as mentioned in note 2 above, by no means all do so on the sentient grounds that Singer (1976), for example, and I favour.

10 Clark (1977) argues on flourishing in relation to animals. See also Attfield (1983:151–4) and Taylor (1986).

11 See Naess (1973), Dobson (1990:121–2), Sale (1984), Norton (1987) and Attfield (1983:149–50) on the intrinsic value of diversity.

12 Brennan (1988) suspects deep ecological appeals to scientific claims about diversity in nature do not hold up – see pp. 43–4, 119, 122–3. Further, he argues that if diversity *is* an ecological reality this is not a sufficient basis for it to be of value – see pp. 152 and 164.

13 Naess (1984) and Norton (1986 and 1987) propose that species have an intrinsic value. See also Eckersley (1992:46–7) and Feinberg (1980:171–3, 204–5). Attfield (1983:150–1, 155–6) is a critic of the idea.

14 On wholes or systems as having a value in themselves see Goodpaster (1978), Rodman (1977) and Callicott (1980). A scientific basis for ethical claims on holism is often made; see Lovelock (1979), Capra (1985) and Callicott (1985). See the discussion in Attfield (1983:156–60, 179–82). Brennan (1988) argues that the scientific basis claimed by ethical holists and their ethical claims

themselves are faulty. In this chapter I reject ethical holism. In chapter 6 I reject ontological or explanatory holism which fetishizes the natural.

15 The idea that the system as a whole provides conditions optimal for life comes through strongly in the influential 'Gaia' thesis advanced by Lovelock (1979). For an accessible introduction to 'Gaia' see Dobson (1990:42–7) and Dobson (1991:264–8). Again, I discuss in this chapter why I think holist Gaia-type ideas are ethically dangerous. In chapter 6 I explain why I think they are flawed as explanations of society–nature relations.

16 See Dobson (1990:24–8), Sale (1984 and 1985), Bookchin (1982).

17 For an argument for non-interference see Regan's (1981) 'preservation principle' rejected, rightly in my view, by Brennan (1988:198).

18 On community and obligations in environmental ethics see Leopold (1968:203), Callicott (1979), Attfield (1983:157–8).

19 See Rawls (1971) and communitarianism of which recent advocates include MacIntyre (1981) and Sandel (1982).

20 Many of these criticisms come up in advocacies and criticisms of utilitarianism. See the collections edited by Frey (1984), Sen and Williams (1982) and Smart and Williams (1973). See also Griffin (1986) on well-being and Kymlicka (1990:ch. 2) for a good critical introduction in the context of political theory. Many of my points below are responses to Kymlicka's neat summary of criticisms of utilitarianism. Attfield (1983) and Singer (1976) are proponents of utilitarian arguments in the field of environmental ethics. I focus on humans in the discussion that follows because many of the allegories and analogies in the literature are specifically related to humans. However, what I am defending are criteria of sentience which involve animals as well as humans.

21 Kymlicka's discussion (1990:30–5) distinguishes sentient arguments based on either (1) what he calls 'equal consideration of interests', that each individual's life matters, or (2) 'teleological utilitarianism', that maximizing the total amount of happiness in the abstract is most important. I favour the first because the whole point about sentient arguments is that they are concerned not about just well-being but about the well-being of *individuals*. It is not happiness we have duties to, but the happiness of people. I return to this on point 3 below on indefensible well-being.

22 Kymlicka (1990:27) distinguishes between 'direct utilitarianism' in which agents pursue actions which they think will satisfy their preferences and 'indirect utilitarianism' in which actions which increase happiness may involve following not directly utilitarian rules or habits. I favour the latter because it is more likely to produce beneficial sentient consequences.

23 On obligations to the dead see Kymlicka (1990:17) and O'Neill (1993b).

24 For more on trees and their moral standing see Stone (1974).

Chapter 4

1 One established area of study is in tracing the long-running roots of modern environmentalist ideas in Judaeo-Christian, romantic, scientific and political perspectives on nature. See Pepper (1984:chs 2, 3, 4 and 7), O'Riordan (1981:ch. 1), and Thomas (1983). My focus here will be more specifically

on sociological analyses of the recent revival of environmental issues in the 1970s and 1980s.

2 See Badham (1984:ch. 3) on the shift from liberal to late capitalism.

3 On disorganized capitalism and its political implications see Lash and Urry (1987), Offe (1985b) and Crook et al. (1992). It ought to be said that I do not fully share the characterizations of economic, social and political transformations in capitalist societies posited in these studies, although there is not sufficient space to detail why here.

4 See Gorz (1982) on the unemployed as new political agents, an issue discussed further in chapter 7. The 'new middle class' are discussed below (see note 22) and in chapter 7.

5 See also Eyerman and Jamison's (1991) concept of 'cognitive praxis'.

6 Smelser has an over-cumulative and reactive concept of social movement action. Social movements may develop without going through all the conditions that Smelser posits and they may create, as much as be a response to, conditions such as societal strain.

7 On new social movements as new see Offe (1985a), Dalton et al. (1990) and Pakulski (1991). Scott (1990) is a critic of the idea that they are new.

8 See Bahro (1986), Kelly (1984) and Goodin (1992:chs 3 and 4). I discuss these issues further in chapter 7.

9 American resource mobilization theorists put similar arguments. For resource mobilization theory see McCarthy and Zald (1979) and Jenkins (1983).

10 For a political angle in explaining the rise of social movements see Nedelmann (1987).

11 For discussions of the relationship between corporatism and new social movements see Scott (1990:144–9), Crook et al. (1992:ch. 5), Wilson (1990), Schmitter (1974), Pizzorno (1981) and Kitchelt (1990).

12 See Jehlicka (1992), Kaldor et al. (1990), Crook et al. (1992:157–9).

13 Environmental social movements did not take hold on the same scale in Sweden, they argue, because these dimensions of knowledge were sucked up into mainstream political culture.

14 They are thinking here of publications like Carson (1962), Commoner (1972), Bookchin (1971) and Goldsmith et al. (1972).

15 For other environmental doubts about science see Beck (1992) and Giddens (1990 and 1991). Dickens (1993) provides an empirical critique of their views, arguing that people are not as sceptical about modern science as they suppose. I propose below that modern science, whatever people think of it, is not such an enemy of the environment as some greens over-simplistically assume it to be.

16 See Capra (1985), Merchant (1990) and Atkinson (1991). See also Marcuse (1969) for a similar view of science. Yearly, it should be noted, does not get into these arguments.

17 See O'Neill (1993a:ch. 9). O'Neill's views on this are similar to mine and I draw on his critique for some of my points below.

18 This idea of a hierarchy of needs comes from Maslow (1954).

19 On the importance of material possessions to personal identity see Dittmar (1992).

20 For a brief review of other empirical critiques of the post-materialist thesis see Lowe and Rudig (1986:517).

21 For a general introductory discussion of these points in relation to new social movements see Crook et al. (1992:ch. 5). Heath et al. (1985) try to show where class still holds up as a basis for political alignment.

22 On middle-class support for environmentalism see Cotgrove (1982), Cotgrove and Duff (1980), Eckersley (1986 and 1989), Rudig et al. (1991), Newby (1980), Lowe and Goyder (1983), Morrison and Dunlap (1986) and Offe (1985a). Not all the evidence supports a middle class–environmentalism link. See, for example, Van Liere and Dunlap's review of studies (1980) which suggest that there is little consistency among the environmentally concerned on occupational status, residence or party allegiance but that the environmentally concerned do tend to be young, well-educated and politically liberal. Two of these factors – youth and education – come up a lot in empirical evidence on support for environmentalism. On education see also Cotgrove (1982), Kriesi (1989) and Eckersley (1989). On age see also Dalton (1988).

23 For a discussion of many of the debates around changes in political alignment and behaviour see Heath et al. (1991).

24 See Lowe and Rudig (1986:531–7), Jehlicka (1992), Crook et al. (1992:ch. 5) and Müller-Rommel (1989) for comparative discussions.

Chapter 5

1 I am not only concerned in this chapter with *political* principles and organization but with *social* life and organization too. However 'political theory' is often used to refer to normative thinking about political and social matters and it is in this broad sense that I use it. This chapter differs from the normative chapters 2 and 7. Chapter 2 on sustainability was concerned with the institutions of a green society. Chapter 7 on green politics is concerned with the best strategies through which they can be reached. This chapter looks at perspectives through which such questions about ends and means are best thought through.

2 See, for example, Porritt (1986) and Dobson (1990).

3 Natural limits are discussed in chapter 1 on industrialism and non-humans in chapter 3 on green philosophy. I do not argue in chapter 3 that *all* of nature has intrinsic value or moral standing. I extend this only to animals. However, the inclusion of even these is still revolutionary for traditional political theory.

4 The problems with decentralism on green grounds are discussed in chapter 2 and those with non-interference in chapter 3. Difficulties with seeing equality and diversity as 'natural' are also mentioned in chapter 3.

5 The environmental merits of centralized co-ordination are discussed in chapter 2 and those of selective growth in chapters 1 and 2.

6 For other discussions of ecology in relation to traditions in political theory see Eckersley (1992), Hay (1988), Dobson (1990:ch. 5) and Pepper (1984:ch. 7).

7 I have discussed some of the problems with extending obligations to entities beyond animals and with shared community arguments for holding obligations in chapter 3 above.

8 See Leeson (1979). Benn (1977) discusses freedom. On the consequences for
   the environment of pursuing individual self-interests see Hardin (1977). See
   also Sagoff (1988:146–70). John Stuart Mill (1982), it should be noted, was a
   liberal with a richer conception of human improvement than one based just
   on material advancement.

9 Both of these strands were discussed in chapter 2 above. My argument, it
   should be noted, is that decentralization, while it has some environmental
   advantages, is not adequate to the resolution of environmental problems.
   Centralized co-ordination provides better prospects. I have argued,
   though, that centralized co-ordination can and should be combined with
   mechanisms of democratic accountability and checks, balances and restraints of precisely the sort insisted on in normative liberal political theory.

10 See Pepper (1984:204–13). Bramwell (1989) discusses ecological elements in
   Nazi ideas. On liberal criticisms see also note 15 below and further references
   in the discussion that follows.

11 Eckersley (1992:11–17) calls them survivalists. *Some* of the arguments and
   spirit of their approach has influenced my arguments for central co-ordination in chapter 2 above. See also Beck (1992) for warnings about political
   centralization and potential totalitarianism arising out of ecological emergency in modern 'risk' societies.

12 Much as this sounds like the classic liberal theory of Hobbes it is important
   to note that human nature is not necessarily fixed in these perspectives or
   assumed to be inherently self-interested. Nor is central state power seen as
   ideally desirable. The picture of human nature and state power is a pragmatic
   reaction to existing circumstances and foreseeable prospects for change
   rather than a general or universal theory.

13 See also discussions in Goodin (1992:158–68) and Ostrom (1991). These
   bring out the international dimensions of these issues. Goodin makes reference to the 'prisoner's dilemma' which is relevant here.

14 For a debate on population within environmentalism see Ehrlich (1970) and
   Commoner (1972).

15 For liberal, neo-liberal and conservative fears about totalitarianism in green
   political theory see Benn (1977), Whelan (1989), Lal (1990) and McHallam
   (1991). Whelan and Lal argue that environmentalists exaggerate ecological
   problems and that capitalism and markets, rather than the state, are the best
   way of solving such problems so far as they do exist. Environmental scares
   are promulgated by state officials bent on global domination. They are secret
   socialists who have lost the struggle for state socialism and are now trying to
   impose their objectives through ecological politics.

16 I discuss these weaknesses of neo-liberalism on freedom further in Martell
   (1993).

17 See Weston (1986), Ryle (1988), Bell (1987), Gorz (1980), Williams (1989),
   Frankel (1987), Bahro (1984), Pepper (1993), Worthington (1984), Eckersley
   (1992:chs 4–6) and Stretton (1976).

18 On ecology in the early Marx see Dickens (1992:especially ch. 3), Benton
   (1989 and 1993: especially ch. 2), Lee (1980) and Soper (1991). The key text
   they focus on is Marx's 'Economic and Philosophical Manuscripts' (Marx
   1975). I will discuss the contribution of Marx to ecology further in chapter 6.

19 This does not mean I favour an economy without a role for markets or
   capitalist ownership. I can see a case for preserving market exchange and a
   role for market criteria in economic decision-making and a place for some

private capitalist ownership. However I would see both as having a more diminished and diluted role than in contemporary market and capitalist economies. Neither does it mean that by collective ownership I necessarily mean state ownership. I favour ownership and control of companies by boards made up of all interests affected by the operations of the company and I see this as one possible form of ownership, albeit a major one, alongside others in the economy. See Devine (1988) and Nove (1983:200–1).

20 See Wright (1986) and Schecter (1994) for two very accessible and readable discussions of the variety of forms of socialism. These bring out, in particular, marginalized decentralist and pluralist traditions in socialist thought.

21 For Mill's views on feminism see Mill (1980). On socialism see Mill (1976). For his work on the steady-state economy see Mill (1979).

22 See Benton (1993:ch. 2), Clark (1989), Eckersley (1992:ch. 4) and O'Neill (1993b). I have focused on the young Marx as it is in his writings that green Marxists tend to see most prospects for an ecological theory of the relationship between society and nature. For discussions of Marx more generally and of the mature Marx on the environment see Grundmann (1991a and 1991b), Parsons (1978) and Tolman (1981).

23 See Benton (1993:ch. 2) for a critical discussion of the human–animal distinction in Marx. Dickens (1992:85–8) defends Marx against this criticism and also discusses the previous criticism considered above. Dickens argues that Marx's idea of the 'humanisation of nature' is more benign than Benton makes out. However, I am not convinced that Marx is not primarily concerned with the betterment of human qualities with little concern for what he sees as basically base characteristics in animals.

24 This is not to say that I am against a return to Marx in other areas. The failure of the political economy of socialism should not be allowed to slip into a rejection of Marx's political economy of capitalism, for example. I am in favour of a return to Marx in areas such as the analysis of capitalist economies, but I do not think it is likely to be very helpful in relation specifically to ecological theory.

25 See Ryle (1988), Bahro (1984), Williams (1989), Frankel (1987) and Eckersley (1992:ch. 6).

26 See Segal (1987) for a very critical and polemical but accessible discussion of the ideas of difference feminism.

27 For general introductions to eco-feminism see Plumwood (1986 and 1988), Plant (1989), Warren (1987 and 1990), Ruether (1975), Griffin (1978), Merchant (1990 and 1992:ch. 8), Caldecott and Leland (1983), Diamond and Orenstein (1990), Shiva (1988), Mellor (1992), Dobson (1990:ch. 5), Dobson (1991:48–52, 100–4, 258–62), *The Ecologist* (1992), Collard and Contrucci (1988) and Salleh (1984). The discussion in this chapter focuses on eco-feminist arguments which overlap with radical difference feminism. Some eco-feminists however, Val Plumwood for example, would probably not disagree with my qualifications on radical difference eco-feminism.

28 This is not to say that patriarchy has not been far more responsible for the subjection of women than egalitarian feminism. Neither is it to do down egalitarian feminism. I am only trying to point out a negative side-effect of an approach in feminism which is otherwise fundamental to the positive advancement of women's position in society.

29 In addition, for reasons outlined in chapter 2, I disagree with Dobson's view that in so far as ecology does imply social and political arrangements they

should be left-liberal-anarchist. I think ecology implies the need for centralized co-ordination and intervention which may sometimes go against this.
Centralized co-ordination is more environmentally adequate, and decentralized communes do not have a monopoly on being 'green'.

Chapter 6

1 See Catton and Dunlap (1978 and 1980) and Dunlap and Catton (1978a,
   1978b, 1983, 1993).
2 An exception is development sociologists' highlighting of the significance of
   states' natural resources for influencing development.
3 See, for example, Capra (1985), Lovelock (1979) and Naess (1989).

Chapter 7

1 For advocacies or discussions of such a position see Schumacher (1973:pt II
   ch. 1), Pepper (1984:ch. 8) and O'Riordan (1981:section 9.3).
2 For discussions of the German green party and debates within it over party
   organization and coalitions see Cohen and Arato (1984), Hülsberg (1988),
   Kelly (1984), Bahro (1986), Dominick (1993), Frankland and Schoonmaker
   (1992), Poguntke (1993), Scott (1990:ch. 4), and Goodin (1992:chs 3 and 4).
   Kelly and Bahro were two of the centrally involved figures in these internal
   struggles. Both argued for 'fundi' positions against coalition with the SPD
   although on the rote system for circulating the party's MPs Kelly was more
   of a 'realist'.
3 See also Pepper (1991, an empirical study of green communes in Britain) and
   Roszak (1979).
4 See Frankel (1987), Goodin (1992) and Ryle (1988) for criticisms along these
   lines.
5 See Foreman and Haywood (1989, a 'field guide' to monkeywrenching),
   Abbey (1990, a novel on ecological sabotage), Dobson (1991:225–32, containing extracts from the aforementioned references) and Goodin
   (1992:132–8, a discussion of some of the philosophical issues around the
   'nonviolence' of monkeywrenching). I am discussing sabotage here rather
   than non-destructive direct action practised by groups like Greenpeace on
   which I have more favourable opinions.
6 Political sociologists and socialist theorists have long tried to identify the
   social constituencies for political ideologies and movements. See Hindess
   (1987) for a critical overview of some such attempts.
7 For another supporter of green involvement in political coalitions see
   Goodin (1992:108–11, 169–76). Goodin is opposed to the 'purism' of
   anti-coalition fundamentalists.

References

Abbey, Edward 1990: *The Monkey Wrench Gang*. Utah: Dream Garden Press.

Abercrombie, Nicholas, Hill, Stephen and Turner, Bryan 1980: *The Dominant Ideology Thesis*. London: Allen and Unwin.

Adams, W. M. 1991: *Green Development: Environment and Sustainability in the Third World*. London: Routledge.

Allaby, M. 1989: *Thinking Green: An Anthology of Essential Ecological Writings*. London: Barrie and Jenkins.

Allaby, M. and Bunyard, P. 1980: *The Politics of Self-Sufficiency*. Oxford: Oxford University Press.

Althusser, Louis 1984: *Essays on Ideology*. London: Verso.

Atkinson, A. 1991: *Principles of Political Ecology*. London: Bellhaven Press.

Attfield, Robin 1983: *The Ethics of Environmental Concern*. Oxford: Blackwell.

Badham, Richard 1984: The Sociology of Industrial and Post-Industrial Societies. *Current Sociology*, 32, 1, Spring, 1–141.

Bahro, Rudolf 1978: *The Alternative in Eastern Europe*. London: New Left Books.

Bahro, Rudolf 1982: *Socialism and Survival*. London: Heretic Books.

Bahro, Rudolf 1984: *From Red to Green*. London: Verso.

Bahro, Rudolf 1986: *Building the Green Movement*. London: Heretic Books.

Barkenbus, J. 1977: Slowed Growth and Third World Welfare. In D. Pirages (ed.) *The Sustainable Society: Implications for Limited Growth*. New York: Praeger Publishers.

Barrett, Michèle 1980: *Women's Oppression Today: Problems in Marxist Feminist Analysis*. London: Verso.

Barry, Brian 1977: Justice Between Generations. In P. M. S. Hacker and J. Raz (eds) *Law, Morality and Society*. Oxford: Clarendon Press.

Beck, Ulrich 1992: *The Risk Society: Towards a New Modernity*. London: Sage.

Bell, Daniel 1973: *The Coming of Post-Industrial Society*. New York: Basic Books.

Bell, Stephen 1987: Socialism and Ecology: Will Ever The Twain Meet? *Social Alternatives*, 6, 5–12.

Benn, Stanley, 1977: Personal Freedom and Environmental Ethics: The Moral Inequality of Species. In G. Dorsey (ed.) *Equality and Freedom*, vol. II. New York: Oceana.

Bentham, Jeremy 1960: *An Introduction to the Principles of Morals and Legislation*. Oxford: Blackwell.

Benton, Ted 1989: Marxism and Natural Limits: An Ecological Critique and Reconstruction. *New Left Review*, 178, 51–86.

Benton, Ted 1991: Biology and Social Science: Why the Return of the Repressed Should be Given A (Cautious) Welcome. *Sociology*, 25, 1–29.

Benton, Ted 1993: *Natural Relations: Ecology, Animal Rights and Social Justice.* London: Verso.

Bhaskar, Roy 1989: *The Possibility of Naturalism.* Hemel Hempstead: Harvester Wheatsheaf.

Bhaskar, Roy 1991: *Philosophy and the Idea of Freedom.* Oxford: Blackwell.

Bookchin, Murray 1971: *Post-Scarcity Anarchism.* San Francisco: Ramparts.

Bookchin, Murray 1980: *Toward an Ecological Society.* Montreal: Black Rose Books.

Bookchin, Murray 1982: *The Ecology of Freedom.* Palo Alto: Cheshire Books.

Bookchin, Murray 1990: *Remaking Society: Pathways to a Green Future.* Boston: South End Press.

Bowles, Samuel and Gintis, Herbert 1976: *Schooling in Capitalist America.* London: Routledge and Kegan Paul.

Boyle, G. and Harper, P. (eds) 1976: *Radical Technology.* London: Wildwood House.

Bradley, T. and Lowe, P. 1984: *Locality and Rurality: Economy and Society in Rural Regions.* Norwich: Geo Books.

Bramwell, Anna 1989: *Ecology in the 20th Century: A History.* Cambridge: Cambridge University Press.

Brennan, Andrew 1988: *Thinking About Nature.* London: Routledge.

Burch, William R., Jr 1970: Resources and Social Structure: Some Conditions of Stability and Change. *Annals of the American Academy of Political and Social Science,* 389, 27–34.

Burch, William, R., Jr 1976: The Peregrine Falcon and the Urban Poor: Some Sociological Interpretations. In P. J. Richardson and J. McEvoy (eds) *Human Ecology: An Environmental Approach.* North Scitrate, Mass.: Duxbury Press.

Buttel, Frederick H. 1987: New Directions in Environmental Sociology. *Annual Review of Sociology,* 13, 465–88.

Button, J. 1989: *How to be Green.* London: Century.

Caldecott, Leonie and Leland, Stephanie (eds) 1983: *Reclaim the Earth.* London: The Women's Press.

Caldwell, M. 1977: *The Wealth of Some Nations.* London: Zed Books.

Callenbach, Ernst 1978: *Ecotopia: A Novel About Ecology, People and Politics.* London: Pluto.

Callicott, J. Baird 1979: Elements of an Environmental Ethic: Moral Considerability and the Biotic Community. *Environmental Ethics,* 1, 71–81.

Callicott, J. Baird 1980: Animal Liberation: A Triangular Affair. *Environmental Ethics,* 2, 311–38.

Callicott, J. Baird 1985: Intrinsic Value, Quantum Theory and Environmental Ethics. *Environmental Ethics,* 7, 257–75.

Capra, Fritjof 1985: *The Turning Point: Science, Society and the Rising Culture.* London: Flamingo.

Carson, Rachel 1962: *Silent Spring.* Boston: Houghton Mifflin.

Catton, William R., Jr 1976: Toward Prevention of Obsolescence in Sociology. *Sociological Focus,* 9, 89–98.

Catton, William R., Jr 1992: Separation Versus Unification in Sociological Human Ecology. In Lee Freese (ed.) *Advances in Human Ecology* vol. 1. Greenwich, Conn.: JAI Press.

Catton, William R., Jr and Dunlap, Riley E. 1978: Environmental Sociology: A New Paradigm. *The American Sociologist,* 13, 41–9.

Catton, William R., Jr and Dunlap, Riley E. 1980: A New Ecological Paradigm for Post-Exuberant Sociology. *American Behavioral Scientist*, 24, 15–47.

Clark, John 1989: Marx's Inorganic Body. *Environmental Ethics*, 11, 243–58.

Clark, Stephen R. L. 1977: *The Moral Status of Animals*. Oxford: Clarendon Press.

Cohen, Jean and Arato, Andrew 1984: The German Green Party. *Dissent*, 31, 327–32.

Cole, H. S. D., Freeman, C., Jahoda, M. and Pavitt, K. L. R. 1973: *Thinking about the Future: A Critique of the Limits to Growth*. Brighton: Sussex University Press.

Collard, Andrée and Contrucci, Joyce 1988: *Rape of the Wild: Man's Violence Against Animals and the Earth*. London: Women's Press.

Commoner, Barry 1972: *The Closing Circle: Confronting the Environmental Crisis*. New York: Bantam.

Conroy, C. and Litvinoff, M. 1988: *The Greening of Aid: Sustainable Livelihoods in Practice*. London: Earthscan.

Cotgrove, Stephen 1982: *Catastrophe or Cornucopia: The Environment, Politics and The Future*. Chichester: John Wiley and Sons.

Cotgrove, Stephen 1991: Sociology and the Environment: Cotgrove Replies to Newby. *Network*, 51, October, 5.

Cotgrove, Stephen and Duff, Andrew 1980: Environmentalism, Middle Class Radicalism and Politics. *Sociological Review*, 28, 333–51.

Cronon, W. 1983: *Changes in the Land: Indians, Colonists and the Ecology of New England*. New York: Hill and Wang.

Cronon, W. 1990: *Nature's Metropolis: Chicago and the Great West*. New York: Norton.

Crook, Stephen, Pakulski, Jan and Waters, Malcolm 1992: *Postmodernization: Change in Advanced Society*. London: Sage.

Crosby, A. 1986: *Ecological Imperialism: The Biological Expansion of Europe 900–1900*. Cambridge: Cambridge University Press.

Dahl, Robert E. 1985: *A Preface to Economic Democracy*. New Haven: Yale University Press.

Dalton, R. J. 1988: *Citizen Politics in Western Democracies*. Chatham, N.J.: Chatham Publishers.

Dalton, R. J. and Kuechler, M. (eds) 1990: *Challenging the Political Order: New Social and Political Movements in Western Democracies*. Cambridge: Polity Press.

Daly, H. 1973: Introduction. In H. Daly (ed.) *Toward a Steady-State Economy*. San Francisco: W. H. Freeman.

Davies, J. C. 1962. Towards a theory of revolution. *American Sociological Review*, 27, 5–19.

Devall, Bill and Sessions, George 1985: *Deep Ecology: Living as if Nature Mattered*. Layton: Gibbs M. Smith.

Devine, Pat 1988: *Democracy and Economic Planning*. Cambridge: Polity Press.

Diamond, Irene and Orenstein, Gloria F. (eds) 1990: *Reweaving the World*. San Francisco: Sierra Club Books.

Dickens, Peter 1992: *Society and Nature: Towards a Green Social Theory*. Hemel Hempstead: Harvester Wheatsheaf.

Dickens, Peter 1993: *Who Would Know? Science, Environmental Risk and the Construction of Theory*. Brighton: Centre for Urban and Regional Research, University of Sussex.

Dickson, D. 1974: *Alternative Technology and the Politics of Technical Change.* Glasgow: Fontana.

Die Grünen 1983: *Programme of the German Green Party.* London: Heretic Books.

Dijkink, G. and van der Wusten, H. 1992: Green Politics In Europe: The Issue and the Voters. *Political Geography*, 1, 7–11.

Dittmar, Helga 1992: *The Social Psychology of Material Possessions: To Have is To Be.* Hemel Hempstead: Harvester Wheatsheaf.

Dobson, Andrew 1990: *Green Political Thought.* London: André Deutsch.

Dobson, Andrew (ed.) 1991: *The Green Reader.* London: André Deutsch.

Dominick, Raymond 1993: *The Environmental Movement in Germany: Prophets and Pioneers.* Indiana: Indiana University Press.

Duncan, Otis Dudley 1959: Human Ecology and Population Studies. In P. M. Hauser and O. D. Duncan (eds) *The Study of Population.* Chicago: University of Chicago Press.

Duncan, Otis Dudley 1961: From Social System to Ecosystem. *Sociological Inquiry*, 31, 140–9.

Dunlap, Riley E. 1980: Paradigmatic Change in Social Science: From Human Exceptionalism to an Ecological Paradigm. *American Behavioural Scientist*, 24, 5–14.

Dunlap, Riley E. and Catton, William R., Jr 1978a: Environmental Sociology: A Framework for Analysis: In Timothy O'Riordan and Ralph C. d'Arge (eds), *Progress in Resource Management and Environmental Planning*, vol. 1. Chichester: John Wiley and Sons.

Dunlap, Riley E. and Catton, William R., Jr 1978b: Environmental Sociology. *Annual Review of Sociology*, 5, 243–73.

Dunlap, Riley E. and Catton, William R., Jr 1983: What Environmental Sociologists Have in Common (Whether Concerned with 'Built' or 'Natural' Environments). *Sociological Inquiry*, 53, 113–35.

Dunlap, Riley E. and Catton, William R., Jr 1993: The Development, Current Status, and Probable Future of Environmental Sociology: Toward an Ecological Sociology. *Annals of the International Institute of Sociology*, 3.

Durkheim, Emile 1933: *The Division of Labour In Society.* New York: The Free Press.

Durkheim, Emile 1950: *The Rules of Sociological Method.* New York: Free Press.

Eckersley, Robyn 1986: The Environment Movement as Middle Class Elitism: A Critical Analysis. *Regional Journal of Social Issues*, 18, 24–36.

Eckersley, Robyn 1989: Green Politics and the New Class: Selfishness or Virtue? *Political Studies*, 37, 205–23.

Eckersley, Robyn 1992: *Environmentalism and Political Theory.* London: U.C.L. Press.

The Ecologist, 22, 1, January/February 1992. Special issue on ecology and feminism.

Ehrenfeld, David 1978: *The Arrogance of Humanism.* Oxford: Oxford University Press.

Ehrlich, Paul 1970: *The Population Bomb.* New York: Ballantine Books.

Ekins, Paul (ed.) 1986: *The Living Economy: A New Economics in the Making.* London: Routledge and Kegan Paul.

Elkington, J. and Burke, T. 1987: *The Green Capitalists: Industry's Search for Environmental Excellence.* London: Gollancz.

Elkington, J. and Hailes, J. 1988: *The Green Consumer Guide: From Shampoo to Champagne: High Street Shopping For a Better Environment*. London: Gollancz.

Elliot, R. and Gare, A. (eds) 1983: *Environmental Philosophy*. Milton Keynes: Open University Press.

Environmental Fund 1977: *Behind the 'Food Crisis'*. Washington D.C.: The Environmental Fund.

Enzensburger, Hans Magnus 1974: A Critique of Political Ecology. *New Left Review*, 84, 3–31.

Eyerman, Ron and Jamison, Andrew 1991: *Social Movements: A Cognitive Approach*. Cambridge: Polity Press.

Feher, F. and Heller, A. 1983: From Red to Green. *Telos*, 59, 35–44.

Feinberg, J. 1980: *Rights, Justice and the Bounds of Liberty*. Princeton: Princeton University Press.

Field, Donald R. and Burch, William, R., Jr 1988: *Rural Sociology and the Environment*. Westport, Conn.: Greenwood Press.

Fisher, Anthony 1981: *Resource and Environmental Economics*. Cambridge: Cambridge University Press.

Foreman, Dave and Haywood, Bill (eds) 1989: *Ecodefense: A Field Guide to Monkeywrenching*. Tucson: Ned Ludd Books.

Forrester, Jay 1970: *World Dynamics*. Boston: Wright-Allen Press.

Fox, Nick 1991: Green Sociology. *Network*, 50, May, 23–4.

Fox, W. 1984: Deep Ecology: A New Philosophy of Our Time? *The Ecologist*, 14, 5–6.

Frankel, Boris 1987: *The Post-Industrial Utopians*. Cambridge: Polity Press.

Frankland, Gene and Schoonmaker, Donald 1992: *Between Protest and Power: The Green Party in Germany*. Boulder, Col.: Westview.

Freeman, A. Myrick III, Haveman, Robert H. and Kneese, Allen V. 1973: *The Economics of Environmental Policy*. New York: Wiley.

Freudenburg, William R. and Gramling, Robert 1989: The Emergence of Environmental Sociology. *Sociological Inquiry*, 59, 439–52.

Frey, R. 1984: *Utility and Rights*. Minneapolis: University of Minnesota Press.

Garner, Robert 1993: *Animals, Politics and Morality*. Manchester: Manchester University Press.

Giddens, Anthony 1971: *Capitalism and Modern Social Theory*. Cambridge: Cambridge University Press.

Giddens, Anthony 1990: *The Consequences of Modernity*. Cambridge: Polity Press.

Giddens, Anthony 1991: *Modernity and Self-Identity: Self and Society in the Late Modern Age*. Cambridge: Polity Press.

Golding, Martin 1972: Obligations to Future Generations. *The Monist*, 56, 85–99.

Goldsmith, Edward et al. 1972: A Blueprint for Survival. *The Ecologist*, 2, 1, January, *passim*.

Goldsmith, Edward et al. 1988: *The Great U-Turn: De-Industrialising Society*. Bideford: Green Books.

Goodin, Robert E. 1992: *Green Political Theory*. Cambridge: Polity Press.

Goodpaster, Kenneth 1978: On Being Morally Considerable. *Journal of Philosophy*, 75, 308–25.

Gorz, André 1980: *Ecology as Politics*. London: Pluto.

Gorz, André 1982: *Farewell to the Working Class: An Essay in Post-Industrial Socialism*. London: Pluto.

Gorz, André 1985: *Paths to Paradise: On the Liberation From Work*. London: Pluto.

Gribbin, John 1979: *Future Worlds*. London: Abacus.

Griffin, J. 1986: *Well-Being: Its Meaning, Measurement and Moral Importance*. Oxford: Oxford University Press.

Griffin, Susan 1978: *Woman and Nature: The Roaring Inside Her*. New York: Harper and Row.

Grint, Keith 1991: *The Sociology of Work: An Introduction*. Cambridge: Polity Press.

Grundmann, R. 1991a: *Marxism and Ecology*. Oxford: Oxford University Press.

Grundmann, R. 1991b: The Ecological Challenge to Marxism. *New Left Review*, 187, 103–20.

Habermas, Jürgen 1975: *Legitimation Crisis*. London: Heinemann.

Hardin, Garrett 1977: The Tragedy of the Commons. In G. Hardin and J. Baden (eds) *Managing the Commons*. San Francisco: W. H. Freeman and Co.

Hare, R. M. 1971: *Essays on Philosophical Method*. London: MacMillan.

Harrison, David 1988: *The Sociology of Modernisation and Development*. London: Unwin Hyman.

Harvey, David 1985: *Consciousness and the Urban Experience: Studies in the History and Theory of Capitalist Urbanisation*. Oxford: Basil Blackwell.

Hay, P. R. 1988: Ecological Values and Western Political Traditions: From Anarchism to Fascism. *Politics*, 8, 22–9.

Heath, A., Curtice, J. and Jowell, R. 1991: *Understanding Political Change: The British Voter 1964–87*. Oxford: Pergamon.

Heath, A., Jowell, R. and Curtice, J. 1985: *How Britain Votes*. London: Pergamon.

Held, David et al. (eds) 1983: *States and Societies*. Oxford: Martin Robertson.

Heilbroner, Robert L. 1974: *An Inquiry into the Human Prospect*. New York: Norton.

Hill, Thomas E., Jr 1983: Ideals of Human Excellence and Preserving Natural Environments. *Environmental Ethics*, 5, 211–24.

Hindess, Barry 1987: *Politics and Class Analysis*. Oxford: Blackwell.

Hirst, Paul and Zeitlin, Jonathon 1990: *Flexible Specialisation vs. Post-Fordism: Theory, Evidence and Policy Implications*. London: Birkbeck Public Policy Centre Working Paper.

Hirszowicz, Maria 1981: *Industrial Sociology: An Introduction*. London: Martin Robertson.

Hülsberg, Werner 1988: *The German Greens: A Social and Political Profile*. London: Verso.

Illich, Ivan 1973: *Tools for Conviviality*. London: Calder and Boyars.

Inglehart, R. 1971: The Silent Revolution in Europe: Intergenerational Change in Post-industrial Societies. *American Political Science Review*, 991–1017.

Inglehart, R. 1977: *The Silent Revolution: Changing Values and Political Styles Among Western Publics*. Princeton: Princeton University Press.

Irvine, S. 1989: *Beyond Green Consumerism*. London: Friends of the Earth.

Irvine, S. and Ponton, A. 1988: *A Green Manifesto: Policies for a Green Future*. London: Macdonald Optima.

Jacobs, Michael, 1991: *The Green Economy: Environment, Sustainable Development and the Politics of the Future*. Pluto: London.

Jamison, A., Eyerman, R. and Cramer, J. (with Laessoe, J.) 1990: *The Making of the New Environmental Consciousness: A Comparative Study of the Environmental*

Movements in Sweden, Denmark and the Netherlands. Edinburgh: Edinburgh University Press.

Jehlicka, P. 1992: Environmentalism in Europe. Paper to British Sociological Association Conference, April.

Jehlicka, P. and Kostelecky, T. 1991: The Greens in Czechoslovakia. Paper to Joint Session of Workshops, University of Essex, March.

Jenkins, J. C. 1983: Resource Mobilisation Theory and the Study of Social Movements. *Annual Review of Sociology*, 9, 527–33.

Jones, Alwyn 1987: The Violence of Materialism in Advanced Industrial Society: An Eco-Sociological Approach. *The Sociological Review*, 35, 19–47.

Kahn, Herman, Brown, William and Martel, Leon 1976: *The Next 200 Years: A Scenario for America and the World*. London: Associated Business Programmes.

Kaldor, Mary (ed.) 1990: *Europe From Below: An East-West Dialogue*. London: Verso.

Kavka, Gregory 1978: The Futurity Problem in R. I. Sikora and B. Barry (eds) *Obligations to Future Generations*. Philadelphia: Temple University Press.

Kelly, Petra 1984: *Fighting For Hope*. London: Chatto and Windus.

Kemball-Cook, David, Baker, Mallen and Mattingly, Chris (eds) 1991: *The Green Budget*. London: Green Print.

Kerr, C., Dunlop, J. T., Harbin, F. H. and Myers, C. 1960: *Industrialism and Industrial Man*. London: Heinemann.

Kitchelt, H. 1990: New Social Movements and the Decline of Party Organisation. In Dalton and Kuechler 1990.

Kituse, J. I., and Spector, M. 1981: The Labelling of Social Problems. In E. Rubington and M. S. Weinberg (eds) *The Study of Social Problems: Five Perspectives*. New York: Oxford University Press.

Kneese, Allen V., Ayres, Robert U. and d'Arge, Ralph C. 1970: *Economics and the Environment*. Baltimore: Johns Hopkins Press.

Kneese, Allen V. and Schultze, Charles L. 1975: *Pollution, Prices and Public Policy*. Washington D.C.: Brookings Institution.

Kreuzer, M. 1990: New Politics: Just Post-Materialist? The Case of the Austrian and Swiss Greens. *West European Politics*, 1, 12–30.

Kriesi, H. P. 1989: New Social Movements and the New Class in the Netherlands. *American Journal of Sociology*, 94, 5, 1078–116.

Kumar, Krishan 1978: *Prophecy and Progress: The Sociology of Industrial and Post-Industrial Society*. Harmondsworth: Penguin.

Kymlicka, Will 1990: *Contemporary Political Philosophy: An Introduction*. Oxford: Oxford University Press.

Lal, D. 1990: *The Limits of International Co-operation*. London: I.E.A.

Lash, Scott and Urry, John 1987: *The End of Organised Capitalism*. Cambridge: Polity Press.

Lee, David and Newby, Howard 1983: *The Problem of Sociology: An Introduction to the Discipline*. London: Hutchinson.

Lee, Donald 1980: On the Marxian View of the Relationship Between Man and Nature. *Environmental Ethics*, 2, 3–16.

Leeson, Susan M. 1979: Philosophic Implications of the Ecological Crisis: The Authoritarian Challenge to Liberalism. *Polity*, 11, 303–18.

Leopold, Aldo 1968: *A Sand County Almanac*. Oxford: Oxford University Press.

Lockwood, Michael 1979: Killing Humans and Killing Animals. *Inquiry*, 22, 157–70.

Lovelock, James 1979: *Gaia: A New Look at Life on Earth*. Oxford: Oxford University Press.

Lovins, Amory 1977: *Soft Energy Paths: Toward a Durable Peace*. Harmondsworth: Penguin.

Lowe, P. and Goyder, J. 1983: *Environmental Groups in Politics*. London: Allen and Unwin.

Lowe, Phillip and Rudig, Wolfgang 1986: Review Article: Political Ecology and the Social Sciences. *British Journal of Political Science*, 16, 513–50.

MacIntyre, A. 1981: *After Virtue: A Study in Moral Theory*. London: Duckworth.

McCarthy, J. D. and Zald, M. N. (eds) 1979: *The Dynamics of Social Movements: Resource Mobilisation, Social Control and Tactics*. Cambridge, Mass.: Winthrop.

McHallam, Andrew 1991: *The New Authoritarians: Reflections on the Greens*. London: Institute for European Defence and Strategic Studies.

Maddox, J. 1972: *The Doomsday Syndrome*. New York: McGraw-Hill.

Mann, Michael 1966: The Social Cohesion of Liberal Democracy. *American Sociological Review*, 423–39.

Mannison, Don, McRobbie, Michael and Routley, Richard (eds) 1980: *Environmental Philosophy*. Canberra: Australian National University.

Marcuse, Herbert 1969: *One-Dimensional Man: Studies in the Ideology of Advanced Industrial Society*. New York: Abacus.

Martell, Luke 1993: Rescuing the Middle Ground: Neo-Liberalism and Associational Socialism. *Economy and Society*, 22, 1, February, 100–13.

Marx, K. 1975: The Economic and Philosophical Manuscripts. In L. Colletti (ed.) *The Early Writings*. Harmondsworth: Penguin.

Marx, K. and Engels, F. 1969: *The Manifesto of the Communist Party*. Harmondsworth: Penguin.

Maslow, Abraham H. 1954: *Motivation and Personality*. New York: Harper.

Meadows, D. H., Meadows, D. L. and Behrens W., III 1983: *The Limits to Growth: A Report for the Club of Rome's Project on the Predicament of Mankind*. London: Pan.

Meadows, D. H., Meadows, D. L. and Randers, J. 1992: *Beyond the Limits: Global Collapse or a Sustainable Society: Sequel to the Limits to Growth*. London: Earthscan.

Mellor, Mary 1992: *Breaking the Boundaries: Towards a Feminist Green Socialism*. London: Virago Press.

Melucci, A. 1989: *Nomads of the Present: Social Movements and Individual Needs in Contemporary Society*. London: Radius.

Merchant, Carolyn 1990: *The Death of Nature: Women, Ecology and the Scientific Revolution*. New York: Harper and Row.

Merchant, Carolyn 1992: *Radical Ecology: The Search for a Livable World*. London: Routledge.

Mesarovic, M. and Pestel, E. 1975: *Mankind at the Turning Point: The Second Report to the Club of Rome*. London: Hutchinson.

Michelson, William H. 1976: *Man and His Urban Environment*. Reading, Mass.: Addison-Wesley.

Midgeley, Mary 1983: *Animals and Why They Matter*. Harmondsworth: Penguin.

Mill, John Stuart 1976: Chapters on Socialism. In G. L. Williams (ed.) *John Stuart Mill on Politics and Society*. London: Fontana.

Mill, John Stuart 1979: *Principles of Political Economy*, ed. D. Winch. Harmondsworth: Penguin.

Mill, John Stuart 1980: *The Subjection of Women*, ed. S. Mansfield. Arlington Heights. Ill.: A. H. M.

Mill, John Stuart 1982: *On Liberty*. Harmondsworth: Penguin.

Miller, H. B. and Williams, W. (eds) 1983: *Ethics and Animals*. Clifton, N.J.: Humana Press.

Mishan, E. J. 1969: *The Costs of Economic Growth*. Harmondsworth: Penguin.

Montreal Protocol 1987: Protocol on Substances that Deplete the Ozone Layer. *International Legal Materials*, 26, 1550–61.

Morrison, D. E. and Dunlap, R. E. 1986: Environmentalism and Elitism: A Conceptual and Empirical Analysis. *Environmental Management*, 10, 5, 581–9.

Müller-Rommel, Ferdinand (ed.) 1989: *New Politics In Western Europe: The Rise and Success of Green Parties and Alternative Lists*. Boulder, Col.: Westview Press.

Naess, Arne 1973: The Shallow and the Deep, Long-Range Ecology Movement: A Summary. *Inquiry*, 16, 95–100.

Naess, Arne 1984: Intuition, Intrinsic Value and Deep Ecology. *The Ecologist*, 14, 5–6.

Naess, Arne 1989: *Ecology, Community and Lifestyle: Outline of an Ecosophy*. Cambridge: Cambridge University Press.

Nash, Roderick 1985: Rounding Out the American Revolution: Ethical Extensionism and the New Environmentalism. In M. Tobias (ed.) *Deep Ecology*. San Diego: Avant.

Nash, Roderick 1989: *The Rights of Nature: A History of Environmental Ethics*. Madison: University of Wisconsin Press.

Nedelmann, B. 1987: Individuals and Parties: Changes in Processes of Political Mobilisation. *European Sociological Review*, 3, 3, 181–202.

Newby, Howard 1980: *Green and Pleasant Land? Social Change in Rural England*. Harmondsworth: Penguin.

Newby, Howard 1991: One World, Two Cultures: Sociology and the Environment. *Network*, 50, May, special supplement.

Norton, Bryan G. (ed.) 1986: *The Preservation of Species: The Value of Biological Diversity*. Princeton: Princeton University Press.

Norton, Bryan G. 1987: *Why Preserve Natural Variety?* Princeton: Princeton University Press.

Nove, Alec 1983: *The Economics of Feasible Socialism*. London: Allen and Unwin.

Nozick, Robert 1974: *Anarchy, State and Utopia*. Oxford: Blackwell.

Offe, Claus 1984: *Contradictions of the Welfare State*. London: Hutchinson.

Offe, Claus 1985a: New Social Movements: Challenging the Boundaries of Institutional Politics. *Social Research* 52, 4, 817–68.

Offe, Claus 1985b: *Disorganised Capitalism: Contemporary Transformations of Work and Politics*. Cambridge: Polity Press.

O'Neill, John 1993a: *Ecology, Policy and Politics: Human Well-Being and the Natural World*. London: Routledge.

O'Neill, John 1993b: Future Generations: Present Harms. *Philosophy*, 68, 35–51.

Ophuls, William 1973: Leviathan or Oblivion? In H. Daly 1973.

Ophuls, William 1977: *Ecology and the Politics of Scarcity: A Prologue to a Political Theory of the Steady State*. San Francisco: Freeman.

Ostrom, Elinor 1991: *Governing the Commons: The Evolution of Institutions for Collective Action*. Cambridge: Cambridge University Press.

O'Riordan, Timothy 1981: *Environmentalism*. London: Pion (2nd edn).

Outhwaite, William 1987: *New Philosophies of Social Science: Realism, Hermeneutics and Critical Theory*. London: MacMillan.

Owen, Dennis 1980: *What is Ecology?* Oxford: Oxford University Press.

Paehlke, Robert 1989: *Environmentalism and the Future of Progressive Politics*. New Haven: Yale University Press.

Pakulski, Jan 1991: *Social Movements: The Politics of Social Protest*. Melbourne: Longman Cheshire.

Parfit, D. 1984: *Reasons and Persons*. Oxford: Oxford University Press.

Parsons, Howard 1978: *Marx and Engels on Ecology*. Westport, Conn.: Greenwood.

Partridge, Ernst (ed.) 1981: *Responsibilities to Future Generations*. New York: Prometheus.

Pearce, David (ed.) 1991: *Blueprint 2: Greening the World Economy*. London: Earthscan.

Pearce, David, Markandya, Anil and Barbier, Edward B. 1989: *Blueprint for a Green Economy*. London: Earthscan.

Pepper, David 1984: *The Roots of Modern Environmentalism*. London: Croom Helm.

Pepper, David 1991: *Communes and the Green Vision: Counter-Culture, Lifestyle and the New Age*. London: Green Print.

Pepper, David 1993: *Eco-Socialism: From Deep Ecology to Social Justice*. London: Routledge.

Piore, M. and Sabel, C. 1984: *The Second Industrial Divide: Possibilities for Prosperity*. New York: Basic Books.

Pirages, D. 1977: *The Sustainable Society: Implications for Limited Growth*. New York: Praeger Publishers.

Pizzorno, A. 1981: Interests and Parties in Pluralism. In S. Berger (ed.) *Organising Interests in Western Europe: Pluralism, Corporatism and the Transformation of Politics*. Cambridge: Cambridge University Press.

Plant, Judith (ed.) 1989: *Healing the Wounds: The Promise of Ecofeminism*. London: Green Print.

Plumwood, Val 1986: Ecofeminism: An Overview and Discussion of Positions and Arguments. *Australian Journal of Philosophy*, 64, 120–38.

Plumwood, Val 1988: Women, Humanity and Nature. *Radical Philosophy*, Spring, 16–24.

Poguntke, Thomas 1993: *Alternative Politics: The German Green Party*. Edinburgh: Edinburgh University Press.

Porritt, Jonathon 1986: *Seeing Green: The Politics of Ecology Explained*. Oxford: Blackwell.

Porritt, J. and Winner, M. 1988: *The Coming of the Greens*. London: Fontana.

Rawls, John 1971: *A Theory of Justice*. Oxford: Oxford University Press.

Raz, J. 1986: *The Morality of Freedom*. Oxford: Oxford University Press.

Redclift, Michael 1984: *Development and the Environmental Crisis: Red or Green Alternatives?* London: Methuen.

Redclift, Michael 1987: *Sustainable Development: Exploring the Contradictions*. London: Methuen.

Regan, Tom 1981: The Nature and Possibility of an Environmental Ethic. *Environmental Ethics*, 3, 16–31.

Regan, Tom 1988: *The Case for Animal Rights*. London: Routledge.

Regan, Tom and Singer, Peter (eds) 1976: *Animal Rights and Human Obligations*. Englewood Cliffs, N.J.: Prentice-Hall.

Rodman, John 1977: The Liberation of Nature. *Inquiry*, 20, 83–145.

Roszak, Theodore 1979: *Person/Planet: the Creative Disintegration of Industrial Society*. London: Victor Gollancz.

Routley, Richard and Routley, Val 1978: Nuclear Energy and Obligations to the Future. *Inquiry*, 21, 133–79.

Rudig, W., Bennie, L. and Franklin, M. 1991: *Green Party Members: A Profile*. Glasgow: Delta.

Ruether, Rosemary Radford 1975: *New Woman New Earth: Sexist Ideologies and Human Liberation*. New York: Seabury.

Ryle, Martin 1988: *Ecology and Socialism*. London: Century Hutchinson.

Sagoff, Mark 1988: *The Economy of the Earth: Philosophy, Law and the Environment*. Cambridge: Cambridge University Press.

Sale, Kirkpatrick 1974: Mother of all: an introduction to bioregionalism. In S. Kumar (ed.) *The Schumacher Lectures: Volume II*. London: Blond and Briggs.

Sale, Kirkpatrick 1980: *Human Scale*. New York: Coward, Cann and Geoghegan.

Sale, Kirkpatrick 1984: Bioregionalism – a New Way to Treat the Land. *The Ecologist* 14, 167–73.

Sale, Kirkpatrick 1985: *Dwellers in the Land: The Bioregional Vision*. San Francisco: Sierra Club Books.

Salleh, Ariel Kay 1984: Deeper than Deep Ecology: The Ecofeminist Connection. *Environmental Ethics*, 6, 339–45.

Salt, Henry S. 1980: *Animal Rights Considered in Relation to Social Progress*. London: Centaur.

Sandel, Michael 1982: *Liberalism and the Limits of Justice*. Cambridge: Cambridge University Press.

Saunders, Peter 1990: *A Nation of Home Owners*. London: Unwin Hyman.

Sayer, Andrew 1984: *Method in Social Science: A Realist Approach*. London: Hutchinson.

Schecter, Darrow 1994: *Paths Beyond Marxism and Social Democracy*. Manchester: Manchester University Press.

Schmitter, P. C. 1974: Still the Century of Corporatism? *Review of Politics*, 36, 85–131.

Schumacher, E. F. 1973: *Small is Beautiful: Economics as if People Mattered*. London: Sphere.

Scott, Alan 1990: *Ideology and the New Social Movements*. London: Unwin Hyman.

Segal, Lynn 1987: *Is the Future Female? Troubled Throughts on Contemporary Feminism*. London: Virago.

Sen, A. and Williams, B. (eds) 1982: *Utilitarianism and Beyond*. Cambridge: Cambridge University Press.

Shiva, Vandana 1988: *Staying Alive: Women, Ecology and Development*. London: Zed Books.

Sikora, R. I. and Barry, B. (eds) 1978: *Obligations to Future Generations*. Philadelphia: Temple University Press.

Simmel, Georg 1950: The Metropolis and Mental Life. In K. Wolff (ed.) *The Sociology of Georg Simmel*. New York: The Free Press.

Simon, Julian L. and Kahn, H. (eds) 1984: *The Resourceful Earth: A Response to Global 2000*. Oxford: Blackwell.

Singer, Peter 1976: *Animal Liberation*. London: Cape.

Singer, Peter (ed.) 1985: *In Defence of Animals*. Oxford: Blackwell.

Smart, J. J. C. and Williams, B. 1973: *Utilitarianism: For and Against*. Cambridge: Cambridge University Press.

Smelser, Neil J. 1963: *Theory of Collective Behaviour*. New York: Free Press.

Soper, Kate 1991: Greening the Prometheus: Marxism and Ecology. In P. Osborne (ed.) *Socialism and the Limits of Liberalism*. London: Verso.

Spretnak, Charlene and Capra, Fritjof 1986: *Green Politics: The Global Promise*. London: Paladin.

Stone, Christopher 1974: *Should Trees Have Standing?* Los Altos, Calif.: William Kaufman.

Stretton, Hugh 1976: *Capitalism, Socialism and the Environment*. Cambridge: Cambridge University Press.

Sylvan, R. 1984: A Critique of Deep Ecology. *Radical Philosophy*, 40 and 41.

Taylor, P. 1986: *Respect For Nature: A Theory of Environmental Ethics*. Princeton: Princeton University Press.

Tester, Keith 1991: *Animals and Society: The Humanity of Animal Rights*. London: Routledge.

Thomas, Keith 1983: *Man and the Natural World: Changing Attitudes in England 1500–1800*. London: Allen Lane.

Thompson, Paul 1983: *The Nature of Work*. London: MacMillan.

Tilly, Charles 1978: *From Mobilisation to Revolution*. Reading, Mass.: Addison Wesley.

Tokar, Brian 1987: *The Green Alternative: Creating an Ecological Future*. San Pedro: R. and E. Miles.

Tolman, Charles 1981: Karl Marx, Alienation and the Mastery of Nature. *Environmental Ethics*, 3, 63–74.

Tönnies, F. 1963: *Community and Society*. New York: Harper and Row.

Touraine, Alain 1971: *The Post-Industrial Society*. New York: Random House.

Touraine, Alain 1981: *The Voice and the Eye: An Analysis of Social Movements*. Cambridge: Cambridge University Press.

Trainer, Ted 1985: *Abandon Affluence!* London: Zed Books.

United States Council on Environmental Quality 1980: *The Global 2000 Report to the President: Entering the Twenty-First Century*. Washington, D.C.: C.E.Q.

Van Liere, K. D. and Dunlap, R. E. 1980: The Social Bases of Environmental Concerns. *Public Opinion Quarterly*, 44, 181–97.

Ward, B. and Dubos, R. 1972: *Only One Earth: The Care and Maintenance of a Small Planet*. London: André Deutsch.

Warren, Karen J. 1987: Feminism and Ecology: Making Connections. *Environmental Ethics*, 9, 3–20.

Warren, Karen J. 1990: The Power and Promise of Ecological Feminism. *Environmental Ethics*, 12, 125–46.

Weber, Max 1930: *The Protestant Ethic and the Spirit of Capitalism*. London: Unwin University Books.

Weir, D. and Shapiro, M. 1981: *Circle of Poison: Pesticides and People in a Hungry World*. San Francisco: Institute for Food and Development Policy.

Wells, David 1978: Radicalism, Conservatism and Environmentalism. *Politics*, 13, 299–306.

Weston, Joe (ed.) 1986: *Red and Green: A New Politics of the Environment*. London: Pluto.

Whelan, R. 1989: *Mounting Greenery: A Short View of the Green Phenomenon*. London: I.E.A.

Williams, Raymond 1989: Socialism and Ecology. In R. Williams *Resources of Hope*. London: Verso.

Wilson, F. L. 1990: Neo-corporatism and the Rise of New Social Movements. In Dalton and Kuechler (1990).

World Commission on Environment and Development (W.C.E.D.) 1987: *Our Common Future*. Oxford: Oxford University Press.

Worster, D. 1986: *Rivers of Empire: Water, Aridity and the Growth of the American West*. New York: Pantheon.

Worster, D. (ed.) 1988: *The Ends of the Earth: Perspectives on Modern Environmental History*. Cambridge: Cambridge University Press.

Worthington, Richard 1984: Socialism and Ecology: An Overview. *New Political Science*, 13, 69–83.

Wright, Anthony 1986: *Socialisms: Theories and Practices*. Oxford: Oxford University Press.

Yearly, Steven 1991: *The Green Case: A Sociology of Environmental Issues, Arguments and Politics*. London: Harper-Collins.

Young, J. 1989: *Postenvironmentalism*. London: Belhaven Press.

Young, Oran R. 1989: *International Co-operation: Building Regimes for Natural Resources and the Environment*. Ithaca, N.Y.: Cornell University Press.

Index

UNIVERSITY OF WOLVERHAMPTON
LIBRARY

114/124
112/113